Wissenschaftliche Untersuchungen
zum Neuen Testament

Herausgegeben von
Martin Hengel und Otfried Hofius

124

Lauri Thurén

# Derhetorizing Paul

## A Dynamic Perspective on Pauline Theology and the Law

Mohr Siebeck

LAURI THURÉN, born 1961; 1984 Master of Theology, Åbo Academy University; 1987–88 Fulbright grantee at Graduate Theological Union, Berkeley, CA; 1988 Licentiate of Theology, Åbo Academy University; 1990 Doctor of Theology, Åbo Academy University; 1983–93 Pastor at Lutheran Evangelical Association of Finland; 1985 and 1991 Assistant of Exegetics, Åbo Academy University; 1993–96 Junior Research Fellow, Academy of Finland; since 1987 Teacher at University of Turku; since 1994 Docent of Exegetics, Joensuu University; since 1995 Docent of New Testament Exegetics, Åbo Academy University; since 1996 Senior Research Fellow, Academy of Finland.

BS
2655
. L35
T48
2000

Die Deutsche Bibliothek – CIP-Einheitsaufnahme

Thurén, Lauri:
Derhetorizing Paul : a dynamic perspective on Pauline theology and the law / Lauri Thurén. – Tübingen : Mohr Siebeck, 2000
  (Wissenschaftliche Untersuchungen zum Neuen Testament ; 124)
  ISBN 3-16-147290-X

© 2000 J. C. B. Mohr (Paul Siebeck), P. O. Box 20 40, D-72010 Tübingen.

This book was printed by Gulde Druck in Tübingen on non-aging paper from Papierfabrik Weissenstein in Pforzheim and bound by Heinr. Koch in Tübingen.

Printed in Germany.

ISSN 0512-1604

# Preface

After several years of developing and applying modern approaches to First Peter and other 'Catholic' epistles, and after seeing what interesting views such perspectives can provide, it seemed natural to turn to Paul. This study arose from a certain dissatisfaction with current Pauline scholarship. Fresh winds blow us away from the old exegetics, which read Paul's letters as dogmatic treatises. But my impression was that this new trend failed to follow through.

The title of this book may be provocative and easily misunderstood. The aim is not to nullify the oratory of the Apostle, nor will it label difficult passages as 'mere rhetoric'. On the contrary, in some cases it will demonstrate how misleading such attempts have been. 'Derhetorization' means identifying the persuasive devices in the text in order to filter out their effect on the theological ideas expressed.

Many modern scholars would agree, that instead of simply trying to describe his theology in his letters, Paul was persuading his addressees. But what does this mean? Persuasion *per definitionem* does not exclude theology, yet it greatly affects the way in which the author presents his thoughts. If Paul's art of persuasion is not understood and deciphered, the view of his thinking will be distorted. Therefore I see a derhetorization of Paul's letters as an important challenge for the Biblical scholarship of the dawning new Millennium.

In other words, Biblical scholarship should not be concerned only with *trivial* issues, but nor should these be disregarded. These basic "three ways" used to include grammar, dialectic, and rhetoric. Each of them is necessary for studying theology, even today.

My gratitude is due to Professors Martin Hengel, Hans Hübner, Heikki Räisänen, and Ed Sanders, who during their visits to Turku convinced me of the fascination of Paul's world of thought, and to Professor Lars Hartman, whose call for realistic ways of reading a text inspired, hopefully also affected, this study.

This volume is dedicated to my Orthodox students at Joensuu University, Finland, and to my Ingrian students at Keltto Lutheran Seminary, Russia. Like the addressees of Paul they all know what it means to live in a religious minority.

Lauri Thurén

# Contents

## Part II
## The Law in Paul's Theology

## Part III
## *Paul Derhetorized?*

# Part I
# The Dynamics of Paul's Writing

Chapter 1

# Towards a Sensible Interpretation of Paul

At the beginning of his literary career Paul wrote to the Thessalonians:

> "From you the word of the Lord has rung out not only in Macedonia and in Achaia, but in every place your faith toward God has gone forth, so that we have no need to speak a word." (1 Thess 1,8)[1]

Then why bother to preach the Gospel, if it is already known everywhere? Of course the apostle did not mean what he said. We all know that the expression is an *hyperbole*.[2] "Taken at its face value, the statement is untrue. But not even the most literal-minded reader of the Bible is going to defend the truth of this statement because he or she, like all of us, knows the author to be saying that..."[3] We can even conceive why Paul wrote in such terms: At the beginning of a letter it is good to flatter the recipients a little. But what about his statement to Corinthians:

> "For I decided not to know anything among you, save Jesus Christ, and him crucified." (1 Cor 2,2)[4]

Of course he knew many other things, too; this comment does not refer to agnosticism.[5] Conzelmann explains that the word 'know' refers to theological knowledge only,[6] and Grosheide translates εἰδέναι here as "to accept as true for oneself and consequently to bring to others".[7] But even this cannot be true! We

---

[1] Similarly Paul claims in Rom 1,8 that the Gospel is known in the whole world (cf. also Col 1,6).

[2] E.g. Marshall (1983, 56) sees here "a pardonable touch of exaggeration". For the figure, see Bühlmann and Scherer 1973, 78.

[3] Thus Gabel and Wheeler (1990, 22) on the hyperbole in 1 Kings 1,40, where the earth is said to have split because of the great rejoicing.

[4] Cf. also Rom 15,18.

[5] Conzelmann 1975, 54, n.17.

[6] Conzelmann 1975, 54.

[7] Grosheide 1953, 59. One may wonder, however, which dictionary did he consult.

know for sure that Paul's proclamation was not so limited even in Corinth; his theology included many other themes than Christology.

Is the apostle deceiving his addressees? By no means. The expression emphasizes the point on which Paul wants to concentrate. The use of the rhetorical device is so obvious that the commentators need not even mention it. In fact, the whole section (1 Cor 1,10–2,16) is so heavily loaded with rhetorical devices[8] and technical terminology,[9] as to indicate that Paul was well acquainted with this art and used it, too. But why does he explicitly claim to have rejected the use of rhetoric (1 Cor 2,1)? Is this also rhetorical?

There seem to be many self-evident rhetorical devices in the Pauline letters, on which scholars rarely dwell. But the very expression "of course" in the interpretation should alarm us. Rhetoric was – and still is – a vast discipline encompassing many different conventions. It comprises not only small technical devices such as those presented above, but compositional and contentual strategies as well. Not all of these devices are so familiar to us.

We can smile at a call to stop missionary activity, based on 1 Thess 1,8, or at the claim that since 1 Cor 2,2 does not fit with the rest of the letter, Paul was an inconsistent, vague thinker, or that, for the same reason, his theology developed further after his arrival in Corinth, or that the sentence belongs only to the contingent part of his preaching.

It is possible, however, that Paul and his original addressees would smile at us for the very same reason, were they aware of many of the problems of modern Pauline scholarship. Expressions and thoughts, which were never meant to be taken at their face value, may have prompted sophisticated but wholly erroneous theological and historical reflections. This is due not only to the scholars' ignorance of ancient rhetorical and epistolary conventions, but also to their attitude to the text itself.

The objective of this study is to participate in the new wave of Pauline studies aimed at a more realistic understanding of the apostle and his thought. In recent decades there have been clear signs of a growing discontent with traditional Pauline scholarship. Theological analyses, supported by narrow historical clarifications, seem far removed from the real Paul, his life and his writings.

---

[8] A. Eriksson (1994, 58–62) enumerates as examples *anaphor* (1,12.20.26), *parallelism* (1,.22.25), *asyndeton* (1,13.14.20), *gradatio* (1,12.22.25.27–28), *accumulatio* (1,20.26.30; 2,3.7.9), *apostrophe* (1.10,26; 2.1), *auctoritas* (1.19,31; 2.9), *homoioteleuton* (1.18,20,22, 29,30; 2,6.12.27–28), *paronomasia* (1,12.30), *hyperbole* (1,13), *interrogatio* (1,13), *dubitatio* (1,20), *antithesis* (1,17.18.22–23.24.27; 2,4.6.12.13.15), *exemplum* (2,1) and refers to Weiss's analysis of the rhetorical composition in 1,26–29 (Weiss 1897, 210).

[9] E.g. πειθός (v.4), ἀπόδειξις (v.5, Cf. Conzelmann 1975, 55, n. 26).

Due to this dissatisfaction, the study of Paul, his letters and his theology is currently in turmoil. New perspectives and methods, such as sociological, psychological, and rhetorical, are challenging and even replacing traditional approaches to Pauline theology.[10] They enable the scholars more accurately to evaluate e.g. his attitude toward Judaism, and to take into better account the wide context of his texts.

Some exegetes have, however, observed that the new approaches have yielded less than they promised to a deeper understanding of the apostle's thinking.[11] In particular there is little discussion of the relationship between the new approaches and theology.[12] Despite many advantages, such as a wider perspective, they still concentrate on the historical "context", which means that the focus stays outside the texts. Hypotheses can indeed be proposed about the background and development of certain ideas, but they alone do not suffice to identify and comprehend a possible system of religious ideas in and behind the texts.[13]

It would be fruitful, if the new approaches merged with the old, essential questions. In other words, when new ways of reading Paul, such as literary and rhetorical criticism or epistolography, and the study of his texts in their environment can be reasonably combined with a theological or ideological interest in his texts, a more sensible view will ensue. Due to different philosophies behind the new and old perspectives, the task is, however, not a simple one.

In the following chapters of Part One, I shall first consider the adequacy of, and conditions for, studying Pauline theology. The fundamental difference between a static and a dynamic view of his texts in such studies will then be illuminated. In my opinion, only the latter provides us with a suitable perspective for Paul's thinking. I shall then determine the grade of dynamics in Paul's texts.

In Part Two, these principles will be applied to a specific issue in Pauline theology, the question of the law. In my view, this controversial question demonstrates how the new, dynamic basic view of the text may influence our understanding of Paul. I hope that the interpretation of both single passages and

---

[10] For the rise of this line see Dunn 1983. Scroggs (1988, 18) includes among those using such approaches "most of the main line biblical scholars working [in Northern America] today".

[11] Scroggs 1988, 22.27; Beker 1980, 352.

[12] Thus Hübner 1987, 327–28.

[13] The question whether or not Paul had any coherent theology will be discussed throughout this book.

complex ideological issues connected to the problem will benefit from the approach. Finally, some overall conclusions will be offered.

Chapter 2

# Was Paul a Theologian?

Major problems in current Pauline scholarship are whether there is a theology of Paul, and, if so, what is its real nature. These questions have been difficult to approach, since they have wide religious and theological implications.

On the one hand, scholars wrestling with the presentation of Paul's theology see the task as immense. On the other, as a result of the "contextual"[1] studies, many exegetes are increasingly persuaded that Paul was merely a situational thinker or a practical pastor, and possessed only a vague theology, if any. Therefore, a principal discussion about the possibilities and relevance of studying Paul's theology must be undertaken.

In this chapter, I shall briefly describe various traditional interpretations and the "quantum leap"[2] which Pauline scholarship has made in recent decades, including some new approaches to Paul's theology. The adequacy of, and possibilities of detecting, such a theology will then be treated.

## A. The Dogmatic Interpretation

Paul's writings and thoughts have traditionally constituted the foundation of Christian doctrine. The Protestant churches in particular have built their theologies from reflections upon Paul's letters. His ideas have become a "canon in a canon", on the basis of which other Biblical texts are judged.

Paul's status as the great theologian of the Early Church is partly based on the belief that his letters contain timeless, universal theology, which can easily be applied to the needs of Christianity throughout all ages.[3] The historical

---

[1] Due to its popularity, I use the term in this, unfortunate, broad sense, although it has little to do with the actual con*text*.

[2] Cf. W. Wuellner on the cover of Norman Petersen's book "Rediscovering Paul" (1985).

[3] Already the fact that Paul's letters have been incorporated in the Canon in such a large collection indicates, that his thoughts have been seen as central for the Christian faith and Church. The end of Colossians (4,16) is interesting in this sense: If the letter is adjudged as authentic, viz. written with Paul's authorization (Schweizer 1976, 20–27; Hartman 1985, 200–201), even Paul himself saw his letters as possessing such a value. It is even possible that

occasions of the letters have served only as catalysts, which provoked Paul to formulate this universal theology. But what if the Paul so depicted was only a reflection of e.g. Augustine's or Luther's own ideology?[4] Obviously the temptation to take a stand for or against the traditional Protestant interpretation of Paul will bias any attempt to approach him without prejudice.

Oddly enough, the critical exegesis until recently supported this basic view. The scholars have assumed that although each letter has a context, its effect can be eliminated by historical and idea-historical explanations. A proper understanding of Paul required only a thorough historical study of the situation of each letter, combined with a systematic perspective. When the circumstances of the addressees and antagonists were recognized, and the situation of the apostle was identified, the scholars considered it possible to arrive at a better characterization of the deeper content and structure of Paul's thoughts. Such structures were worth seeking, since Paul was assessed as an eminent thinker and theologian.[5] However, exegetes have rarely been unanimous about the content of this theology.

The theology (or theologies) found in Paul's texts made him an authority in the eyes of the Church. In separate issues it was, of course, feasible to consider, whether the apostle was a child of his time,[6] but such exceptions only confirmed the rule. A scholar's critical attitude toward the apostle on minor points only made the central Pauline theology, as described by the same scholar, more valid for all ages.

Simultaneously, the emphasis on Paul's theology meant an unacceptable exaggeration of his historical position in Early Christianity. A glance at some important isagogical handbooks shows, that exegetes of this century have mostly seen the thoughts of Paul as the theological, and even historical, centre of the New Testament.[7] Other texts are commonly related to his writings; they

---

the apostle participated in the editing of the Corpus Paulinum (Trobisch 1989, 119–36 and Hartman 1986). At least soon afterwards some people thought so (Beker 1980, 356, referring to the "sound doctrine" of 1 Tim 1,10 and 2 Tim 4,13).

[4] A hallmark article in this discussion was Stendahl 1976 (first version published 1960).

[5] Räisänen (1987, 1–2) enumerates some amusing credits given by modern scholars to the apostle's philosophy and theology. On the other hand he, however, states that Paul is no longer regarded as a systematic thinker (1987, xi).

[6] Cf. e.g. the explanations in different commentaries on his rule on female preachers in 1 Cor 14,33b–36: Despite often contradictory arguments the hermeneutical result is always the same.

[7] See e.g. Köster 1980, 698–735.

are assessed as the post- or pseudopaulinic aftermath of the thinking of the apostle.[8] The works dealing directly with Pauline theology have the same tone.

The great studies of Paul also show what kind of religious, philosophical and ethical structures have been perceived in his letters. To mention but a few famous scholars, Albert Schweitzer[9] reads Paul as a mystic, Rudolf Bultmann searches for actualizing and normative theology in Pauline texts,[10] and Hans Conzelmann seeks a theological interpretation far beyond what the apostle actually says.[11] The borderline with hermeneutics is often blurred in such studies: Paul's ideas easily transcend the historical circumstances and thereby become important and binding even on "us". Bultmann rightly states that a scholar can never be without his own hermeneutical preoccupation: "In Wahrheit gibt es *keine neutrale Exegese.*"[12] But his solution is to make the unavoidable bias a virtue and an integral part of the scholarship.[13]

When reading these great exegetical thinkers one can hardly avoid the question: Whence do their theologies actually emerge? It may be naive to ask, whether the apostle himself would have approved of the theological and philosophical reflections which the scholars present as Pauline. Maybe this was not their task, perhaps they excavated unconscious theological principles? Schlier acknowledges the problem and therefore seeks to write not the theology of Paul, but only a Pauline theology.[14] We can, however, inquire, what is the relationship of these thoughts to documents produced by Paul, and whether they promote our understanding of their original purposes.

The answer is often negative. The "theologies of Paul" may well be religiously valuable, relevant, or poignant. But their connection to the Pauline texts is indistinct. Francis Watson has fittingly stated that, although it is

---

[8]   The Pauline orientation of New Testament exegesis is evident especially in the way people read non-Pauline texts therein. In his respectable commentary on 1 Peter L. Goppelt (1978) represents this ideology (for more on the Paulinistic fate of 1 Peter, see Elliott 1976, 243 and Thurén 1995b, 20, n. 23). 2 Peter is attacked more aggressively by Käsemann. His theological criticism (1964) is based on the notion that the letter falls short of the Pauline standards! The fate of the letter of James in the Western Churches and even in modern exegetics (see Thurén 1995a) is also enlightening. See the bitter comments by Donelson on the fate of the Pastorals, too (1986, 1–2.68).

[9]   Schweitzer 1930.

[10]   Bultmann 1951–52.

[11]   Conzelmann 1969.

[12]   Bultmann 1975, 258, his emphasis.

[13]   Bultmann 1975, 257–61.

[14]   Schlier 1981, 9–23.

legitimate to look for theology in the New Testament texts, the search can be shown in practice often to have led to misunderstanding.[15]

It would seem that the scholars only modified some traditional religious interpretations of the apostle or constructed alternatives to them. In the background, however, there is a similar view of Paul as *the* thinker of Christianity. His message has been conveyed in slightly different ways; it has served as a source of various religious principles. Exegetics has thereby been used as a tool to create different Paul-based, nobler forms of Christianity. Seen from afar, Käsemann, Bultmann, and Schweitzer represent the same tradition as Luther, Augustine, and Marcion.

## B. The "Contextual" Alternative

In recent decades there has been a new turn in Pauline scholarship.[16] American and South African exegetes in particular have been disappointed by traditional theological studies, and the scholarship has resorted to new methods. The focus has shifted from theology to the context of Paul, which however is seen in a much broader sense than earlier.

These scholars have emphasized that Paul wrote each of his letters for a specific purpose and a specific audience. He did not formulate his thoughts like Seneca for a broad audience among the upcoming generations.[17] It seems reasonable, that the occasion for writing was usually a practical exigency rather than theological or philosophical contemplation. The theology in the texts may simply reflect the occasional circumstances characterized by non-religious factors. On the other hand, in case of obviously religious matters, it has been emphasized that it is misleading to rationalize the intuitions of Paul, viz. make theology of them.[18] Scholars have therefore turned their attention to areas long neglected.

As a result of this new "contextual" preoccupation, it has become increasingly difficult to discern any timeless, general, or even coherent theology in the Pauline texts. The more we perceive the external and internal thrusts, which provoked the formulation of each letter and the thoughts therein, the harder it becomes to see those thoughts as universal or harmonious. Moreover, tensions

---

[15] Watson 1986, 180.

[16] See e.g. Dunn 1983; Beker 1980, 352–53 and Seifrid 1992, 2–3.

[17] Cf. Deissmann 1926; Beker 1980, 352–53.

[18] Thus already Andrews 1934, 37.

between and within the letters have gradually demolished the picture of Paul as a great theologian.

The interpretation of Romans illustrates this turn in Pauline scholarship. Whereas the earlier scholars assessed Romans as the testament or dogmatics of Paul,[19] and thereby as a sort of hermeneutical key-text of the New Testament, it is currently fashionable to speak of the liberation from a "Lutheran captivity" of the letter.[20] Exegetes are increasingly aware of the dynamic nature of the text: The apostle did not write to the Romans only in order to inform the addressees about his theology or dogmatics, but had a practical purpose. Whether this purpose was to prepare a mission to Hispania, to rehearse for negotiations in Jerusalem, to reunite the Jewish and Gentile Christian groups in Rome, or only to amend his poor reputation,[21] or a combination thereof, the contents and the theology expressed in the letter plausibly serve the goal.[22]

This new approach to Paul is not based on new historical information about the apostle. Instead, a change in the goals of the scholarship can be discerned. Moreover a new focus in the study of history yields these results.

The first difference involves the scholars' attitude to their material: they attempt to be more neutral. The goal is not so much as earlier to produce direct raw material for hermeneutics or to operate as godfathers of the Church, supporting or tearing down a religious system of dogmas. Instead, scholarship seeks to be descriptive and analytical. Traditional hermeneutical needs have been set aside. Thus, according to one position, we need no longer look to Paul for answers to, or even inspiration for solving, the central problems of humanity.[23] According to another opinion, Paul's thoughts could be utilized in the political and social discussion without a specific religious context.[24] Paul is then seen as a thinker, but not primarily a theologian.

---

[19] See Donfried 1991, xli. As recently as 1971, Kuss still held this view (1971, 163.202–203).

[20] Stendahl 1976; cf. also Stowers 1982, Watson 1986, 179–181; Elliott 1990, 292.

[21] Different explanations are presented in e.g. Elliott 1990, 21ff; Jervis 1991; Wedderburn 1991. See also Donfried (ed) 1991a and below, section II 3Aa.

[22] According to Boers, the letter is "as direct, and as hard-hitting, a moral confrontation as is Galatians" (1982, 194–95).

[23] Watson (1986, 181) poses a radical question: Should Paul's thoughts continue to serve as a major source of modern theological discussion? Most scholars however, dare not go this far, since they would thereby foul their own nest.

[24] Petzke 1975. E. Schüssler-Fiorenza (1988, 16–17) prefers to focus on the problems raised by liberation theology. Some modern South African scholars involve exegetics in the political discourse; see Botha 1994 and articles in Olbricht and Porter (eds.) 1996.

The second change involves the way of studying history, and thereby the context of Paul's writings. As in general historical studies, some scholars concentrate on circumstances, conventions, norms, and normal life, on sociological and psychological regularities, instead of on separate events and the history of ideas. The significance of such dimensions for Paul's thinking has been increasingly emphasized.

A typical new approach is sociological. Pauline theology is examined over against his social frame of reference, taking account of common social regularities.[25] It is characteristic to see Christianity as a typical Jewish reform movement, which gradually developed into a sect. Paul's thoughts were generated to meet the needs of this transformation.

This is claimed by e.g. F. Watson, who postulates that Paul's poor progress in the Jewish mission forced him to move to the Gentile mission. However, in order to succeed, he had to modify his product and make it more attractive. Therefore he changed his theology concerning the Torah. This, in turn, caused difficulties with the traditional theology. The development followed a typical pattern of how a sect is created.[26] One can only conclude that it was not based on ingenious theological thinking.

Watson does not thereby deny the existence of Pauline theology.[27] He claims only that theology was but a secondary phenomenon, tailored to meet practical needs. First there was a social demand, then Paul had to devise a theoretical, theological explanation as if to legitimize a solution, which he would propose in any case. E. P. Sanders arrives at a more psychological result, which however in this sense resembles that of Watson: First there was a solution (Christ is the saviour), then a plight was produced (the need for salvation by Christ).[28] This model also enables us to explain the inconsistencies in Paul's theological statements: since the social requirements for the message varied in different cities, so did the theology.

Most of the contextual approaches are sound and reasonable *per se*. But serious questions can be raised: Do they really help us to understand Paul? Do they provide us with an alternative to the older theological studies? Are they even in principle capable of so doing?

---

[25] Holmberg (1990) offers a good overview of sociological research into the New Testament.

[26] Watson 1986, 28–40.177–78.

[27] Watson 1986, 180–81.

[28] Sanders 1977, 474–511.

Some scholars again give a negative answer. They accuse such approaches to Pauline theology of "contextualism".[29] This signifies, that the thoughts and ideas of the apostle are explained solely from the "context"; thereby the real ideology /philosophy /theology is totally excluded. If Paul's thoughts and their structure can be wholly explained by contextual factors, their theoretical value is diminished so that they can hardly be discerned without the context. Thus the hermeneutical value of any essence in Paul is also lost.[30]

In fact, some of the "contextualist" exegetes actually do assess their own results in this way. Already in 1973 W.G. Doty could look back and say of Paul's ethics:

"One of the most important reclamation projects in the history of biblical research was the reclaiming of Paul as a situational or contextualist theologian and ethicist rather than as a dogmatic moralist... [He is] not an abstract thinker... but involved with his addressees in the process of dialogic piecing together of concrete ethical responses in each situation."[31]

In 1982 Hendricus Boers went one step further:[32]

"...Paul's writings are not products of theological reflection, and can thus not be interpreted theologically. There is no such thing as a theology of Paul, although many New Testament scholars have written "theologies" *based on* Paul. The letters individually and as a group do not have *theological* integrity. They are written from out of fundamental religious/pastoral concerns."[33]

The emergence of the contextual approaches means that scholarship has abandoned the assessment of Paul as a creator of great theological systems in favour of an emphasis on Paul as a pastor dealing with concrete questions, motivated by psychological and sociological factors. In current discussion it is reiterated *ad nauseam* that Paul was not a systematic theologian, since he had practical goals.[34] The study of his theology is even proclaimed "dangerous".[35]

---

[29] Cf. Scroggs 1988, 17.

[30] Scroggs 1988, 18–19.

[31] Doty 1973, 37.

[32] Cf. also Schlier 1981, 9.

[33] Boers 1982, 195 (his emphasis). According to Boers, there is no point in attempting to interrelate Paul's statements in the text, or to search for an implicit theology under the text. Paul's logic was mythical, and cannot be translated into "theological modes of thinking".

[34] See e.g. B.W. Longenecker 1996, 94–97; Tomson 1996, 258–70; Barclay 1996, 287–88.

[35] Longenecker 1996, 94.

But whereas the first alternative alienated from the historical Paul, the latter can be criticized for the opposite.[36] The joy of realizing that Paul wrote about practical situations seems to have overwhelmed the scholars. For the context, no matter how deep, broad, and well-known, always remains but one perspective on the text. I maintain that enthusiasm for a method often seems to have resulted in uncritical, biassed application of its results.

My first criticism of the contextual studies is practical: The scholars have too narrow a knowledge of the method utilized; they lack the necessary expertise. Therefore a modern model is often applied one-sidedly to the text so as to distort it. Only too often "the data have to give way for the model".[37] This can however be avoided by deeper studies of the method, and by a more meticulous application thereof.

The second comment concerns the limits of the approach and the historical dimension. When, for example, a sociological theory is applied, only sociological results can be expected. However, their significance for other questions and dimensions is difficult to determine. Although sociology seems adequately to explain the thoughts of Paul, nevertheless it cannot exclude or supersede results achieved by other perspectives.[38] In practice, it is difficult reliably to weigh the actual historical importance of the results of one method against those of another. How can we say, for example, whether Paul was driven by psychological or sociological factors rather than by theological reflections? One cannot directly jump from what the man writes to what he is.[39]

Thus, when we search for e.g. the origins of Paul's thoughts about the Torah, historical, sociological, psychological, or rhetorical[40] explanations – albeit valid and correct – do not alone suffice for understanding of his views and the

---

[36] Thus Witherington warns of replacing "a theological or ethical reductionism with a sociological reductionism" (1995, x).

[37] Holmberg 1990, 106 on Watson; cf. the criticism of J. Elliott's sociological analysis of 1 Peter (1981) by B. Olsson (1984).

[38] As an analogy we could imagine the cause of the Reformation in Sweden. This event can be explained from an economic perspective: The Hanseatic merchants in Lübeck had financed the revolution of Gustav Vasa, who was now deep in debt. When he heard of the new Lutheran Church order, which enabled him to use the properties of the Church to pay his debts, he decided to convert the state to Lutheranism (Grimm 1954, 241–43). Although this reasoning may be right *per se*, it hardly suffices to explain the whole Reformation in Sweden.

[39] Longenecker's argument is revealing: "...for Paul sees the issue to be not so much one concerning doctrine and right thinking *per se*; behind this presentation lies a more fundamental concern..." (1996, 94). Against this reasoning I claim that, first, we cannot conclude directly from Paul's words what he actually thinks, and second, we cannot easily measure which things were "more fundamental" for him. See also below section II4A.

[40] Cf. below section I 3B.

reasons why and how they were invented.[41] If Paul was prompted to give practical guidance, and yet wrote in surprisingly theological terms, compared with other NT authors, this can be interpreted in the opposite way, too.

This leads us to the third, most serious question, which concerns the type of argumentation used when theological inferences are derived from contextual studies. From the point of view of argumentation theory, such statements are *argumenta ad personam*.[42] It is simply false argumentation to judge a thought or ideology on the basis of the personal attributes, the history, or the situation of its advocate. The thoughts themselves must be studied.

In practice the situation is less serious: The modern contextual information can be used to fill the gaps in our knowledge. Yet it must be borne in mind that criticism of Paul's thinking can never be based on such grounds.

The shortcomings and exaggeration of some scholars should not, however, prompt us to understate or reject these methods. It is evident that – when utilized with proper sophistication – they enrich the picture of the historical Paul and the development of his thought. They help us to realize better than before that the apostle did not *write* timeless dogmatics, which could be systematized with some minor contextual corrections. Scholars should now perceive more than previously that Paul wrote his texts in complex, many-sided tensions of starting-points and goals.

This, however, by no means proves that the historical Paul *was* a contextual thinker without a clearly organized, coherent theology, or that he did not have a theology. It only suggests that when attempting to outline such a possible theology, more aspects ought to be considered with greater care.

## C. Back to Theology

The new contextual methods emerged in order to explain the motivation and background of theological thoughts occurring in the letters of Paul; the context of the apostle is clearer than before. But these alternative and additional models are of little help for *understanding the thoughts* of the apostle. However, especially the contents of his thought – irrespective of the context – have made him a target of constant interest and a source of theological inspiration. Paul

---

[41] In a similar way, a study of Wittgenstein's life and social circumstances undoubtedly adds an interesting perspective to his production. Yet it is hardly suited to a philosophical scrutiny thereof.

[42] For this type of fallacy, see Perelman 1969, 111–12.318; Toulmin, Rieke, and Janik 1984, 144–45.

has been studied throughout the ages because of the theology in his letters, irrespective of how and why it developed. The quality of the text itself is such as to invite this kind of interpretation. Therefore a separate goal of exegetical studies should be to clarify these theological ideas and the possible system behind them. The exegesis ought still to explain, under what conditions, and to what extent, it is possible to delineate coherent theological thoughts in his texts. From this perspective, the contextual factors are only of marginal interest – no matter how much we know about the circumstances in Paul's life, which possibly impinged on the development of his theology. Therefore we ought to proceed from the context to the text itself.

Then instead of asking, whether the theology of Paul was a secondary explanation of a religious experience or a product of social needs (the answer to this question is hard to control),[43] it is more important to discover on what grounds and to what extent is it possible to outline a coherent theology in his texts, and to determine its nature.[44]

This leads us to a fundamental question: What kind of Pauline theology should be studied? For the more the context is disregarded as suggested, the further from the historical Paul we proceed. In fact, there are at least three legitimate options: The theology of the historical Paul, the theology in the Pauline letters, and the theology emerging from the Pauline letters.[45]

a) It is difficult to study the theology of the *historical Paul*. Despite the diverse sources, it is astonishing, how much less critical the exegetes have been in this issue than when reconstructing the thoughts of the historical Jesus. The fact remains that we cannot enter the brains of the historical apostle in order to study his theology or his intentions. We only have his texts, which tell us what he seems to have wanted his addressees to think he thought[46] – and a feeling that the man is earnest and sincere.

We must also take into account, far more seriously than before, that Paul presumably did think and proclaim many ideas as central, but they were not so

---

[43] Beker 1980, 358.

[44] Cf. J.Becker's statement: "Bei aller Vielfalt paulinischer Äusserungen gibt es natürlich elementare Linien und Grundentscheide, die sich durchhalten, weil sie von einem gemeinsamen Denkansatz herkommen." (Becker 1989, 395).

[45] E.g. Wright believes that "Pauline theology" can be studied (1992, 1–4), but finds only two alternatives: historical exegesis and "serious constructive 'Pauline Theology'" (1992, 260).

[46] Cf. Scroggs 1988, 26–27.

controversial as to be featured in any of his letters.[47] As an example we may take the doctrine of God the Father/Creator.[48] This does not involve an underlying religious, non-argumentative logic suggested by Patte,[49] but ideas communicable and crucial in Paul's (possible) system of religious thought. It is surprising how little interest Paul's actual *theo*logy (Theo-logie in German) has attracked.[50]

Further, we do not know how fragmentary the canonized letter-corpus is, but this aspect too should be taken into account.[51] In any case, modern exegesis must discard a romanticized view, according to which the collection just happened to come together. It is more plausible that there were people who gathered and edited these texts,[52] and in so doing sought to convey a certain picture of the apostle.[53]

This means that it is – in principle – a mistake to speak of Paul's thoughts or intentions, if the historical apostle is meant. This is not mere pedantry. First, "the biblical Paul is not the historical Paul".[54] Second, even if we possess genuine, unchanged Pauline documents, it is important to realize that the author does not always think exactly along the lines which he would have his audience to believe. We as readers are targets of the author's rhetoric; it is difficult to stand aloof from the act of persuasion. The apostle does not stay as a calm object; he requires authority and easily causes reactions *pro* and *con*.

The historical Paul's thoughts can, however, be discerned fairly accurately behind his texts, since we also have some information on his life and career. If there is consistency between what he said and what he did, this might reveal more about his actual, historical theology.

---

[47] Seifrid (1992, 259) states that "everything that appears in the letters we possess is the result of Paul's selection of arguments from a broader range of possibilities, the extent of which we will never fully know", but does not regard this as a major obstacle.

[48] Cf. Dahl 1975; Beker 1980, 355–67. The de-theologizing, Christologizing tendency is obvious in e.g. many translations of Phil 2,11 – the closing phrases of the hymn are reversed so that it no longer ends with the glory of God the Father (see e.g. Gute Nachricht; Pyhä Raamattu 1938 and 1992; Bibelen 1978).

[49] Patte 1983, xvii. See closer below section I 2D.

[50] Moxnes 1980 and Wright 1992 are some exceptions.

[51] Cf. Beker 1980, 353.

[52] For the question of the editing of Corpus Paulinum, see Trobisch 1989 and footnote 3 in section I 2A above.

[53] Again, the studies of the Gospels have been more critical. Nobody takes them as biographies or neutral descriptions of Jesus' thoughts. The collection of Paul's letters provides us with more direct information, the historical integrity of which ought however also be more critically assessed.

[54] Trobisch 1989, 137.

It is also possible to grasp something about his "unwritten theology" because of an interesting but neglected source. Paul's letters often contain sentences, which are so condensed, that they are difficult to understand (e.g. Rom 1,3–4;[55] 1 Cor 15,56). The original context is missing. It may well be that such "kernel sentences" are summaries of Paul's (or somebody else's) teaching or tradition, of which we have too little knowledge. However, the doctrines or ideas mentioned were presumably so well known to the original addressees, that a short reference sufficed. By studying these 'tips of icebergs' one could approach even such teaching of Paul, as was not acute in any of the situations of his letters, but still important, even crucial, for him. Similarly, contemporary Jewish teaching, which does not contradict Paul's thoughts, might help us to discern his theology.

b) An alternative target is somewhat easier: To sketch a picture of the *theology in the Pauline letters* – or the theology of the author implicit in these texts.

According to many literary critics, any text lives its own life independent of its author. The text is not only an historical document, but 'speaks' to any reader, even beyond the original situation.[56] The text itself can contain ageless and profound claims, ideas, and structures of ideas, which can be reliably demonstrated and studied – irrespective of whether the author himself/herself ever consciously discussed them. In principle they can affect any reader – the original audience included. Particularly this literary character of Paul's letters has promoted their general acceptance, use, and canonization. Therefore it is not "wrong" to study the Pauline theology in his texts even if the historical Paul was never a systematic theologian. However, the interpreter should then realize and articulate what he/she is doing.

c) The previous perspective can then escalate into a third goal, to use Pauline texts as raw material and background for new theological ideas and systems. As such I would consider e.g. Schweitzer's or Bultmann's theological presentations. They are also feasible interpretations of the text, provided we bear in mind that they no longer represent the theology of the historical Paul, nor even

---

[55]  See Eskola 1992.
[56]  See e.g. Iser 1972; 1978. Concerning Paul see Scroggs 1988, 227–28.

the texts as historical documents.[57] At some point, however, the interpreter arrives at the limit: A text does not allow whatever interpretation.[58]

But already earlier, the limits of exegetics are transgressed and we have reached the realm of hermeneutics. Strictly speaking, the only controllable target for an exegetical scholar is to examine the theology in the texts. Such a study can offer material for hermeneutical considerations as well, but the primary goal is to discover what the texts – and the Paul of the texts – wanted to say, and whether there is a coherent theological system behind them, on the ideological level. Furthermore, inferences can be drawn and suggestions made about the thoughts of the historical Paul, insofar as these can be credibly reconstructed.

To sum up: Exegetics should also be used to verify on which of the three levels of Pauline interpretation each presentation operates. This may provide material for those who are interested in studying the thoughts of the historical Paul, that of one of his letters or a combination thereof, and thereby also yield new hermeneutical interpretations. The new interpretations and the exegetical study should, however, be clearly separated; *vestigia terrent*. In order to avoid producing only a reflection of the scholar's own personal theology, Paul's importance to modern churches or theology should be left intact. This principle, in turn, can enable exegetes to achieve a more neutral descriptive and analytical study of the Pauline letters. It could diminish the tendency to harmonize them or render them even less consistent. Instead, in a non-hermeneutical study we adopt a less biassed approach to the different themes, tensions and discrepancies, in order to arrive at a more reliable interpretation.

But despite the difficulties, it still is a matter of great interest, what the historical Paul thought, just as in the case of the historical Jesus. The goal of a such a theological study is to pursue a system of his religious thoughts beyond the texts and the acute situation. Knowing that Paul wrote his texts for concrete, pastoral situations, and that he attached great weight to religious experiences and mysticism, we may still assume that he indeed had an organized, coherent theological system of thoughts, which is partly reflected in his texts.

The actual letters, despite their pastoral purpose, do not imply that Paul was incapable of explaining his theological ideas; on the contrary. Compared with other New Testament authors his texts indicate highly theological thinking.

---

[57] Hartman (1993, 155) critically remarks: "But perhaps such theological reconstructions have a skeleton which is less Pauline than, let us say, a Lutheran reading of Heidegger. Paul is, however, made to provide the flesh – and its authority. Is such a freedom vis a vis the historical meaning permissible? If so, why? Or, if not, why?"

[58] See Eco 1990.

From the way the theology is applied in the letters it would be possible to delineate the ideological structure behind them. Although such structure was not necessarily complete, there is no reason to doubt that it existed.[59]

The "Nachwirkung" of his letters point in this direction, as confirmed by a comparison with other New Testament texts. There has never been similar interest in the theology of Peter or James. Paul really seems to have had a special interest in theological questions, and a tendency to theologize practical issues, to approach even practical questions from a theological point of view. Even in acute crises his response was usually theoretical and ideological.

Thus we can invert the picture: Instead of boldly alleging that Paul was not a theologian or dogmatician but simply reacted to practical situations, it is fairer to say that the theological nature of his reactions to practical situations reveals to us his tendency to think and formulate different issues in theological terms. In other words, Paul had such a passion for theology that it becomes visible in different situations.

## D. New Approaches to Pauline Theology

If the old solution, to reconstruct a great theology far removed from history, is abandoned, but we are still reluctant to accept the simplistic conclusion, viz. that Paul was opportunistic and changed his position and theology according to practical needs, what can be done instead? How do we find the theologian behind the mystic, the politician, and the pastor? Some scholars have again embarked on this enterprise. These new studies share with the contextual scholarship the search for descriptive neutrality, the fear of harmonization and ideologization. Yet the focus returns to the thoughts, viz. the theology, of the apostle.

a) One model for overcoming the tensions and perceiving some coherence in Paul's thoughts bifurcates the texts in a new way, compared with e.g. the old Bultmannian *kerygma-dogma* -division. Daniel Patte utilizes a structuralistic approach and arrives at a division between a system of convictions, viz. *convictional logic*, behind the text, and *argumentative logic*, viz. faith and

---

[59] According to Wright (1992, 263) Paul "is no less a theologian for being a tactician, a pragmatist, a rhetorician..."

theology.[60] This indicates that problems ensue when the differences between these universes are not observed. However, two objections can be raised.

First, just as is the case with Boers' idea of a mystical logic, or references to Paul's Semitic turn of mind,[61] which we as Western-educated people do not understand, we can against Patte's concept of convictional or mythical logic in Paul cite F. Siegert's analysis of Romans 9–11.[62] Siegert examines Paul's argumentation (not simply his logic)[63] by using Ch. Perelman's modern argumentation theory. It becomes evident that the argumentation technique in Paul closely corresponds to that of modern – *or* ancient Jewish – argumentation; there is in principle nothing specific or wrong with his "logic". This means that we cannot bury our problems by referring to an exotic mode of argumentation.

Second, as Hans Hübner has shown, there is no principal difference between Patte's solution and Bultmann's old scheme.[64] Nevertheless, Patte also offers many valuable notions, e.g. that Paul's vocabulary has different meanings in different contexts.[65]

b) J. Christiaan Beker also aims at a bifurcation, but seeks a more flexible version. He tries to define *contingent* and *coherent* material in the texts. He refers to a net of theological convictions and symbolic relations.[66] The unifying factor is an apocalyptic interpretation of the Christ-event; but Beker rejects the thought of any single concept, such as justification, as a key to the whole of Pauline theology.

The criticism which Beker levels against different "centers" of Pauline theology also applies to his own view of apocalypticism as a unifying factor. There is much material in Paul, which is not related to apocalypticism.[67] Even the division between the contingent and the coherent material is difficult to discern in practice, since clear guide-lines and definitions are lacking.

---

[60] Patte 1983, xvii; 12–29. According to him, "systems of convictions have their own logic, their own organization which we call *convictional logic* so as to distinguish it from the rational logic of an argument – which we call *argumentative logic*" (1983, 41, his emphasis). Patte also identifies convictional logic with mythical logic (1983, 366–67).

[61] Boers 1982, 195–96.

[62] Siegert 1985.

[63] On the difference between formal logic and theories concerning actual human argumentation see Thurén 1993, 470–77.

[64] Hübner 1987, 151–61.

[65] Patte 1983, 202.

[66] Beker 1980.

[67] Cf. Scroggs 1988, 20.

However, Beker has promoted the study of Pauline theology in many ways on the theoretical level, and many of his insights can be accepted.[68]

c) Hübner represents another solution to the tensions between the letters. According to him, the solution is a *development* of Pauline thinking.[69] It is not plausible that Paul's theology was fixed and immutable. Instead, he reflected his insights in practical situations. By focussing on the history of both the apostle himself and the circumstances of each letter we can see what situations invited Paul to theological progress. Hübner goes so far as to see Paul's gravity in his ability to be flexible and react to different situations.[70] Thereby e.g. the contentual tension between Galatians and Romans can be explained on historical grounds, viz. the progress in Paul's theology.[71]

But is Hübner making a virtue of necessity? What differentiates this image of Paul from an opportunist? Has not Hübner in fact portrayed a situational thinker after all? Was Paul ready to change everything in his theology in a similar way, or was there something constant?[72]

In principle the personal development of an author is reflected by his views, and there are clear signs thereof also in Paul's thoughts. This cannot, however, be used as an argument in evaluating the existing thoughts, since it builds only upon hypothetical and uncontrollable suggestions about the personal history of the apostle. In addition, as stated above, to explain central Pauline ideas in this way comes close to *argumentum ad personam*.[73] Just as in the case of scholars who refer to Paul's specific "logic", the problems are solved with a neat, but hypothetical explanation. And, according to Heikki Räisänen, even this does

---

[68] Thus Beker e.g. fittingly emphasizes that the structures of thought which we find behind Paul's texts must stay as close to the text level as possible. Otherwise they are not credible and useful for a practical study of the Pauline texts and thereby of all his thoughts (Beker 1980, 355).

[69] Becker (1989) correspondingly finds different phases in Pauline thinking: the emphasis varies from the early Anthiochian period to the Galatian and Roman periods. However, he rejects Hübner's thesis of real development (Becker 1989, 419): "Es hat auch wenig Sinn, zwischen Gal und Röm noch Spuren einer Entwicklung angezeigt zu sehen. Die Unterschiede bestehen wohl nur aus polemischen Akzenten, wie sie den Gal prägen, und Vertiefungen, wie sie der Röm enthält."

[70] Hübner 1993, 28–29.

[71] Hübner 1993, 233–34.

[72] For arguments against too heavy development, see Hengel and Schwemer 1997, 11–15.301–310.

[73] Cf. above the end of section I 2B.

not suffice: Paul did not change his views well enough, since the same tensions found between Galatians and Romans persist also within the latter.[74]

d) A fourth solution, presented by Räisänen, comes in principle close to Derrida's *deconstruction*.[75] He does not attempt to explain the tensions and discrepancies found in the Pauline texts. Instead, such difficulties are illustrated as clearly as possible. The purpose is not to show that Paul did not possess any theology, but to see it in a more realistic light.[76]

After pungent criticism of previous scholarship, and after identifying some sore points in the Pauline theology, Räisänen has however to surrender. The texts of Paul remain inconsistent and the theology vague, although some coherence can be found.[77] This solution has often been countered by referring to the difference between Paul's culture and ours. To find inconsistency and contradictions is said to result from too academic and theoretical a study.[78] This objection, however, is untenable, since corresponding criticism against Paul was levelled already by his contemporaries.[79]

Thus the possibility of identifying contradictory thinking in Paul has to be left open, but as a solution to problems of interpretation, it remains but a "last resort".[80] It is safer to leave a question unanswered than to harmonize the problematic sections, if a plausible answer is not found. Yet if we as interpreters do not understand the text, the fault is not necessarily in the text. We should also ask whether the obstacle is in the interpreter, viz. our own approach to the text.

Summing up, the very rise of new, "postmodern" theological approaches to Paul's theology indicates the importance of the topic. Scholars attempt to escape the unrealistic portraits offered by the older works, which prompted contextual studies through sheer frustration. But the new "theologies" have not completely succeeded, since the basic problem has not been solved.

I maintain that many of the current difficulties in understanding Paul are due to an unrealistic, *static* view of the nature of the texts, which is common to both

---

[74] Räisänen 1987, xvi–xviii.

[75] For applying deconstruction to the New Testament, see Seeley 1994.

[76] Räisänen 1987, 1–11.

[77] Räisänen 1987, 264ff.

[78] So e.g. Wright 1992, 4–7.

[79] See below section I 4. Further, to claim that certain amount of inconsistency is natural for Paul means that he indeed was only a situational thinker.

[80] Dunn 1985, 523; cf. Seifrid 1992, 70.

old and more recent methodology. Therefore, we ought to consider a dynamic aspect of his letters.

Chapter 3

# From a Static to a Dynamic View of Paul's Text

## A. Two Perspectives

It is characteristic both of the conventional, and of most of the new theological studies, to observe the Pauline texts as if they were a stock of material, from which diverse thoughts and conceptions can be derived. Paul expresses his thoughts and views to the addressees of his letters in various situations. Scholars think that by taking these situations into account, they can construct a total picture of what Paul thinks from what he says. As Lars Hartman says, "Theologians are tempted to regard Bible texts as boxes full of theology."[1]

Such a view reflects a one-way model for communication, in which the author has in mind certain thoughts, which he then delivers to the audience through the text. The author informs them. The role of the text in this model is *static*. When using this model, it is convenient to make ideological or theological summaries: The scholar selects a topic and gathers together relevant expressions from various texts by the author. When these thoughts are then matched by taking the context into account, viz. decontextualizing them,[2] the result is the actual theological view, which was in the mind of the author.

A static view is common to both a conservative and a more progressive way of reading Paul. Material can be produced for the analysis and the synthesis from comparable texts. What Paul says about something is totally equivalent to his view on the matter, be the opinion coherent or disjointed.[3]

Modern studies of language and communication do not regard this model as particularly useful. Like the idea of a "literary" translation, it simply does not

---

[1] Hartman 1993,127.

[2] Scroggs (1988, 18–19), however, expresses some doubts about such a procedure, but concedes that it is possible. See also Räisänen 1990, 88.

[3] Cf. Bultmann 1976, 39: "Wie er schreibt, so ist es gemeint." Cf. also Bultmann 1975, 254–57.

work in the real world.[4] Instead, scholars increasingly emphasize the pragmatic aspect.

In this model of communication, it is acknowledged that the author does not use the text only to *inform* the addressees about his opinions.[5] Instead, the goal is usually to *affect* the addressees, to provoke a response in them, and thereby to influence their thoughts and actions. The text thereby serves as a vehicle or tool, which should promote the goals as well as possible.

Within the medium chosen, diverse means are utilized. The ideological thoughts, the way they are presented, arranged, and emphasized are but a few. Other factors are often at least as important. For instance, the style can greatly affect the addressees' thoughts and emotions, and even serve as one of the predominant devices of a text.[6]

The text does not function as one-way communication. A more fitting term is *interaction*. For example, the different parts of the text affect the addressees envisaged by the author. This audience, in turn, affects the way the author can express himself in the parts of the text. Thus e.g. at the beginning of the letter he must be cautious and positive, in the end more outspoken.[7] Or since different letters, e.g. Romans and Galatians, had very different goals, even the theological utterances utilized vary.

According to F. Watson, modern exegesis in its search for theology has concentrated – wrongly – on what Paul says and not on what he does.[8] Watson focussed the social aspect of the apostle's career, but we could make the notion even more appropriate by incorporating the perspective of modern text-analysis and ask, what Paul does *in and by his texts*.[9]

The *performative* nature of the text becomes evident. According to the Speech Act theory,[10] the text not only contains a message, but also performs certain functions. The thoughts, even the theology expressed in the text, are but a means to attain this goal. This does not necessarily indicate that the theology

---

[4] See Breuer 1974; Warning 1975; Wuellner 1978, 8–11; Combrink 1996, 273–84. However, the change of paradigm, which occurred decades ago in Bible translation and general literary studies, has had little impact as yet on the study of Biblical theology.

[5] Or perhaps all his opinions are not revealed.

[6] See Thurén 1996, where I claim that the style actually is a major, maybe the main, issue in 2 Peter.

[7] See Thurén 1990, 40.53.

[8] See Watson 1986, 22; so also du Toit 1994, 403.

[9] Cf. Wright 1992, 8: "Scholars have often failed to think clearly about what precisely Paul is *doing* in any particular passage."

[10] See Austin 1976.

of the author is only a means. His goal may well also be to affect the theology of the addressees. Even such "theoretical" goals are possible.

By using theological ideas, like other devices, the author intends to complete the task which he has undertaken. We can also speak of a *volitional* aspect and ask, what is the author trying to achieve with the text, what is his actual aim.

In a text-book the level of dynamics may be low, and the persuasion covert. I maintain that the Pauline texts are essentially different, and refer not only to the effect of the context. Since Paul's communication was guided by efforts not only to present his religious ideas but also to use them in order to influence his audience, it is questionable, whether we can take his expressions at their face value. I am not referring only to simple misconceptions of a stylistic device as presented in the beginning of this study, but the whole text.

The goal of any of Paul's letters was hardly to let the addressees *know* what Paul thought or how he felt. Therefore we do not directly know what Paul thinks from what he says, nor can we easily draw a psychological portrait of him. What has been said above about a dynamic approach to any text applies also to Paul. Even his letters did not seek merely to make his addressees *believe* what he wanted them to believe about his thoughts. The eventual goal was far more practical: to persuade, to *modify* the addressees' thoughts, values, and behaviour. And in persuasion, almost everything is allowed.

If this can be demonstrated in Paul's texts, then the strategic goals and tactical moves confuse and exaggerate the thoughts presented, as compared with neutral description. There he, just like any other author, utilizes devices on different levels – e.g. *insinuatio* – to affect the addressees in the way designed. In front of another audience or in another situation he would express himself differently. Only when this is fully recognized, can we start looking for what he really means.

Therefore, an analysis of Paul's theological universe must be able to penetrate this rhetoric. No sound comparison between religious ideas presented in his texts or even different parts of a single letter can be made without a proper study of their function in the total persuasive strategy.

Such a dynamic approach to the theology of Paul does not necessarily solve the problems inherent in his texts; it is possible that the result is the opposite. Nevertheless, the study can be focussed on the real issues by eliminating misunderstandings, which are due to the interpreters' unduly static comprehension of the nature of the texts. This provides us with a more sensible basis.

Thus when searching for a theology, we must be aware that we are posing the "wrong question" to the text. We are reading it for another purpose than that for which it was originally written. We need a more realistic Pauline theology, but it is difficult indeed to ask a static question of a dynamic text. This is the heart of academic theology. Yet the difficulties inherent in the wrong questions should be recognized and considered.[11]

Therefore the study of the theology behind a text, and the scrutiny of the tensions therein require more than a contextual correction. We have to understand, for what purpose the author writes as he does, and how this purpose modifies his explicit "thoughts". Only thereby can we hope to discern any ideological pattern behind what is said.

In practice, the change from a static to a dynamic view of the text is less dramatic. Since the dynamic model is a very natural way of reading a letter, it has always been used to some degree, often unconsciously, when studying Paul, as the simple examples above referring to 1 Thess and 1 Cor demonstrate. This realization has not, however, sufficiently affected the theological interpretation of the letters.[12]

The studies which have already been done in this field give us a good start. Yet the task of examining the Pauline letters from a dynamic perspective in order to grasp the apostle's thoughts behind the texts is immense; it is a challenge for a wide, long-term exegetical project. As du Toit fittingly states, "much solid work has still to be done. In some respects we are only starting".[13]

To sum up, it is my thesis that Paul attempts to expresses himself purposefully in different situations, using certain theological *topoi* in the way he sees as most effective considering the final target.[14] Not only the situation or context, but especially the strategic goal of a letter affected the way in which Paul expressed his ideas. We have to admit, that Paul did not provide us with an objective presentation of his theology or ideas. 1 Thess 1,8 is not an exceptional phrase in Pauline writings. Instead, he typically presented his thoughts in the form which he adjudged the most suitable in order to influence and persuade his audience. Due to this goal-oriented point of departure, Paul's ideas seem to be

---

[11] For example, the parable of the rich man and Lazarus (Luke 16,19–31) does not directly provide us with material for deducing, what was Jesus' or the evangelist's view on heaven or the life after death (cf. Schweizer 1982, 173): "...weil sie nicht dogmatisch über das Jenseits belehren."

[12] Whereas some people are ready to disregard all theology in Paul's letters because of their situational character, others still use them as a static source of ideological or theological statements, viz. to find dogmatic structures or, if Paul proves to be very inconsistent, at least religious intuitions.

[13] Du Toit 1994, 403.

[14] In an important article Betz (1986) discusses Paul's own utterances about his relation to rhetoric. For discussion see below, section I 4B.

different even within the same letter.[15] This does not however indicate that he is an opportunist or even 'situational' as a thinker, or that he lacks a clear theology. For most authors do likewise. Whether or not the apostle was opportunistic depends on the degree to which he modifies his thoughts. The issue is crucial: How much did the dynamic nature of Paul's texts affect what he wrote?

## B. Some Approaches to Textual Dynamics

Before looking for indicators of the dynamic nature of Paul's writings, some words on methodology are necessary. In order to approach the function of a text, its parts, its thoughts and its vocabulary, controllable and solid methods are needed. Therefore we must resort to studies of the conventions of human communication and interaction, such as pragmatics, rhetoric, and argumentation analysis.

In New Testament exegesis these fields are rapidly growing, and we shall soon possess an abundance of e.g. rhetorical analyses of the Pauline letters.[16] Most of this literature seeks to identify contemporary rhetorical conventions therein. As such this enthusiasm indicates the rhetorical nature of Paul's texts.

However, these studies are often (rightly) seen as one of the contextual approaches,[17] which makes them problematic for our needs. We know that in antiquity the study of this field flourished in logic, rhetoric, and – what is specific for our goal – epistolography. The Hellenistic and even Jewish cultures were largely infiltrated by rhetoric. Certainly many expressions, tactical and strategic moves in Paul's texts can be explained by such contemporary customs. But ancient rhetoric is almost as good a tool for analyzing modern speeches, too. It is easy to study music,[18] art,[19] architecture, or advertisements and give Latin or Greek labels to features in them. This only demonstrates the universal

---

[15] E.g. the old "indicative-imperative" -pattern is a simple attempt to handle with Paul's tactical moves.

[16] For the literature up to 1993, see Watson and Hauser 1994, 178–202. Cf. also Porter 1997, 533–85.

[17] Scroggs 1988, 18.20, followed by Räisänen 1990, 87–88. To see rhetoric as dealing with the context is correct insofar as we speak of the historical, formal, low level or first-order rhetoric. The goal of such rhetorical criticism is to learn, what contemporary techniques and modes of expression the apostle used, and to identify them in the texts.

[18] See Albert Schweitzer's famous studies on J.S. Bach (1990; originally published 1908), where he also analyzes the rhetoric of Bach's works.

[19] See Carraci *et al.* 1990.

nature of conventions in communication, not an historical dependence on Quintilian or Cicero. Correspondingly, not every rhetorical feature in Paul's texts must be due to their cultural context.

Exegetics, however, does not need to rely solely on ancient material, since most rhetorical conventions are universal. Thus they need not be regarded as the context, viz. culture-bound "external" conventions. They belong to the text itself. In fact, in current scholarship also another type of rhetoric is utilized.[20] Standard rhetorical studies outside Biblical exegesis can be called general or second-order rhetoric. Its point of departure and goals are wider and it befits the task attributed to rhetoric above. When we search for the functions of different expressions, sections and thoughts in Paul's letters, both modern and ancient approaches to human communication and interaction can be utilized. The communication and interaction present in Paul's texts are examined *per se,* irrespective of the apostle's training, although it is interesting to find contemporary technical rhetorical terminology in his texts.

Thus rhetoric can be generally defined as the art of persuasion, where strategic and tactical devices are used to influence the audience. The consideration of the dynamic aspect when searching for the underlying system of thoughts therefore requires that the text be *de-rhetorized*. This means in short, that we must identify the persuasive devices in the text and to filter out their effect on the ideas expressed. Such derhetorization means that a rhetorical dimension is added to the contextual one. We are thereby aided to understand the theology / system of religious thoughts beneath the surface level.

Two specific areas in the study of persuasion, which have proven useful for New Testament exegesis are the modern *study of argumentation* and *epistolography*. Even argumentation analysis does not concentrate on the question, whether Paul represented a certain "rabbinic" or Hellenistic argumentation, but the argumentation *per se* is examined.[21] Proper argumentation analysis can reveal hidden, implicit premises and rules of decision, which are necessary for identifying the system of thoughts behind a text. Epistolography provides us with a tool for perceiving the formal conventions of letter-writing, which also affect Paul's mode of expression. These customs naturally guide the way in which the apostle expresses himself.

There is an increasing tendency to study the Pauline letters with the help of these three and corresponding approaches, but they have seldom been applied

---

[20] For discussion, see Porter 1993, 100–22; Thurén 1990, 42–64; 1993, 470 n. 24.

[21] See Thurén 1993. Thurén 1995b is the first full-scale analysis of the structure of argumentation in a Biblical text. It is also used to construct an ideological, viz. theological, system in 1 Peter.

to the understanding of his theology. On the contrary, rhetoric is still often seen as an alternative, albeit an exclusive one, to theology.[22]

## C. The Dynamic Nature of Paul's Writing

Returning to the question about the dynamics in Paul's texts, I claim that if his ideas are presented therein through heavy rhetoric, a comparison between different letters, and even parts of a single letter, may cause serious misinterpretations without a thorough derhetorization. The failure to recognize this phenomenon has, according to this assumption, caused unnecessary problems and blurred essential issues in modern exegesis.

To substantiate the thesis, evidence of the dynamic nature of Paul's writings needs to be demonstrated. Only then is it reasonable to discuss some crucial theological issues in his production. To assess the dynamic nature of Paul's texts, we start with his own confessions.

Sometimes Paul explicitly admits that the rhetorical, dynamic form of his speech also affects its content.

In 1 Cor 9,19–23 Paul explains: "I have become all things to all men so that by all possible means I might save some", and gives five examples of what he has become although he is not such: A slave to all men, a Jew to the Jews, having the law to those having the law, not having the law to people not having the law, weak to the weak.[23] This indicates a pragmatic attitude to behaviour and theology: the goal seems to be more important than the content. And indeed, Paul goes on to maintain that one should run in such a way as to obtain

---

[22] Thus Dunn (1996b, 315) wonders "to what extent, if at all, should we discount Paul's language [in Gal 2,11–14] as rhetoric?" and concludes that the dispute between Peter and Paul "is no mere rhetorical flourish". Similarly Hays (1996, 158), although identifying "considerable rhetorical power" in Paul, consoles us that "Paul is not merely employing cheap rhetorical tricks". The language of these scholars indicates an outdated view of rhetoric (see e.g. Botha 1988), although real problems between rhetoric and theology do exist; see below.

[23] Cf. Marshall 1987, 300–17. See also Richardson 1980 and Willis 1985. Mitchell (1991, 134 esp. n. 416) and Schrage (1995, 347) rightly claim that the expression "all things to all men" may have been formulated by Paul himself. However, it could *per se* be an extreme version of the accusation that he is a chameleon. The apologetic nature of the whole section 9,19–23 supports this interpretation (cf. Hurd 1965, 128 and Berger 1984, 361). Therefore it is natural to think, that Paul is defending himself against charges, as he does in 2 Cor (cf. Betz 1986, 40–47). Paul's only argument for saving his ethos is that his flexibility is well meant. This suffices to convince Mitchell (1991, 134) that there is no insinuation whatsoever in Paul. But is he applying some Hellenistic pattern? For this question, see below section I 4C.

the prize and not aimlessly (1 Cor 9,24.26), which can be taken as confirmation of this interpretation.

The same idea is reiterated later: "I try to please everybody in every way" (1 Cor 10,33). While this general principle is hardly confined to separate issues, it implies that Paul heavily adapts his behaviour, speech, and even theology to the audience.[24] He even recommends a somewhat similar attitude to his audience in Rom 14: One should abstain from one's own freedom from cultic rules in order to avoid hurting others.

In 1 Cor it is easy to discern, what this pragmatic adaptability meant for Paul. He explains that one should not eat meat, which is explicitly said to be sacrificial. Although the idols are artefacts, they are real demons for people who believe in them (1 Cor 10,15–33). Correct theological insights in this issue seem to be of little importance. Paul's practical flexibility and dynamics impel Conzelmann to expostulate that the Apostle's "thoughts tumble over each other" and that he is "seemingly" contradictory.[25] While having difficulty in perceiving a contradiction in 1 Cor 10,[26] I cannot deny that Paul's flexible principle here and in Rom 14 is in diametrical opposition to his intransigent attitude to cultic matters in Galatians!

Sometimes Paul admits explicitly that he uses heavy rhetoric. When describing his own communication, Paul can speak of the rhetorical technique of *immutatio vocis* (Gal 4,20) – modulation prompted by the desire to persuade.[27] He also reveals some of his tactics: In 2 Cor 7,8–12 Paul describes his risky rhetoric, which has succeeded: he has caused pain to Corinthians in order to win them. On the other hand, in 10,9–11, where he discusses the discrepancy between his epistolary and his oratorical presentation, he claims that he is not trying to frighten his addressees with his letters.

---

[24] Conzelmann (1975, 179) admits that 1 Cor 10,33 "has the same sort of opportunistic sound as 9:20–22", but rejects the idea because of "Paul's self-understanding as a whole". He also refers to Paul's own defense: Paul claims to have a good purpose in his flexibility. I do not find these arguments convincing: maybe they just affirm an opposite view of the Apostle's "self-understanding".

[25] Conzelmann (1975, 172–72) on the other hand, recognizes the strong rhetorical colour of the passage (1975, 174 n. 38).

[26] It is hard to believe, that Paul's argument is based on a division between gods and demons, which are also dangerous (as e.g. Lang 1986, 128 and Schrage 1995, 444–46 claim). Why would he then allow eating of all meat, unless it is specifically described as sacrificial (1 Cor 10,25–28)? More likely, the section is a non-theoretical explanation of the defects of sacrificial meat. Although the "weak" individuals are wrong in principle, their salvation is not to be jeopardized. Therefore Paul supports their position and reminds the "wise" that even they cannot totally master the situation.

[27] Cf. Lausberg 1960; Martin 1974.

In 1 Cor 14,16–17 Paul happens to reveal his pragmatic, functional view of praising the Lord. Praise is not merely a spontaneous expression directed to heaven; instead it has an immanent function: "If you are praising God [only] with your spirit... you may well be giving thanks enough, but the other man [who does not understand] is not edified". Thus at least one reason for praising God is to *influence the hearers.*[28]

But more than that, in the above quotations Paul explicitly acknowledges that he is not completely frank or even theologically solid in his texts. His practical goals override strict theological positions, and in order to win over the audience great flexibility is allowed. Sometimes he can deny such opportunism, but he can also accept the accusations and just say that he has a good purpose after all. If this is true, does not the theology of Paul need serious reconsideration?

There is even evidence that the practical goal and the devices utilized exerted too strong an influence on what and how Paul wrote. His message was sometimes misunderstood due to the excessive rhetoric. His search for persuasive effectiveness caused him constant problems. He often has to explain his words, which the audience misinterpreted because of their misunderstanding of his rhetoric.

First, in 1 Cor 5,9–13 Paul has to correct his unduly strong words about associating with sexually immoral people, which the addressees seem to have taken too literally.[29]

Second, one of the main problems in 1 Cor, that the addressees do not expect a resurrection of the dead, may have a similar origin: If Paul preached to them about baptism in the balanced way of Col 2,12 (baptism means death with Christ, but also resurrection with him) and the Corinthians took it too literally, he must now correct himself.[30] At least later, in Rom 6,3–4, the picture of baptism is no more in balance – instead of speaking of resurrection with Christ, Paul adds an exhortation to live in Christ.

---

[28] It is interesting to compare this attitude with Paul's own praise of God, especially in the opening sections of his letters. As part of typical *exordium* or letter-opening, praise has a pragmatic function even there.

[29] Fee, however, believes that there was no misunderstanding. Paul's opponents had only attempted to show how ridiculous the teaching of the Apostle was. (Fee 1987, 222).

[30] The Corinthians may have thought that the resurrection took place already at baptism, and should no more be expected. See below section II 3Ab and Cb.

Third, 2 Thess 2 may correct a misunderstanding based on Paul's rhetoric in 1 Thess: Some people seem to think that Jesus will come very soon, and now it is explained that this not what Paul meant.[31]

Fourth, there is a striking contrast between 1 Thess 1,8 (the example quoted in the beginning of this book) and 2 Thess 3,1: "Pray for us that the message of the Lord may spread rapidly and be honoured just as it was with you." Maybe the Thessalonians took his kind words at face value after all, which resulted in laxity, and Paul has to urge them to spread the message again.

These examples give us a glimpse of the characteristics of Paul's rhetoric: He is not only flexible in adapting his message; he also tends to exaggerate the message in order to make it more effective, to the extent that people take him too literally and thereby misunderstand him.

Paul was sometimes criticized for not being a proper rhetorician (2 Cor 10,10),[32] but was his rhetoric also condemned by his addressees as too insinuating, flexible or sophisticated?

2 Cor 1,13–18 reflects criticism of Paul's sincerity,[33] and on the basis of 2 Cor *in toto*, Betz suspects that Paul was accused of being "a sophist and fraud".[34] Gal 1,10 too, not to mention 1 Cor 9,22,[35] may imply doubt of Paul's sincerity.[36] Bruce enumerates many other sections, where Paul was "charged with altering his message to please his constituency".[37] Although none of these verses definitely prove such charges, they all point in the same direction. It would be odd, if Paul defended his sincerity on many occasions, if there were no accusations.

Finally, it is easy to recognize minor features where Paul uses exaggeration or understatement or otherwise lets the rhetoric colour his message. In most of these cases the influence of a dynamic attitude to communication is evident. Some of these verses have been taken too literally; such attempts to explain these natural flourishes as if they were ingenuous statements may be amusing, but sometimes also misleading.

---

[31] Cf. Bruce 1982, 164. The correction is not isagogically important, since it does not indicate who is correcting 1 Thess.

[32] "For they say, 'His letters are weighty and strong, but his bodily presence is weak, and his speech contemptible.'"

[33] Chadwick 1954/55, 262–63. According to Martin (1986, 19–20) Paul is here accused of deliberate obscurity or of saying the opposite of what he had in mind.

[34] Betz 1986, 40.

[35] See below section I 4.

[36] Thus Ridderbos 1953, 55–56; Guthrie 1973, 64; Longenecker 1990, 18. Betz (1979, 55–56) doubts this, saying: "not every rhetorical denial is an accusation turned around."

[37] Bruce 1982, 27: Rom 1,14; 1 Cor 4,1–4; 9,16.17; 15,9.10; Gal 1,15–17; 2,7–10.

These simple citations prompt us to search for more subtle, sophisticated rhetorical devices and modes of expression, which may have gone unnoticed and which thereby may have biassed our understanding of larger, theological issues, too. These examples are not to be confused with metaphors, like in Philemon 12 ("I am sending him – my heart – back to you").

"We *always* thank God for *all* of you, mentioning you in our prayers, we *continually* remember your work..." (1 Thess 1,2–3)[38]
"We worked *night and day* not to be a burden..." (1 Thess 2,9)
"*Night and day* we pray *exceedingly abundantly* that we may see you again" (1 Thess 3,10)[39]
"I *always* thank God for you" (1 Cor 1,4)
"I *constantly* remember you in my prayers *at all times*" (Rom 1,9–10)
"In *all* my prayers for *all* of you I *always* pray with joy" (Phil 1,4)

"You have been enriched *in every way* (1 Cor 1,5)[40]... you do not lack *any* spiritual gift (7)... I came to you... in much *trembling*" (2,3)
"*Everything* is permissible for me" (1 Cor 6,12)
"I praise you for remembering me in *everything* and for holding to the teachings *just as I passed them* on to you" (1 Cor 11,2)[41]
"I consider *everything*... σκύβαλα that I may gain Christ"[42] (Phil 3,8)

"I hear that... there are divisions among you, and *to some extent* I believe it" (1 Cor 11,18)[43]
"From now on we know *no one* κατὰ σάρκα" (2 Cor 5,16)

---

[38] O'Brien (1980, 56) clarifies this and many of the following explanations by claiming, that when saying "I always pray for you" Paul actually means: "I remember you in my regular times of prayer". I find the explanation artificial, as if we with the phrase "I am always thinking of you" really referred to certain standard times of remembrance. More likely, the expression is a (too) common exaggeration.

[39] According to Bruce (1982, 68–69) Paul "is fond of compounds expressing superlativeness".

[40] The rhetorically unconscious comments are whimsical: Conzelmann (1975, 26) explains that the expression "*naturally* must not be pressed", since the "motif is *of course* transformable according to the particular context" (my emphasis). Schrage (1991, 114) tells us not to put the expression "auf die Goldwaage", and Grosheide (1953, 26) would translate ἐν παντί "all that is here under discussion". It is more likely that Paul is here exaggerating and flattering his audience for the sake of *captatio benevolentiae*.

[41] Conzelmann (1975, 182), followed by Schrage (1995, 499) recognizes here a *captatio benevolentiae*.

[42] Elsewhere Paul assesses it as a privilege to be a Jew: Rom 9–11; 1 Cor 11,22. On "gaining Christ" Hawthorne (1983, 139–40) says that Paul is "somewhat caught in the web of his rhetoric".

[43] Grosheide (1953, 266) here finds nothing rhetorical, but ponders whether Paul's sources are less reliable than usual or whether he suspects the message due to its form. Lang (1986, 148) too takes the expression literally: Paul finds the message somewhat exaggerated. This is, however, hard to swallow in the light of 1 Cor 1,10–13, where Paul seems to take the information very seriously.

"I would like to learn *just one thing* of you" (Gal 3,2)[44]
"As long as the heir is a child, he is *in no respect* different from a slave" (Gal 4,1)[45]
"I will not venture to speak of *anything* expect what Christ has accomplished through me..."
(Rom 15,18)

"We wanted to give to you... even our *lives*" (1 Thess 2,8)
"You have all you want... you are kings... we have been made a spectacle for the whole
universe" – *see whole the 1 Cor 4,8–13*[46]
"In fact, you put up with anyone who enslaves you or exploits you or takes advantage of you
or lords it over you or slaps you in the face" (2 Cor 11,20)[47]
"You who abhor idols, do you rob temples?" *and three other questions* (Rom 2,21–23)[48]

Many of these statements occur in the beginning of the letters, in the *exordia*,
the rhetoric of which calls for a specific treatment.

Finally, we may glance at one of the first guides to the study of Pauline
theology, 2 Pet 3,16. The author states that people who are ἀμαθεῖς, unlearned
or uninstructed, easily distort Paul's thoughts, with fatal results. What kind of
instruction is meant? Is it "instruction in faith"[49], "traditional teaching"[50] or
"instruction, which gives steadfastness"[51]? Or does the author refer to one of the
most natural meanings of the word, namely basic instruction given at school?
In that case, he could well mean education in grammar and rhetoric. If the last
option is at least partly the case, 2 Pet 3,16 acknowledges the nature of Paul's

---

[44]  The expression has many ancient parallels, see Betz 1979, 132 n. 42.

[45]  Betz (1979,203) acknowledges that the expression is hyperbolic. Following him,
Longenecker (1990,162) states that it "is, *of course,* a hyperbole for the sake of the
illustration" (my emphasis).

[46]  Conzelmann 1975,87: "Paul resorts to irony." According to Schrage (1991, 331) the
section (6–13) is "rhetorisch sehr kunst- und wirkungsvoll".

[47]  The entire 2 Cor 11,16–12,10 has been widely recognized for its sophisticated rhetoric.
For an overview, see Martin 1986, 357–60.

[48]  According to Räisänen Paul here characterizes Judaism as a whole, but his "description
leaves, from the historical point of view, much to be desired" (1987, 98–101). This is an
example of rigid misreading of Paul's rhetoric as if it claimed to be objective description. In
the same way, we should read Jesus' corresponding utterance in Matt 7,3–5 ("Why do you
look at the speck of sawdust in your brother's eye and pay no attention *to the log in your own
eye*") as his sincere description of his listener's outlook. It is more likely that both Paul and
Jesus use hard metaphors in order to prick the audience's conscience. Paul's accusation
belongs to the rhetoric of a prosecutor, not of a judge. Dunn (1988,113–15) notices that the
section has perplexed many scholars and states: "It is the rhetorical flourish which constitutes
the exaggeration and it would be unlikely to mislead Paul's listeners", referring to several
ancient parallels. See further below, section II 4B.

[49]  Bauckham 1983, 331.

[50]  Kelly 1981, 373.

[51]  Reicke 1964, 183.

rhetoric, referring to inherent possibilities of misunderstanding. Then this statement serves as a warning against reading Paul with no or too little education and sense of rhetoric.

James 2,14–26 might well be another correction to a naive understanding of Paul's heavy rhetoric, where the conception 'faith' is misunderstood.[52]

To sum up, there are good reasons to believe that Paul was fluent in rhetoric and used many different devices, tactics and strategies. More important, he was also wont to allow his reason for writing and his persuasive goals to influence what and how he wrote. Sometimes this caused misunderstanding, which he must later correct, and even criticism. Traces of corresponding problems and attempts to resolve them can be found also in after-Pauline texts.

Thus, it is hardly surprising that later interpreters in Christian churches – and even modern exegetes – were led astray by the exceptionally dynamic nature of Paul's texts. This ought to make us more aware of his techniques and suspicious of rhetorical moves even where technical terminology is not utilized.

---

[52] However, since the section involves other problems, too, it deserves a more thorough discussion. See Thurén 1995a.

Chapter 4

# Was Paul Sincere?

## A. Questioning Paul's *Ethos*

The assessment of Paul's texts as dynamic gives rise to a difficult question: How should this recognition affect our own way of reading Paul? Disregarding the techniques of persuasion in minor details, which *per se* may mislead the reader, we still have to ask, whether they indicate a greater discrepancy between what Paul explicitly says and what he actually thinks or intends. Was the apostle honest and sincere? Or did he modify his thoughts – not only the mode of expression, but also the message and even the implicit theology – in order to meet the needs of the rhetorical exigency?

The dynamic nature of a text can be illustrated with a scale. At one extreme, we have an author who totally ignores the needs and expectations of his audience and states only the bare facts. At the other, the author deliberately adjusts everything he says to suit his readers, being ready to compromise his own position in order to gain acceptance or to provoke a desired reaction. Every author can be placed on this scale. Somewhere there is a point, after which the author can be assessed as unreliable and dishonest.

Thus our question is: where on the scale should Paul be placed? The question involves not only the interpretation of his theological statements, but a more intriguing issue, his general trustworthiness or *ethos*.

The question has seldom been stated. In 1939, W.L. Knox claimed that Paul was indeed opportunistic in his theology.[1] "Any system of thought and language that expressed the position of Jesus as the Lord was equally acceptable."[2] In practice this meant, that after recognizing the Palestinian version of Christianity as unconvincing to the Gentiles, Paul modified his theology in order to suit new requirements. This view resembles a modern sociological explanation for the

---

[1] Knox 1939; reprinted 1961.
[2] Knox 1939, 178.

development of Pauline theology by F. Watson,[3] remotely also Hübner's more theologically, viz. ideologically, oriented theory thereon.

However, although disastrous for Paul's reputation as a proper theologian, Knox's thesis does not *per se* postulate or even suggest that Paul was not sincere or "serious", as H. Chadwick rightly notes.[4] Chadwick himself comes closer to our question in an article about 1 Cor 9,22. He raises the question, whether the Apostle "was not so much concerned about the 'truth' of what he said, but only with 'gaining' his hearers". Chadwick refers to several verses indicating that such allegations were often made by Paul's opponents. Paul reacted strongly simply because the accusations contained "some element of truth".[5]

Chadwick seeks support for the thesis in Paul's statements on marriage in 1 Cor 7, on libertinism in 1 Cor 6, on *gnosis* and on spiritual gifts.[6] He concludes that "Paul had an astonishing elasticity of mind, and a flexibility in dealing with situations requiring delicate and ingenious treatment", reducing "to an apparent vanishing point the gulf between himself and his converts". Paul differs radically from the defenders of orthodoxy, who try to distance authentic Christianity from any sectarians.[7]

Chadwick adds, that his notions about the nature of Paul's thinking have far-reaching importance. However, perhaps due to the lack of suitable methodology in studying Paul's techniques of "gaining his hearers", Chadwick's thesis has had little effect on scholars, although it has not been convincingly refuted either.

Rhetorical criticism offers an accessible approach to the problem, as it is particularly concerned with how the "gaining" of the audience proceeds. However, if rhetoric remains on a "contextual" level, identifying ancient rhetorical techniques in the texts, it – like sociological criticism – avoids the core of the problem.

Many scholars actually limit the effect of rhetoric to this rather technical level. For instance J. Becker, when studying theology of Gal, uses rhetoric only for formal observations.[8] Yet it is interesting to note that Becker later assesses the situation of Gal as "emotionally loaded" and rightly states: "Wer Paulus

---

[3] Watson 1986.
[4] Chadwick 1954/55, 276.
[5] Chadwick 1954/55, 261–63; for the discussion, see above section I 3C.
[6] Chadwick 1954/55, 263–70.
[7] Chadwick 1954/55, 275.
[8] Becker 1989, 288–94.

verstehen will, muss also zwischen seinem Sachanliegen und seinen polemischen Attacken unterscheiden."[9]

It is even more difficult to make assessments on the emotional level. Does Paul show us his genuine feelings? What if in e.g. Galatians Paul deliberately portrayed a furious apostle by using the appropriate rhetorical devices?[10] If this is true, we cannot know, whether Paul actually was carried away by powerful emotions. Emotionally loaded expressions in no way prove that the author has lost control; on the contrary. But if Paul's theologically odd expressions have tactical goals, and if even his emotionally impressive statements are carefully calculated, rhetorical criticism reiterates the profound question already posed by Paul's antagonists: Is the man trustworthy at all?

The question means that, when seeking for Paul's theological insights, we have not adequately defined his relationship to persuasion by identifying rhetorical structures and devices, and trying to minimize their effect on the ideological content of the texts. We also need to grade the dynamics of his theology. If the man is too clever a rhetorician, his *ethos* comes under suspicion.

Especially in religious speech, the *ethos* is crucial. The conviction that the preacher earnestly believes in what he says is often more important than the content of a sermon. Whereas Paul has sometimes obviously been misunderstood because exaggerations were taken as his solemn beliefs, it is also fatal for his religious influence and theology, if he proves to be a sophist without any firm stance. If the man resembles a hero in a Hollywood film, who keeps an eye on his watch while passionately kissing a woman, who can trust him in deep religious matters?

The task of a critic is to see beyond the rhetorical moves of the author, not to be subject to them. But then again, there is also a risk of being over-critical: If Paul really was so serious that he almost went out of his mind, how should he have expressed himself in order not to pass as a mere rhetorician?

## B. Attempts to Save Paul's Reputation

The ideas that Paul was an opportunist or that he produced texts, which were excessively dynamic, can be refuted on the grounds that rhetoric was merely his tool, used for a limited purpose only. This would place him toward the simple

---

[9] Becker 1989, 321. Thereby he wants to solve theological problems, such as the tension between utterances about the Torah in Gal 3,19 and Rom 7,12.

[10] See below section II 2Aa. See also Thurén 1999.

and honest end of the scale, meaning that the grade of dynamics in his texts was low, provided his rhetoric is correctly understood. According to this position, the presentation of the plain truth was for Paul more important than the most effective persuasion, even though he honoured some basic rhetorical elements.[11]

Thus Schrage gives us an emphatic warning: "Eine der Sache und nicht der blossen Pragmatik und Funktion verplichtete *theologia crucis* ist denn doch noch etwas anderes als eine *theologia rhetorica...*"[12] But this outburst of the old theologian remains "mere rhetoric" as he adduces no arguments for the discussion between theology and the mode of its expression.[13]

More analytic argumentation for this opinion is provided by one of the fathers of rhetorical criticism, Betz, who also claims that Paul's maxim was: Rhetoric should never override theology. According to Betz, Paul rejects empty rhetoric in 1 Thess 2, mere persuasion and magical manipulation in Gal 1,10 and 5,7, and the latter also in 3,1; 4,7–8. Instead, Paul's argumentation is rational and presents the truth. Betz, however, admits that even such contradiction is a typical rhetorical device (*synkrisis*).[14]

The nature of Paul's rhetoric is discussed thoroughly, according to Betz, in 1 Cor. In 2,1–12 Paul distinguishes between the rhetoric of the most effective persuasion and the rhetoric demonstrating power and truth – a division known in ancient philosophical discussion.[15] For himself, Paul "clearly" chooses the latter. In 2 Cor 10–11, Paul defends his performance as a speaker: He is accused of lacking typical rhetorical virtues, of not being βαρύς and ἰσχυρός, but answers with marvelous sarcastic rhetoric, claiming to be a "layman of speech".[16] In the Letter of Reconciliation Paul however uses typical *protreptic* rhetoric, stating that his risky tactics have succeeded (2 Cor 2,3–9; 7,8–13).[17]

---

[11] Further, it would be natural, if especially the Canonical edition of his letters attempted to present his theology in such a manner, that they could be easily taken as binding on, and normative for, later Christianity.

[12] Schrage 1991, 81. He continues: "Einig ist man sich ohnehin darin, dass künstliche ManIriertheit, affekterregendes Raffinement, pathetische oder propagandistische Manipulation oder ein besonders an Stileleganz oder am Hörervergnügen orientiertes Interesse bei Paulus fehlen." Yet he does not deny the rhetorical character of the Pauline letters.

[13] Similarly, Mitternacht (1999, 290) and Kuula (1999, 33) fear that focusing on Paul's rhetoric when studying his theology may destroy proper criticism of the latter. My fear is different: it is dangerous to make compromises concerning any of the three ways (rhetoric, dialectic, grammar) in order to support some theological hypothesis.

[14] Betz 1986, 22–24.

[15] Betz 1986, 36.

[16] Betz 1986, 41–43.

[17] Betz 1986, 45.

Thus, according to Betz, Paul well knows the rhetorical techniques and traditions of his time,[18] yet clearly takes a stand against any persuasion which compromises the truth.

In my opinion, the arguments which Betz presents cannot be used in support of a low dynamic grade or great sincerity on Paul's part, on the contrary. For if a rhetorician says that he is not trying to cozen his audience, is he to be trusted? This is what he was trained to say. As stated above, the very fact that Paul needs so forcefully to deny the persuasive and dynamic nature of his texts and its effect on his message, seems suspicious. Just consider the following examples, some of which are found also in Betz:

> "By the appeal we make... we are not trying to trick you. On the contrary, we speak... not trying to please men but God... You know we never used flattery" (1 Thess 2,3–5)[19]
> "Christ did not send me to preach... with wisdom of words" (1 Cor 1,17; cf. also 18–25)
> "When I came to you, brothers, I did not come to proclaim with eloquence... My message and my preaching were not with wise and persuasive words" (1 Cor 2,1.4)[20]
> "We are not writing to you anything different from what you read or from what you can recognize" (2 Cor 1,13)[21]
> "We are not καπηλεύοντες[22] God's message... but we speak with sincerity" (2 Cor 2,17)
> "I may not be a trained speaker" (2 Cor 11,6; cf. also the accusation in 10,10).[23]

Why does Paul emphasize, in different situations, the simple, frank, un-rhetorical nature of his presentation? Sometimes he claims not to be an orator at all, and where this would be too hard to believe, at least says that his texts include no *insinuatio* whatsoever.

---

[18] In his commentary on Galatians (1979), Betz himself however seems to know only the judicial rhetoric of the handbooks.

[19] Bruce (1982, 26–27) explains, that due to "so many wandering charlatans" Paul had to emphasize his integrity, and that he was frequently accused of opportunism, yet there was no reason for suspicion. Cf. also Morris 1959, 70–74 and Holtz 1986, 69–77.

[20] I find it difficult to follow Schrage (1991, 224–27.231–36), who like Betz (1986, 36–38) argues that Paul here takes a stand in a discussion about the type of rhetoric appropriate in religious matters. What orator would admit that he is using persuasive rhetoric? Yet Betz and Schrage do not deny the rhetorical character of Paul's statement, whereas other scholars naively accept Paul's claim. Thus e.g. Lang (1986, 35–37) affirms: "Paulus vertraute bei seine Predigt auf die Kraft des Wortes vom Kreuz, das keine Unterstützung durch rhetorische oder philosophische Kunstgriffe bedarf."

[21] See Chadwick 1954/55, 262–63; Martin 1986, 19–20, and above section I 3C.

[22] The verb is *hapax Novi Testamenti*; it means an adulteration of the product in order to make a better profit. See Martin 1986, 49–50.

[23] Martin (1986, 342–43) wonders, whether Paul is here talking "tongue-in-cheek"; for a more thorough rhetorical analysis, see Forbes 1986. Earlier the verse was thought to refer to Gnosticism (Bultmann 1976, 205) or other far-fetched issues (see Martin 1986, 343).

Paul's claims hardly deal only with rhetoric in the technical sense. Probably the major issue is exactly what we are interested in: To what degree does the persuasive goal affect the way in which theological issues are presented? Paul emphasizes that – contrary to his opponents' – the success of his message does not depend on its form but on the power of God. While the latter is beyond the scope of our methodology, we have to examine the former.

The undermining of rhetorical capability or willingness to use standard conventions of communication must have a function in Paul's texts. I cannot help thinking, that denial of rhetorical tactics even in Paul is but a simple, common rhetorical device. A natural explanation is that an audience tends to be suspicious of rhetoric, or that they have too often noticed his techniques, or even that he has been criticized for them.[24]

In many instances we have witnessed the apostle's special interest in rhetoric, e.g. his habit of using perplexing exaggeration. In general, modern scholars could demonstrate the use of typical devices and ancient rhetorical terminology in his texts. Therefore, it is plausible that at least some of the original readers, not only Paul's antagonists, did the same. While manifest rhetoric does not work, Paul needs to guard himself[25] and tone down his oratory, as the opposite anti-rhetorical examples show. Paul does not want to lose his ethos nor allow his essential message to be explained away. Therefore he claims that not everything he writes is mere rhetoric.

## C. Adapting a General Pattern?

1 Cor 9,19–23 is the most explicit expression of Paul's flexibility. Modern scholars have attempted to excavate a possible Jewish[26] or Hellenistic[27] background to these annoying words, which would indicate that he was following a standard pattern. The interpretations of the Early Church Fathers discussed by Mitchell are especially interesting.[28] Tertullian, Clement of

---

[24] See above section I 3C.

[25] For another means of keeping rhetoric effective in the eyes of readers aware of standard eloquence, see Thurén 1995a.

[26] Daube 1956, 336–49.

[27] Mitchell refers to the Odysseus legend (Malherbe 1989, 91–119), friendship-conventions (Marshall 1987, 70–90; 306–17), Cynic-Stoic arguments about true freedom (Vollenweider 1989, 199–232), the Proteus legend (Vollenweider 1989, 216–220), a slave leader as a topos (Martin 1990, 86–116), political commonplaces (Mitchell 1991) and Epicurean psychagogic theory (Glad 1995).

[28] Mitchell 2000.

Alexandria, Origen, and John Chrysostom all claim that Paul is following a contemporary custom of adaptation, and even more, a divine pattern of condescension. Thereby Paul imitates the Christ of Phil 2,6–11.[29]

The problem with these witnesses is that, as Mitchell acknowledges, they are making a virtue of a necessity.[30] The Church Fathers could not tolerate an inconsistent and opportunistic Paul. Thus they eagerly defended him against charges of flattery and inconsistency, inverting the charges to a divine pattern of behavior – thereby confirming that such charges did exist! But we do not use Philo as a reliable historical source for the theology of early Israel, since we know that he attempts to explain away anthropomorphisms. Why should we pay more attention to the testimony of the Fathers, who had a corresponding tendency?

The tactics of the Fathers are merely the *status definitionis* of Roman court rhetoric. When the charges cannot be denied, and particularly when the accused has confessed to his behaviour, the defense has to give it another, more acceptable name.[31] But as historical witnesses, the Fathers are biased. And indeed, it seems to be far-fetched to compare the incarnation of Christ in Phil with Paul's case: Christ was hardly accused of opportunism!

A similar problem is inherent in the other 'backgrounds' or 'patterns' presented. They all fit into the same *status*. Thereby scholars rename Paul's behavior and make it seem more acceptable. Thus Mitchell commends Glad for "naming the overall topic more broadly as adaptability, rather than demagoguery or flattery".[32]

It is valuable *per se* to demonstrate that in different Hellenistic traditions great flexibility was allowed for a good purpose. Indeed Paul was perhaps influenced by such thinking. But corresponding references could be made to modern persuasion, too. The different traditions demonstrate little more than the general dynamic nature of human communication.

We cannot however avoid the practical problem at hand: Modern theologians are not alone in wrestling with Paul's "inconsistent" utterances. Not all Paul's original addressees were satisfied with his flexibility either. And, instead of *definitionis*, Paul himself chose another *status*, that of *qualitatis:*[33] He admitted the behaviour with which he was charged, and did not even try to

---

[29] Mitchell 2000.
[30] Mitchell 2000.
[31] Cf. Martin 1974, 32–36.
[32] Mitchell 2000.
[33] Martin 1974, 36–41.

redefine it. He could only argue that he had a good purpose. But does this *status* actually increase his theological ethos?

## D. Against the Wind

Although the above quotations hardly go to prove Paul's sincerity, it is nevertheless possible that the Apostle saw himself as honest with his audience. Actually, speaking of *ethos* and *pathos*, the two alternatives – an orator manipulating the feelings of his audience and a speaker openly and passionately proclaiming his message – do not exclude each other. First, the limit is blurred: an orator can consciously arouse himself to express genuine feelings. Second, even sincere emotions can be verbalized in conventional ways, which have been thoroughly learnt.

I begin with the extreme, and simple, charge brought by Chadwick. According to him, Paul was almost a "weathercock" trying to please his audience. Therefore, Paul did not seek confrontation.[34] However, is not this exactly what he does in the beginning of Galatians?

Paul first uses a for him unusual rhetorical technique of beginning a speech,[35] blaming his audience from the outset ("I am astonished that you are so quickly deserting him who called you in the grace of Christ and turning to a different gospel" Gal 1,6). Then he goes on to curse the antagonists, who were not theologically so far away from his own views.[36] Finally Paul expostulates:

"Am I *now* trying to win the approval (πείθω) of men... Or am I trying to please men? If I were *still* trying to please men, I would not be a servant of Christ." (Gal 1,10)

Contrary to Betz, I cannot regard this outburst as a philosophical statement in a discussion of two types of rhetoric.[37] Instead, two facts about Paul's own attitude can be inferred.

First, Paul indirectly admits having sometimes used highly persuasive rhetoric, modifying his message – even the contents thereof – in order to make

---

[34] This is what Chadwick (1954/55, 275) claims when contrasting Paul with people, who close the door to deviationist sects "with all firmness".

[35] See further Thurén 1999.

[36] "If anyone is proclaiming to you a gospel contrary to that which you have received, let him be accursed" (Gal 1,9).

[37] Betz 1986, esp. p. 23–24. Cf. 1 Cor 2,1.4 discussed above in section I 4B.

it more effective.[38] Even if the statement does refer to his antagonists' accusations,[39] he does not totally reject them.

Second, Paul claims that he has defined for himself the limitations of rhetorical dynamics. In many cases he can be a Jew to a Jew and a Greek to a Greek (1 Cor 9,20–21), but in the case discussed in Galatians such an adaptability would jeopardize his whole mission. Or so he would have his readers think.

Thus it seems, that Paul's habit of going to extremes in order to win the addressees' favour and a "meeting of minds" for the upcoming persuasion, does not *per se* signify an opportunistic attitude. Instead, Paul's usual *captatio benevolentiae* serves as a useful tool, which he may in some instances reject. He can also become unexpectedly "irate" with his audience when necessary.

The example in Galatians indicates that Paul did not want merely to please his audience. Instead, he used rhetoric as a means to win them over. He could dramatize the situation in order to incite his hearers. He attempted to widen the gap between the addressees' slightly inappropriate thoughts and his own convictions. Such a technique is seldom used in rhetoric; it is a risky, but effective means of persuasion.[40] But is it ethical to pretend to be angry in order to play on the emotions of the audience?

## E. Sincerity behind the Rhetoric?

Although Paul does not always flatter his audience, this does not prove that he is sincere in his texts. Whereas cases, where Paul denies the use of rhetoric are not particularly convincing, he would make a more favorable impression, if he claimed that he is sincere, yet simultaneously utilized rhetoric openly in order to persuade.

In order to find such comments, we can look for theologically extreme statements, which Paul seems to use as an ultimate means of persuasion, and for his sore points. One could assume that at least on such edges, or limits of dynamics, Paul lays his cards on the table, viz. presents more than rhetorical

---

[38]   Cf. Ridderbos 1953, 55.56 n. 6, according to whom Paul ironically refers to the preceding verses; opposed by Betz 1979, 56, who claims that Paul refers to his pre-Christian life. However, if Paul was criticized for his rhetoric, and he even admits being rather flexible in many cases, it is likely that he here draws the line on that custom.

[39]   See Ridderbos 1953, 55–56; Guthrie 1973, 64; Longenecker 1990, 18. Betz (1979, 55–56) doubts this, stating that "not every rhetorical denial is an accusation turned around".

[40]   See Thurén 1995a, 283–84; 1998a.

figures. Thereby these would be especially interesting for assessment of the overall sincerity of the apostle, indicating that at least sometimes Paul says what he thinks. This is important, since an ideological structure is worth studying only if there are stable principles.

These requirements are met, when Paul discusses one of the most painful issues for him, the fate of Israel, in Rom 9,1–3:

> "I speak the truth in Christ, I do not lie, my conscience bearing witness in the Holy Spirit... for I could pray that I myself be accursed (ἀνάθεμα)..."

The solemn words convey the impression that the apostle is speaking from his heart. If he is ever to be taken seriously, this is one such occasion. He even risks his own relationship to God in order to convince the addressees of his sincerity.

Yet the rhetorical devices and conventions are openly displayed. According to Dunn, conjunctions are omitted in order that the sentences might be read slowly and solemnly, the double feminine nouns with a similar ending are chosen for aesthetical reasons,[41] the antithetical style and the additional phrases "in Christ" and "in the Holy Spirit" are designed to give extra weight.[42] Rhetoric is thus fully utilized, yet there is no sign that Paul is not deadly serious. On the contrary, the good rhetoric emphasizes that Paul wants to make his opinion absolutely clear because of the importance of the issue.[43]

Similar, albeit less extreme solemn oath formulas can be found – although in fewer words – in many places in the Corpus Paulinum. The rabbis normally abstained from referring to God in such a manner; thus these expressions may have been weighty for Paul:[44]

| | |
|---|---|
| 1 Thess 2,5.10 | "God is our witness"[45] |
| Phil 1,8 | "God is my witness" |

---

[41] Dunn 1988, 522–23.

[42] Dunn 1988,530–31.

[43] I cannot follow Michel (1978, 292), who in v. 2 sees "rhetorische Absicht" and "persönliche Ergriffenheit" as mutually exclusive alternatives.

[44] Billerbeck 1922, 330–32; 1926, 26; cf. also Michel 1978, 81; Hawthorne 1983, 24. Dunn (1988, 28) finds an oath referring to God also in T. Levi 19,3 and Josephus, De Bello 1.595, whereas Martin (1986, 34) discovers this custom only in the OT.

[45] Simultaneously (1 Thess 2,3) Paul affirms that he is not trying to cozen the addressees, which at least partly is a rhetorical trick (see above). However, the appeal to God refers directly to the claim of not being greedy, which was an important issue for Paul. This combination of rhetorical manipulation and sincere statement resembles 2 Cor 12,2–7.

| Rom 1,9 | "God, whom I serve with my spirit, is my witness"[46] |
| 2 Cor 1,23 | "I call God as my witness" |
| 2 Cor 11,31 | "The God and Father of the Lord Jesus, who is to be praised forever, knows that I am not lying"[47] |
| Gal 1,20 | "I assure you before God that what I am writing you is no lie" |

When the formula was used later (1 Tim 2,7), the divine aspect of the oath was omitted:[48] "I am telling the truth, I am not lying"

There is also the interesting claim in 2 Cor 11,10, where not his faith, but his personal pride – another sore point in Paul – is placed in question:[49]

"As surely as the truth of Christ is in me, nobody in the regions of Achaia will stop this boasting of mine."

In these expressions Paul goes to the limit at some points when affirming his sincerity. He swears to God, calling Him as witness and stakes his own relationship to Christ. This tone verges on blasphemy, when Paul in Gal 1,8 exclaims:

"But even if we or an angel from heaven should preach a gospel other than the one we preached to you, let him be accursed (ἀνάθεμα)."

Since Paul here first proclaims a conditional curse on himself, it is difficult to follow Longenecker, according to whom the second cursing of an angel from heaven is ironic, denoting Judaizers referring to the apostles in Jerusalem.[50] Betz is equally far off the mark in maintaining as "virtually certain" that the

---

[46] Dunn feels that the style here is awkward and sincere, instead of being "conscious rhetorical art" (1988, 27). But if an awkward style sounds sincere, it serves well its rhetorical purpose. Cf. the pompous style of 2 Peter (Thurén 1996).

[47] Bultmann 1951–52, 219.

[48] Cf. Dibelius and Conzelmann 1972, 43.

[49] Martin (1986, 347–48) finds the word 'boasting' ironical, and Forbes (1986, 20), referring to ancient rhetorical conventions, argues that Paul's ironical boasting is quite different: actual self-praise (which is meant to be taken seriously) was totally forbidden. Nevertheless Paul *is* boasting. I regard the ironical style partly as a means of *praeteritio*, as is evident in 2 Cor 12,6: I refrain from telling you that I have had great visions... This device is used when the speaker definitely wants to say something despite the circumstances. Irony is then a typical feature. See Lausberg 1960, § 882–86. Forbes (1986, 21) and Martin fall victim to this device: "The third person is a means of reflecting his embarrassment (or reluctance) at boasting of what he has done..." (Martin 1986,398). See also below.

[50] Longenecker 1990, 17.

Apostle refers to common "angelic revelations".[51] The rhetorical effectiveness requires an escalating structure: It would be odd if Paul first (conditionally) cursed himself, but then went on to refer to some hazy angelophanies, which do not need to be taken seriously.

The escalating structure of the parallel Gal 4,14 is more natural: "You welcomed me as God's angel, as Christ Jesus." Correspondingly, in 1,8 Paul seems to regard the cursing of an angel from heaven as even more dreadful (and for persuading the addressees, more effective) than cursing himself. Why? While God's angel in 4,14 is well nigh identified with Christ, the angel from Heaven in 1,8 is hardly a satanic phenomenon, but a representative of the Lord. Or even more, it is used as a way of avoiding a direct blasphemy as in 1 Cor 12,3: "No one speaking in God's spirit can say 'Jesus be cursed (ἀνάθεμα)'."

To speak of angels in order to circumvent God's name is typical of Early Christianity, as a comparison between Matt 10,32 and Luke 12,8 demonstrates.[52] Paul is so certain about his Gospel, that not even God Himself can change it. Thereby the two expressions in Gal 1,8 become parallel: If the real Gospel proves to differ from Paul's version, he is cursed on two grounds. One could hardly imagine more telling ways for Paul to emphasize his message. If the facts he thereby preaches are not true, little remains of his religion.

The above quotations show, that also in his texts Paul was ready to venture all when fighting for his cause. Cursing himself or Christ can hardly be only an insinuating device. Yet his habit of (over)using rhetoric is not denied.

But how does this sincerity on some extreme occasions relate to Paul's use of rhetorical tricks and manipulation of the addressees' thoughts and feelings? The above quotations, albeit well designed, still seem to be straightforward. Yet we have elsewhere seen more insidious sayings by Paul. It would be good to see him combine both aspects: heavy rhetoric, which cannot be taken literally, and heavy theology, which is meant to be the exact truth.

This is actually done in 2 Cor 12,2–7. First Paul boasts about "a man caught up in third heaven", and *not* about himself. Then in 6–7 he then continues:

> "Even if I should choose to boast, I would not be foolish, for I would speak the truth. But I abstain so that no one will think more of me than what he sees in me or hears from me, even the extraordinary revelations."

---

[51] Betz 1979, 33.

[52] According to Luke, The Son of Man will acknowledge people before God's angels. This hardly means that the angels are seen as higher as the Son of Man. More naturally, Luke here avoids uttering God's name, as does Matthew. Cf. Dalman 1930,171–72.

It seems clear that Paul is portraying himself, yet he explicitly denies it (5). The problem is not only that he speaks in the third person à la Caesar in *De Bello Gallico*. Paul is *explicitly lying* to his addressees. The contrast becomes even sharper, when Paul in verse 6 adds one of his oaths: "I speak the truth." Many theological and psychological suggestions have been made to explain, why Paul does so.[53]

However, here we have a simple *praeteritio* (I refrain from saying that...), and it is difficult to believe that Paul's audience felt that the apostle had deluded them, when they realized to whom he referred. As in any *praeteritio*, the use of the rhetorical device is so obvious.

To be sure, what Paul actually affirms when claiming to speak the truth is not the identity of the mystic. Instead he refers to the reality of his own experiences, and in the light of the whole letter, to his message in general. He seeks to distinguish himself from his antagonists, who are labeled as unreliable.

The interesting feature in this passage is that Paul openly combines manipulation of the addressees by rhetorical devices with the claim that he is an honest and sincere preacher. Yet no sensible reader was expected to find this contradictory. For a person with a natural, dynamic attitude to the text, these phenomena simply represent two distinct dimensions of communication.

The issue becomes problematic only when the texts are studied from the 'wrong' perspective, viz. the modern way of seeking theology in Paul, where his utterances are tacitly equated with paragraphs in a lawbook.[54]

Another important means of investigating Paul's *ethos* is to study the coherence between his life and his teachings. Without going deeper into this vast area, we can state that the apostle obviously did not spare himself when working for what he adjudged to be right. In his mission, the man was eager and serious. He used the rest of his life to promote his message.

But in being so eager, Paul allowed himself a full use of rhetorical *insinuatio*, tactics and strategy – he manipulated his addressees with the best means available in order to reach his goal. Even Luke's description of Paul's insidious speech before the Council in Jerusalem (Acts 23,6–9) is well suited the picture, as it is surprisingly different from that of Stephen (Acts 7).[55]

---

[53] For an overview, see Martin 1986, 398–400. Heckel (1993) provides a thorough study of the section 2 Cor 10–13.

[54] However, as we have witnessed, even some of his contemporary readers took too much at face value.

[55] Luke probably has tactical reasons for presenting the two men in such different ways, which cannot be discussed here. But the close correspondence of the Paul portrayed above with that of Acts 23 is interesting.

Paul's use of rhetoric – when it succeeded – did not jeopardize his *ethos* in the eyes of most of the original addressees. They were simply guided in the direction intended by the Apostle, although some of the techniques were glaringly obvious. Only occasionally did the techniques fail, or were criticized by Paul's antagonists.

Obviously many of his original addressees interpreted his techniques in a positive light, since the letters were generally accepted and even later canonized. It is my claim that these readers understood the dynamic character of Paul's texts. This was possible, since after all, the rhetoric he used was conventional.

Yet Paul's rhetoric is problematic for us, who cannot identify with the original rhetorical situation in these texts. When wanting to be analytical, when attempting to understand the communication and interaction in the texts objectively, when seeking the theology beyond the texts, we do not wish to submit to the original manipulation. Thus the gap between us and the original audience is not merely apparent; the main difference consists in our attitude to the text. If already the Corinthian readers sometimes misunderstood Paul's rhetoric, how much greater (*qal wachomer*) is the risk for us!

There is no reason to suspect that Paul was dishonest or compromised his theology for the sake of maximal rhetorical impact. He believed that he had received both his message, and the injunction to proclaim it, in a revelation from Jesus Christ. This Gospel may not be altered. Despite all the heavy rhetoric, or perhaps because of it, Paul's uncompromising theological attitude as displayed in Gal 1 may well represent his general view. This, however, does not mean that the apostle meets the philosophical requirements, which modern readers perhaps unconsciously impose on him.

In other words, Paul may be sincere, but perhaps not with us. We may expect him to write as a dogmatician or at least to be straightforward with his addressees. Starting with such presuppositions we find that the man is not only contradictory (something that was earlier explained with the word 'para-doxical') or ready radically to develop his theology to meet the new socio-cultural needs of his mission, but even more: insinuating, crooked, and dishonest.

Yet we are not forced to abandon our theological questions in order to understand Paul. We only need a better comprehension of his rhetorical techniques. Some of Paul's techniques are easily understood even by modern readers, but I maintain that much has also been overlooked, resulting in misleading interpretations and – among some serious scholars – a deceitful picture of the man himself. In order to understand Paul as his first addressees did, and in order to perceive the theology behind his rhetoric, a correct insight into the persuasive qualities of his texts is required.

We need to be suspicious – perhaps not of Paul, but of the traditional interpretations of Paul. Instead of focusing on what the apostle says, or imagining what he wanted to say, we must discover, what kind of effect he aimed to produce in his addressees. Only thereby can his theological insights be assessed.

To sum up: Can we trust Paul? The answer is yes, if we fully recognize the gap between our questions and the rhetorical situation of the text. This does not mean that we are free to distance our interpretation from Paul's actual sayings, nor does it make his texts more obscure, on the contrary. The situation can be compared with Paul's language: His Greek was analyzed and translated long ago. The time is overdue to begin deciphering his art of persuasion, too.

# Part II
# The Law in Paul's Theology

Chapter 1

# Solutions with Problems

I have argued that Paul's way of communication is strongly rhetorical, and that this must be borne in mind when studying his theological statements. Having dealt with minor examples it is time to turn to a major theme in Pauline exegetics: What is the apostle's view on the *Torah*, the law?[1] I shall ask, what happens if his expressions are derhetorized.

Paul's understanding of the law is one of the most controversial topics in contemporary exegetical research.[2] The interest is fostered by our new understanding of ancient Judaism,[3] but also by new approaches and a new attitude to the apostle's theology.[4] The notion of 2 Peter about the complexity of Paul's writings is taken seriously[5] – uncritical harmonization is no longer an acceptable way of solving the problems. Nor can we e.g. refer to Paul's different, religious logic,[6] which in my opinion simply means spraying religious camouflage over the obvious obstacles in his texts. In the present circumstances, there are four major lines for grasping Paul's view of the law:[7]

---

[1] Once again it must be emphasized that this question is not identical with the query about what Paul *teaches* about the law on different occasions. Nowhere in his texts does the apostle explicitly define his absolute, neutral position. We only have texts written with powerful rhetoric in order to affect specific social groups.

[2] For the current situation and literature until 1994, see Dunn (ed.) 1996, 1–5.309–34; Thielman 1994, 14–47. Cf. also Eskola 1998 and Kuula 1999,8-25.

[3] Promoted especially by E.P. Sanders 1977. For the fall of the "Weberian" view of Judaism, see closer Laato 1991, 16–33.

[4] See above section I 2D. We are not only acquiring more information of the "context" of, and external factors affecting, the apostle's writing. The problems involved in reading his texts are realized more clearly than before.

[5] Räisänen (1987, xii) refers to "a general agreement that Paul's view is very complex and intricate". On 2 Peter, see above section I 3C, end.

[6] E.g. the use of paradox as a standard intellectual tool. See Räisänen 1987, 4. Nevertheless, there are those who disagree (see section I 2D).

[7] For a detailed presentation of such surveys, see Westerholm (1988, 1–101) and Moo (1987, 287–307).

I   The most common solution is to *bifurcate* the concept of law. There are two ways of so doing:[8]

a) According to Dunn, Paul rejects the law only with regard to its social function, as a means of distinguishing Jews from Gentiles. Paul only attacks Jewish misuse of the law.[9] The "works of law" mean only actions which establish this difference. Otherwise the law is to be obeyed.

b) More traditional ways to the same goal postulate a difference between the Mosaic and the Messianic law,[10] between ceremonial and moral law,[11] or between a legalistic use of the law and the law as expressing God's will. The latter means that the law as an obligating and enslaving power has ceased, yet it still expresses God's will even for the Christians.[12]

The problem with any bifurcation is that the divisions cannot be easily documented in Paul's texts.[13] There are no clear criteria for solving which type of the law he is considering in particular cases.[14] Unfortunately one simply cannot prove that Paul would be arguing against a Jewish misunderstanding or an outdated use of the law.[15] Instead, he often discusses the law without any restrictions.

II   The second explanation refers to the *occasion for writing*. Again, two main lines can be distinguished:

a) Drane, Hübner, and Wilckens find a development in Paul's thought.[16] In Galatians, Paul is entirely negative toward the law, but a serious rethinking, caused by different factors, leads to the more balanced view of Romans. This solution, which tends to show Paul as an opportunistic thinker, fails to explain corresponding tendencies within the letters.[17]

b) Beker also refers to the occasion for writing as an explanation for the differences. He does not emphasize development in Paul's thought, but states merely that Paul wrote differently due to the various exigencies in the congregations. For instance the crisis situation in Galatians provoked an

---

[8] Cf. the somewhat comparable presentation by Hong 1993, 12.

[9] Dunn 1988, lxix–lxxii.

[10] Longenecker 1976, 128–32.

[11] Kaiser 1983, 307–14; Schreiner 1989, 47–74.

[12] Hong 1993, 189–91.

[13] Cf. Westerholm's criticism of Dunn (Westerholm 1988, 117–19).

[14] E.g. a linguistic differentiation between νόμος and ὁ νόμος is not viable. See Räisänen 1987, 17.

[15] See Räisänen 1987, xxix.42–50; Westerholm 1988, 130–35, and Thielman 1994, 139.

[16] Drane 1975, Hübner 1978, Wilckens 1982.

[17] See above section I 2Dc and Räisänen 1987, xvi–xviii.9.

aggressive style and correspondingly inconsistent logic.[18] Yet, despite these problems, there is a consistent core in Paul's theology.

One can also directly refer to Paul's emotional state: When writing Galatians he was so anxious that he produced statements, which in a less tense situation he would never recognize as his own words.[19]

III The third solution, advocated by E.P. Sanders and H. Räisänen, is actually *no solution* at all. Paul is simply inconsistent as a thinker. The different expressions cannot be explained only by external factors – Paul could not solve the problems even for himself, and happens to reveal this on various occasions.[20]

This line is free from the harmonizing tendencies often visible in the previous explanations; nevertheless problems ensue from its comparison with actual statements of Paul, as will be argued below. As our "last resort",[21] it should not be "psychologized" away.[22] However, other solutions must first be considered.

IV Westerholm agrees about the obscurities and misleading expressions in Paul,[23] yet finds a clear basic structure: The law is *totally outdated* and superseded by Christ and the Spirit.[24] Paul's writings merely lack "careful order, logic or detachment".[25] Behind some "positive" statements there is a deliberate paradox.[26] But if the solution is so simple, why was Paul unable so express it?

---

[18] Beker 1980, 55–58.104–108. Cf. Becker (1989, 419), who refers to the polemical accent of Gal and the "Vertiefungen" in Rom.

[19] See below section II 2Aa.

[20] See also Goulder 1994,33-37. Kuula, a pupil of Räisänen, offers an updated, but somewhat uncritical version of this thesis (1999).

[21] See above section I 2Dd.

[22] The ancient rhetorical custom of "revealing" the antagonist's hidden, psychological motives was used by Paul (Gal 2,4; 6,13), and likewise by Räisänen about Paul (1987, 232ff). Thielman's attempt to apply the same technique to Räisänen however is not convincing. His suggestion, that the thesis of the Finnish scholar is occasioned by the Christians' shame over their treatment of the Jews (Thielman 1994, 46), is hardly borne out by the history of the Jews in Finland (cf. Illman 1996, 101).

[23] Westerholm 1988, 219.

[24] Westerholm 1988, 195–97. Thurén (1986) expresses similar views.

[25] Westerholm 1988, 219. The reason for this obscurity is the polemical situation, or the nature of Paul's own personality.

[26] Westerholm 1988, 205; the argument which is for Räisänen (1987, 4) too easy an avoidance of problems.

Why do his statements constitute an "extremely complicated problem"[27] for scholars and mislead them?

The basic problem is that Paul speaks about the law in many different ways. Occasionally he can utter reverent words about it (Gal 3,12; 6,2; Rom 2,20; 7,10.12.14 etc.), whereas in other situations the law is compared with miserable *stoikheia* (Gal 4,9) and is seen as a source of evil (Gal 3,19; Rom 5,20; 7,7 etc.). It is hard to determine, whether the law is in force (Gal 5,14; Rom 13,8) or not (Gal 3,25; Rom 7,6), whether it can be fulfilled or not, and what is its relation to the Christian salvation.[28] It is particularly difficult to obtain an earnest and solid theology behind the texts.

Actually, we seem to be left with two basic alternatives. First, we can explain away the problems with some principle, which however is hard to defend against critical questions.[29] Such explanations of problematic verses often become so complicated, or they are based on new, exclusive ideas of the scholar, that it is difficult to believe that they are within the natural understanding of the implied addressees. The alternative is simply to register the problems and conclude that Paul failed to create a new attitude to the law, that he was too irrational and impulsive to pass as a theologian.

Of course a critic must admit, that not *every* problem connected with Paul and the law is due to the text – there is always the possibility that we as readers simply misunderstand something which was taken for granted by Paul's original addressees.

Thus some of the problems can be avoided by mapping the semantic polyvalence of the term *nomos* itself. For example, the *nomos* in Romans 3,21ab may well be used with two meanings: "But now, apart from law, the righteousness of God has been disclosed, and is attested by the law and the prophets." But how were the original readers supposed to choose the right one? What if the apostle is just playing with words in a way, which was not expected to confuse his original readers? It seems that to choose only one alternative may be due to misunderstanding of Paul's way of communication.

This leads us to my main thesis: In Paul's texts there are far more problematic issues inherent in his way of expressing himself. I maintain that many of the difficulties presented in modern exegetical literature also concerning the question of Paul and the law may be attributed to an unnatural, static view of the Pauline letters as texts.

---

[27] Hong 1993, 11.

[28] See e.g. Hong 1993, 11.

[29] Cf. e.g. Räisänen's (1987, xiv) criticism of Hübner's interpretation of Gal 3,19.

In order to find his attitude to the law, and thereby define the real problems, we ought to base our analysis on a dynamic view of his letters.[30] When simple misunderstandings are avoided, the real, essential problems can be better approached and discussed. Thus I use the question about Paul and the law as an example in the call for a more realistic way of reading his texts and of searching for a Pauline theology.

Thereby I just want to avoid problems which arise because modern readers misjudge the literary character of the Pauline letters. Reading the texts from the dynamic perspective does not suggest that obvious discrepancies ought to be explained with rhetoric. Every obscurity simply cannot be labelled as a "rhetorical device" and then given a different meaning. For full controllability, it is most convenient if actual standard rhetorical strategies and devices can be adduced. In such cases we can try to determine, how an expression or section was meant to be understood and what is the idea beyond it. Paul could indeed have used exceptional techniques of persuasion, too,[31] but even then the persuasive strategy must be clearly demonstrable.

Even concerning the law we must ask, whether persuasion sometimes overruled theological clarity[32] or sincerity.[33] Such cases can be carefully studied, but as a general principle it must be kept in mind, that e.g. simplification or exaggeration is not *per se* a sign of insincerity, but a natural part of any argumentation seeking rhetorical effectiveness.

To sum up: Instead of searching for harmonization, theological rationalization, or unnatural systematization (be the result a chaos or a neat system), we ought to recognize the dynamic nature of Paul's expressions concerning the law, derhetorize them, and search therein for a possible invariant system of thought.

---

[30] See above section I 3.

[31] I have suggested that this actually occurs in James (Thurén 1995a).

[32] Thus Gardner 1913, 162.

[33] Cf. above section I 4.

Chapter 2

# The Law in Galatians

Instead of comparing separate, incompatible utterances about the law from different Pauline texts, I start by sketching his views in individual letters.[1] Thereby the specific nature of the texts can be fully observed.[2] Although it has been called "extremely unwise",[3] I begin with Galatians, for several reasons.

First, it is the one text in which Paul's statements about the law have been commonly seen as unique and peculiar. Romans and Philippians, for example, are often said to represent a sounder, more mature or well-thought out version of his doctrine. Without Galatians, where Paul's argument about the law "threatens to undo... the coherent core of Pauline thought",[4] it would be easier to sketch a Pauline doctrine about the law. However, this exceptional text makes the whole topic particularly interesting.

A second reason for focussing on Galatians is that Paul's way of communication in this letter has been diligently studied. Betz's commentary, in which he sought correspondence with ancient rhetoric, prompted rhetorical studies of Gal, and the discussion of the rhetorical character of the text has flourished ever since.[5] This offers us good material.[6]

I shall begin by characterizing some general features in Gal. I shall then proceed from this material to the more ideological, viz. theological, issues in the text.

---

[1] This is emphasized also by Hong (1993, 15) and Thielman (1994, 10–11), whereas his teacher Wright (1992) concentrates on separate key passages.

[2] So also Hong 1993, 15.

[3] So described by Cranfield 1983, 858 and Räisänen 1987, 133. Kuula (1999, 25–29) rightly emphasizes, that Gal should be studied without always other Pauline texts in mind.

[4] Beker 1980, 58.

[5] For detailed survey of rhetorical studies on Gal until 1992, see Watson and Hauser 1994, 194–98; cf. also Porter 1997, 541–47; Mitternacht 1999,153-232.

[6] The purpose of this study is not, however, to arrive at an overview of the rhetorical qualities of Galatians, although many comments will be made. Instead, rhetoric will be utilized as a means for approaching the ideology behind the text.

# A. Galatians as Persuasion

There are many rival theories about the rhetorical status and disposition of Galatians.[7] Different persuasive devices have been identified; many of them closely correspond to ancient customs. Although no unanimity has been achieved, already the fact that so many rhetorical analyses have been written on Galatians indicates that the text bears a strong resemblance to oratory.

The problem is, however, what to do with the results. How do they actually promote a better understanding of the text? In my opinion, this difficulty is due to the narrow theoretical view of rhetoric as a "contextual" approach.[8] With a higher, "second order" view on persuasion, better results will be achieved.

## a. Was Paul too Angry?

The first step when analyzing the persuasive character of Galatians is to study the common claim that the apostle wrote the text when he was too wrathful for proper theology. With this explanation the sharp expressions reflecting Paul's theology in Galatians are often downplayed.

Paul is said to dictate "under considerable emotion"[9], "in a singularly passionate way" so that we learn to know "his fiery temperament".[10] The apostle is distressed by a painful situation and does not know what to do.[11] He writes

---

[7] The suggestions vary between the judicial genre (Betz 1979, Brinsmead 1982, Hester 1984), the deliberative (Kennedy 1984, 145–47; Hall 1987; Vouga 1988; Smit 1989; Longenecker 1990, cix–cxiii) and the epideictic (Hester 1991). For the discussion see Hong 1993, 22–24; Porter 1997, 541–47. Hong warns that one should not try to "push Galatians too far into a specific rhetorical framework" (1993, 25). This, however, is not the goal when seeking the genre of a text. The genre or genus only indicates the overall nature of the aim of the text: What *type of response* the text is designed to produce. This provides a necessary framework for its understanding. See closer Thurén 1990, 71–72.

[8] Cf. the frustrated confession of Dunn about "being less enthused about the value of these disciplines for a theology of Paul". He continues: "In particular it seems to me fairly pointless to argue about whether Paul's letters are 'epideictic' or 'deliberative', or whatever." Dunn 1994, 414. This fully understandable statement is due to the low level rhetoric practiced by many scholars. In Gal, eg. Hong uses rhetoric only to seek the structure of Galatians (1993, 24–25). For another use of the rhetorical genus, see below section II 2 Bc.

[9] Fung 1988, 93.

[10] Ridderbos 1953, 18.

[11] Ridderbos 1953, 170–71.

"mit glühendem Eifer",[12] "im ersten Affekt",[13] in "deep personal anguish",[14] unable clearly to formulate his utterances.

All this is claimed to have a defective impact on his explicit theology. According to one alternative, this indicates that the apostle paid little attention to serious theology, but let his feelings guide his speech. Perhaps he thereby happens to reveal what he really thinks about the law – something he does not dare to do in Rom.[15] Another explanation is that the usually thoughtful apostle was so upset by the new situation in Galatia, that he cannot be held responsible for what he said.[16] In his anger he even seems to have forgotten basic rhetorical skills.

Certainly this is the impression which occurs to the reader of the Epistle. But how do we really know? What if this only what the apostle wants his address-ees to think, and we modern readers are similarly affected?

Let us visualize, how is a listener expected to react when facing a respected speaker who now, surprisingly, is furious. I can imagine two things: First, he/she must take the speaker seriously. There is no room to suspect any rhetorical tricks or calculation, when the speaker's emotions seem strong and genuine. Another point is that the listener cannot remain calm him/herself, but will be emotionally affected. This, however, is precisely the goal of the skilled orator; this is what he/she is trained to produce.[17]

If Galatians is as carefully planned as the modern rhetorical analyses, especially the commentaries of Betz[18] and Longenecker,[19] demonstrate, it would be no surprise if Paul's emotional statements served the *pathos* appeal of the text rather than represented his actual state of mind.[20] Of course it was good for

---

[12]  Rohde 1989, 13.

[13]  Rohde 1989, 11.

[14]  Thielman 1994, 120.

[15]  E.g. Räisänen (1987, 200) claims that Gal 3,19 is written "in heated debate". The statement is "steeped in emotion". Paul dictates in anger and overreacts, and happens to reveal that his "mind was divided with regard to the law"(Räisänen 1987, 132–33).

[16]  Cranfield 1964, 62.

[17]  Martin 1974, 158–66; Kraftchick 1985, 137–43.

[18]  Betz 1979. In March 1996 I asked Prof. Betz in Copenhagen, if his notions on the rhetoric in Gal can be used to determine whether the apostle really was angry. Betz emphatically dismissed such a question as mere psychology. Next year, also in Copenhagen, he however explained that he knows no example in antiquity of an author losing his self-control and thereby revealing his emotions.

[19]  Longenecker 1990.

[20]  Longenecker (1990, cxviii–cxix) rightly counts some expressions in Galatians as aimed at the *pathos* appeal and thereby at persuading the addressees. He, however, does not draw any further conclusions from these observations.

the cause, if the speaker worked himself up into the same emotion.[21] Maybe Paul was just a good father, sounding angry in order to protect his children?

Notwithstanding we must add, that the use of rhetorical devices and strategies in a text does not prove, that the author *could not* have been overwhelmed by the feelings which this technical artifice is intended to display. However, recognition of such clichés makes us wonder, whether the opposite is to be believed.

Let us scrutinize the statements which convey an emotionally heated picture of Paul in Galatians.

In 1,6 Paul begins the Letter with an expression of astonishment (θαυμάζω), instead of his standard εὐχαριστῶ. The normal thanksgiving section is replaced by a rebuke. Longenecker's explanation is typical: "Paul evidently could not think of anything to commend them for, and so enters directly into the issues at hand. He had just received the news... and reacts to that news on the spot." Rohde argues, that Paul here breaks the common epistolary pattern.[22] Ridderbos informs us that Paul's heart is full of pain.[23]

It is evident, that the θαυμάζω expression is intended to signal the importance of the issue. But what does it actually tell us about Paul's feelings? The addressees hardly knew how Paul was wont to begin his letters. Although unique in the *Corpus Paulinum*, the expression is but a conventional letter-opening cliché, a standard rhetorical device designed to signal the author's unhappiness vis-à-vis the addressees' behavior and attitudes.[24] We do not know whether the historical Paul really was astonished or e.g. irritated[25] – the only fact we have is that he uses a persuasive device for a certain purpose.

1,8–9 is a curse, which can be seen as exceptional, and emotionally based. Although certainly a strong, extreme expression, such a threat is by no means unknown to e.g. Quintilian.[26]

1,10 is seen as an "emotional outburst"; Paul "speaks in fervor".[27] However, even here we have technical terminology. The verse serves as a transitional formula between the *exordium* and the *narratio*.[28] In the style of classical

---

[21] Cf. Martin 1974, 161.

[22] Rohde 1989, 38.

[23] Ridderbos 1953, 46.

[24] See Koskenniemi 1956, 65–67; Lausberg 1960, § 270; Betz 1979, 46–47, Longenecker 1990, cv–cvii.14 (who however does not draw any conclusions from this). Whether the expression contains some irony (Betz 1979, 46–47), or not (Mussner 1974,53), is irrelevant.

[25] Mullins 1972, 385.

[26] See Betz 1979, 45–46.

[27] So, according to Longenecker (1990, 18–19) most modern commentators.

[28] Betz 1979, 46.

oratory, Paul rejects "empty" persuasion, claiming to be free of calculated rhetoric, in order to demonstrate his candour.[29] Although the reactions of the first readers are unknown to us, at least many modern commentators have been affected as planned by this device.

In 3,1–5 Paul wonders who has "bewitched the foolish Galatians". Once more he is said to speak "with obvious emotion"[30] and "strong feeling".[31] But again – is Paul really angry? This section, albeit one of the most emotionally colored and apparently straightforward in Paul, is in fact carefully constructed and "loaded with rhetorical figures"[32].

Hardly anybody believes that the questions in 3,1–5 are to be taken at their face value. Paul does not require information; the questions are rhetorical, to provoke a reaction from the audience.[33] The "biting and aggressive" style likewise serves a rhetorical purpose. Betz rightly explains: "This insult, however, should not be taken too seriously. Such addresses were commonplace among the diatribe preachers of Paul's day."[34] He even claims that Paul here presents a "carefully prepared mixture of some logic, some emotional appeal, some wisdom, some beauty, and some entertainment" in order to influence his readers, rather than with too perfect and thereby suspicious logic.[35]

4,12–20 is often described as an "erratic and irrational outburst", "reflecting strong pathos".[36] Paul is said to be overwhelmed by his own emotions. The main argument is that he does not continue with "sachlich-theologische" argumentation, but refers to personal matters.[37] We meet "deep affection, concern, and perplexity".[38] The metaphors "mother" and "children" reveal particular depth of feeling on Paul's part.[39] We are given "a glimpse into the heart of a true evangelist and pastor".[40]

---

[29] See Betz 1979, 54–55; Fung 1988, 49–50.

[30] Fung 1988, 129.

[31] Guthrie 1973, 91.

[32] Longenecker 1990, 99.

[33] For the functions of the rhetorical question, see Wuellner 1986, 49–77.

[34] Betz 1979, 130; cf. also Longenecker 1990, 100. This consolation means, however, only scholars: For the original readers (as well as for modern hermeneutical purposes) the insult should be understood with its full emotional force.

[35] Betz 1979, 129.

[36] Schlier 1965, 208; cf. also Mussner 1974, 304–305; Longenecker 1990, 188; even Betz 1979, 221.

[37] Mussner 1974, 304–305.

[38] Longenecker 1990, 194.

[39] Guthrie 1973, 121; Ridderbos 1953, 170.

[40] Longenecker 1990, 197.

But at least here a warning bell should sound. The speech of a trained orator hardly happens to reveal something about his heart, nor does a carefully prepared letter. Our only picture of the author is that implicit in the text, and serves a purpose: the *ethos* of the author is boosted and the reader is to be emotionally affected by the author's implied emotions.[41] Most commentators seem to have fallen into this trap.

Betz, although also himself describing this section as "lighter", rightly remarks: "What has not been recognized is the rhetorical character of this passage."[42] In particular the stereotypical devices of mother,[43] *immutatio vocis*,[44] and *dubitatio*[45] have duly affected, viz. misled, the scholars. Interestingly enough, Luther, who still possessed a certain medieval perception of rhetoric, states: "He does not miss anything."[46] To pretend to be devoid of arguments is typical for an orator, and a sophisticated device in Paul's strategy.[47]

Summarizing, we can say, that Galatians as a whole is an impassioned, emotionally loaded letter. This can hardly be denied. The examples mentioned above are the most striking, but many minor features in the text support the impression. There is, however, reason to doubt, whether the *author himself* is overwhelmed by emotions. He presents himself in the text as perplexed, uncalculating, straightforward, and impassioned; the Letter seems to be an instant response, a natural primitive reaction, to alarming news from the congregations. Yet a closer look reveals that this purposeful impression is consciously produced by utilizing effective contemporary rhetorical means. One would expect less orthodox ways of expressing perplexity, if the apostle actually was infuriated.

Of course it is possible, that Paul was carried away by his emotions; perhaps he had learned his rhetoric so well that he could follow the rules even in a furious state. But is this plausible? Another explanation is that the apostle knew exactly what he was doing. Irrespective of his private thoughts (which we cannot penetrate), the apostle was able carefully to compose a letter, aimed for maximum effect among the addressees.

---

[41] Kraftchick finds this device often in Gal (1985, 227–28).

[42] Betz 1979,221.

[43] Betz 1979,233.

[44] Betz 1979, 236; Martin 1974, 353–55.

[45] Betz 1979, 236–37; Lausberg 1960, § 776–78; Quintilian, *Inst.*, IX,ii.19.

[46] Paul "as a genuine orator presents his case with great care and faith – all in order to call them back to the truth of the Gospel and to win them away from the false apostles" (Luther 1911 (1535), 652).

[47] Betz 1979, 237.

I make no claim to take the pulse of the historical Paul; correspondingly it cannot be argued that he was merely simulating deep feelings. The intransigence of his theology and his impassioned way of life, both as a Jew and as a Christian, indicate that he was often wholly serious, although no reliable psychological assessment can based on the material we have. But it is important to recognize, that even his most emotional letter shows no sign of lost control. We have reason to believe that the theological content of Gal was far more important to him than the art of persuasion as such, nor is there proof that his emotions blurred that content. Whether or not his theology in Galatians is contradictory and incoherent, it seems clear that Paul's exceptional theological utterances cannot be explained away by referring to his state of mind. The apostle must be held fully responsible for what he dictated.[48]

### b. Coerced by the Villains?

Even if Paul was not confused when composing the Letter, there is another explanation for his eccentric theological statements. The Letter is confusing, since it is a hasty response to an acute situation. The Judaizing antagonists[49] have launched an attack from Jerusalem[50] on Pauline congregations, importing a radically different theology. Paul has to react rapidly and forcefully in order to recover his position[51] among the addressees, and to save the genuine Christian doctrine.[52] This haste explains, why his theology in the Letter is somewhat exaggerated. The theology is less important than winning the battle. This, in turn, indicates either a careless or an opportunistic attitude on the part of the apostle.

But was the situation too urgent to produce proper theology? According to Longenecker, one of our main sources for the situation in Galatians is the opening statement 1,6–9.[53] However, the rhetorical function of these verses,

---

[48]  Thus also Kuula 1999, 33.

[49]  The majority of scholars are inclined to see the antagonists as Judaizing Christians. Other hypotheses (that they are local Jews, Gentile converts, gnostics, zealots, pneumatics etc.) have attracted little support. For an overview, see Longenecker 1990, lxxvii–c; Fung 1988, 3–9.

[50]  Longenecker 1990, xcv. Or at least they may have been in contact with Jerusalem (Fung 1988, 8–9).

[51]  According to Ridderbos (1953, 18) it is a traditional view, that the antagonists were attempting to "cut off the effect of Paul's work", directly challenging Paul's status (Ridderbos 1953, 15; Longenecker 1990, xcv), although they claimed not to be opposing him (Longenecker 1990, xcv).

[52]  Cf. Ridderbos 1953, 15–18.

[53]  Longenecker 1990, xcv; another source is the postscript in 6,11–18.

although within the *exordium*,[54] is already that of a *narratio*: the speaker describes the situation in seemingly neutral terms, in order to prepare for his forthcoming arguments. This is one of the most effective means of persuasion.[55] Therefore, these verses must be read with great suspicion.

For many scholars one of the clearest proofs of the apostle's haste is 1,6 (οὕτως ταχέως), which they take to mean that the exigency of Galatians was acute.[56] However, this expression is of rhetorical origin[57] and "should not be used too quickly to date the letter".[58] It rather refers to the ease, with which the addressees were allegedly won over by the antagonists.[59]

Another sign of the haste is the vicious nature of the antagonists, whose rapid invasion seems to have posed an imminent danger to the congregation. Unfortunately, our only source for the antagonists' conduct is Paul's polemic attack on them, and there are risks in such "mirror reading".[60] It is likely that the one-sided dispute yields an unbalanced picture of the antagonists and even of the whole situation.[61] Longenecker warns us of the difficulty of such an approach, but admits that this is the only way to proceed.[62] Barclay too is aware of the problem. He even acknowledges the rhetorical nature of the text, and provides seven criteria for assessing the reliable facts.[63] However, he fails to see the most obvious factor affecting the description of the antagonists: the technique called *vituperatio*.

Knowledge of vituperatio brings us a means for critical reading of such a polemic. In antiquity, as in modern cultures, there were certain conventional ways of vilifying the antagonists and of adjusting the situation at hand, to suit the wishes of the speaker. A comparison with such conventions explains many things.

---

[54] Cf. Betz 1979, 44–45. Against him I claim that also the epistolary opening phrases 1–5 serve as exordium. Betz' inability to recognize this is due to his understanding of the relationship between rhetoric and epistolography (see Thurén 1990, 60–61).

[55] See O'Banion 1987, 325–51; Thurén 1995a, 271.

[56] See Guthrie 1973, 61; Ridderbos 1953, 15.46–47; Fung 1988, 44; Longenecker 1990, lxv.

[57] Mussner 1974, 53 n. 54.

[58] Betz 1979, 47–48.

[59] Thus Rohde 1989, 38–39.

[60] Barclay 1987, 73–93; Longenecker 1990, lxxxix.

[61] Schmithals (1972, 18) even argues that Paul did not know the situation very well, and Marxsen (1968, 53) claims that he misunderstood the whole thing.

[62] Longenecker 1990, lxxxix.

[63] Barclay 1987, 73–93.

Classical forms of vilification are found throughout the Letter. Du Toit's study has highlighted some common features of this persuasive device in both religious and philosophical treatises.[64] The author was supposed to use standard labels when describing his opponents.[65] In fact, the technique was so well-known to both parties in communication, that no-one took them at their face value.[66] They could be hyperbolical or purely fictive. Thus it is an elementary mistake to regard such stereotypical labels as exact historical information.

Yet this does not mean that the author was dishonest in his search for a maximal effect. He utilized certain devices in order to modify the addressees' attitudes toward the opponents, whom they often already knew. The problem is that later readers, who do not share the original addressees' knowledge of the opponents and the device, easily gain the wrong impression of the situation.

Almost every device presented in du Toit's article on vilification can be found in Galatians.[67] The antagonists are censured for their *hypocrisy* (2,13) and labeled with a ψευδ-prefix (2,4) they are accused of *sorcery* (3,1) and of *moral depravity* (6,12–13, even 2,4)[68] or a *perversive influence* (1,7; 5,10; 5,12);[69] they are presented as *ludicrous characters* (5,12)[70] and threatened with *eschatological judgement* (1,8–9; 5,10).[71] To "reveal" the opponents' *secret intentions* is also an effective means of impugning their trustworthiness (2,4; 6,13).

The purpose of such statements was not to describe the antagonists – the addressees were often already acquainted with them – but to indicate that they are the villains of the piece. Their *ethos* was denigrated in order to dissociate the addressees from them.[72] By such defamation the author seeks to alienate the addressees from the antagonists, to protect them from their influence.

Were the antagonists foreigners? Longenecker presents as a *communis opinio*, that the antagonists were not local, since the apostle so frequently distinguishes them from the addressees. As the strongest evidence he adduces

---

[64] For other literature, see also Thurén 1997, 458 n. 45.

[65] Johnson 1989, 432–33.

[66] See Johnson 1989, 423–33; du Toit 1994, 411.

[67] Another good example is the Letter of Jude, see Thurén 1997.

[68] Du Toit 1994, 405–408.

[69] Du Toit 1994, 409.

[70] Du Toit 1994, 410. He refers to Lütgert (1919, 31ff) as the worst example of deriving historical data from vilifying labels. Lütgert finds the Cybele-cult behind this verse.

[71] Du Toit 1994, 410.

[72] Cf. Du Toit 1994, 412.

the use of the word τινες.[73] However, this is a common device for such a task, having clearly a pejorative function in Galatians 1,7; 2,12.[74]

Hong argues that since the antagonists are mentioned in the third person and the addressees in the second, the former must be intruders.[75] If, however, the separation of the two groups was Paul's main goal, the distinction of the persons tells us nothing about their origin. If the antagonists were a group within the congregation, such a distinction is precisely what Paul would have made in order to protect the addressees from their influence.

Further proof that the antagonists were not natives could be 2,4, in which they are claimed to have *infiltrated* and *intruded* among the addressees to *spy*.[76] But even these images belong to standard labels. Derived from military and political language[77] they are used also in 2 Pet 2,11 and Jude 4. According to this device, the villains are presented as obscure strangers or "undercover agents", whereas the addressees are good citizens. Even these labels tell us more about the goals of the author than the actual circumstances in the congregation. The fact that Paul condemns his opponents as intruders does not mean that they actually were such. Thus Munck's thesis, that the antagonists were Paul's own converts, who under the influence of the OT and the news from Jerusalem were attracted by Jewish customs, cannot be easily refuted.[78]

We can conclude that these stereotypical devices provide us with little factual information about the antagonists. It is possible that they were dishonest, hypocritical newcomers to the congregation with evil intentions. But this cannot be proven from the text. Instead, the technique used tells us a significant feature of Paul's purpose: to dramatize the situation and to alienate the antagonists from the addressees, in order to exclude their influence. But the very same labels could have been used by the opponents about Paul himself.

To sum up: The Letter may give the impression of haste, but nothing in the situation directly implies that Paul was in too much of a hurry to think before writing.

---

[73] Longenecker 1990, xciv.

[74] Cf. Du Toit 1994, 406. For more on alienation as a persuasive device in Gal, see du Toit 1992, 279–95.

[75] Hong 1993, 117.

[76] Longenecker (1990, 51) claims that these are "of course" Paul's own terms, meaning that the opponents did not so regard themselves, and in a sense this may be true. However, the terms themselves are hardly of Pauline origin.

[77] Betz 1979, 89–91.

[78] Munck 1959, 131. This is of course not to say that Munck is necessarily right.

*c. The Antagonists' Theology Defined?*

We have reason to believe, that just as Paul's stereotypical words concerning the antagonists' ethics, motives, or social status were presumably not meant to be a neutral description, so his inferences concerning their theological standpoint are exaggerated. Although the antagonists' doctrine could not be derided as easily as their way of life – there was always the risk of Paul losing his own credibility – even a theological description thereof can be skewed. As with any caricature, this could be easily seen by the audience, without ruining the goal. There is no reason to think either that the speaker believes in the caricature or that he is lying to the audience.

Paul's description of the antagonists has often been interpreted as a characterization of Judaism. But is this reasonable?

By rhetorical polarization and *synkrisis*[79] Paul highlights the antithesis between salvation through the law and the central elements of Christianity. In many instances Paul claims that righteousness through the law excludes Christ, grace, faith, and promise: Gal 2,6. 21; 3,2–5. 6. 11. 12. 17. 18. 21f; 5,4.

Räisänen shows how this antithetical technique has led Christian exegetes to produce "a desolate picture of 'late Judaism'", which is still widely accepted, although it is only a "vicious *caricature*".[80] He first acknowledges that Paul only speaks of Christian Judaizers, not of Jews, and asks, whether Paul is at all to be blamed for the later Christians' distorted picture of Judaism.[81] But he nevertheless concludes: "Paul either (implicitly, at least) gives an inaccurate picture [of Palestinian Judaism], or else bases his view on insufficient and uncharacteristic evidence."[82]

But we find no indication that Paul would have tried objectively to describe the faith of his Judaizing opponents, let alone Palestinian Judaism, or that he would accidentally convey a distorted picture of Judaism to his original addressees. It is not Paul, but the modern exegetes' unnatural, static way of reading his writings, which conveys the impression of a postulated religion attempting to gain righteousness through the law. Galatians does not visualize Jewish soteriology.

Speaking of the views of his opponents, Paul does not actually attribute to them the overstated legalistic soteriology which he is discussing. On the contrary, they are said *not* to fulfill the law, and are alleged to be interested in circumcision *not* in order to gain salvation, but to avoid persecution because of

---

[79] For the device and its use in Hebrews, see Evans 1988; Seid 1996.
[80] Räisänen 1987, 164–65.168, my emphasis.
[81] Räisänen 1987, 162.168.
[82] Räisänen 1987, 177.181.184.188.

Christ (6,12–13). If Paul sought to imply that his opponents agreed with the position, which is presented in the Letter as an antithesis to his own theology, he would hardly describe them in this way.[83]

Instead, the "legalistic" soteriology is composed and presented by Paul himself. It reflects a pedagogically overstated, theoretical view of the possible consequences of the antagonists' theology. In order to counteract an adversary's ideas, it often suffices to exaggerate and redefine them, to reveal their "true nature". This may not be fair, but is at least good rhetoric.

This is exactly what Paul is doing with his opponents. He sees the antagonists' theology as "yeast", and his mission is to show, how it can "leaven the whole batch of dough" viz. the Christian theology (or the addressees' faith) (Gal 5,9).

Thus, although recent research helps us to perceive the burlesque nature of a postulated Jewish idea of salvation through the law without God's participation, it cannot be explained without a glance at the persuasive techniques of Galatians. By driving the views of his opponents *ad absurdum* Paul portrays the possible result of their theology. Only thereby can he show why the opponents' teaching is incompatible with his own. The later interpreters' understanding of the Pauline caricature is another story.

Summing up thus far, we cannot conclude from the information in Galatians, that the superficial situation in the congregation was particularly dramatic. The individuals whom Paul opposes were probably not religious and ethical monsters; their version of Christianity hardly differed much from that of Paul. It is possible but not certain that they came from elsewhere – perhaps they merely represent ideas inherent in the congregation. Probably neither they nor Paul's (other) addressees saw the situation as urgent.

Consequently some commentators argue that there is no evidence that the opponents presented themselves as especially hostile to Paul.[84] Whereas Jewett believes that they were merely pretending to be on Paul's side,[85] Howard wonders whether they even had any intention of opposing the apostle.[86] At least it is probable, that the antagonists saw themselves as representatives of orthodox Christianity.[87]

---

[83] Du Toit (1992, 157–61) argues that the verse consists of a rhetorical contrast and ought to be translated: "For those of the circumcision want to have you circumcised, not so much because they wish to uphold the law, but rather because they would like to boast in your physical state."

[84] See especially Howard 1979, 1–19.

[85] Jewett 1971.

[86] Howard 1979, 1–19.

[87] Betz 1979, 89–91.

### d. Galatians as Dramatization

Why then is Galatians such a frantic letter? As a literary phenomenon, the emotional, aggressive and dramatizing character of Galatians is primarily a matter of *style*. The apostle's actual feelings are not necessarily exactly the same as those which he displays in a literary product. The scholars' failure to perceive this is attributable to negligence of style in modern exegetical research. As stylistic studies formerly tended to be technical classifications of devices, paying little attention to the style's pragmatic function, even the emergent rhetorical research has put this subject at a disadvantage.[88]

In fact, stylistic matters should often be given priority when studying New Testament texts, as they can reveal the author's goal. The style of particularly a rhetorically conscious text was never fortuitous; instead it was an important means of persuasion. Thus stylistic features should not be seen naively as errors.

In Galatians, the agonizing style is well suited to the rhetorical exigency, as is the pompous style of 2 Peter. It was the apostle who sought trouble and controversy. It is obvious that Paul himself assessed the situation as serious. The seemingly slight shift in the teaching – the question of certain religious rites – was for him theoretically crucial.

The argumentative situation is however difficult, since the addressees fail to follow this reasoning. Paul meets the exigency with oppressive rhetoric, polarizing and dramatizing the situation. He paints a stark picture and forces a choice between the alternatives. This requires him to alienate the addressees from the antagonists as effectively as possible (exactly what he accuses his antagonists of trying to do in 4,17), and to widen the theological gap as much as he can. Some specific tools for this purpose can be detected.

α) *Labeling the Opponents*. From the aforesaid heavy use of vilification as a device we have already concluded, that Paul assumes that the addressees did not look askance on his antagonists or their theology. They did not find the situation as especially critical or dramatic. The device is thereby also a tool for *dramatizing* the situation, for seeking confrontation with the opponents.

β) *Mighty Expressions*. When in 1,16–22 Paul highlights the different origin of his Gospel, it is evident that he emphasizes his independence from the apostles in Jerusalem, and the distance between him and them.

---

[88] I have discussed this issue more thoroughly in Thurén 1996.

But the point is often not so much what Paul says, but how he says it: Paul recommends an uncompromising attitude. The dissuasive, emotional emphasis is evident in the gently modifying expressions of the *narratio*. Thus when Paul proclaims that he "opposed [Kephas] κατὰ πρόσωπον, *to his face*" (2,11), the point is not that he and Peter had different opinions, but the thespian, aggressive way he conveyed this to Peter.[89] Similarly, in 2,5 Paul adds a stark, almost melodramatic adverb: "We did not give into them πρὸς ὥραν, *even for a moment*."[90]

The confrontation is depicted by the use of hyperbole, at its best or worst. Whoever does not agree with Paul is immediately ἀνάθεμα, *cursed* (1,8–9). Paul received no Christian education whatsoever from any man (1,12ff). He was very advanced in Judaism and persecuted the Christians καθ᾽ ὑπερβολήν (1,13–14) etc.

γ) *Absolute Theology.* 5,2–3 and 5,9 express the same absolute, climactic attitude concerning theology: "If you let yourselves be circumcised, Christ will be of no use to you at all." The slightest deviation from Paul's doctrine will prove fatal, since "a little yeast leavens the whole batch of dough". What the addressees (and possibly the antagonists) see as complementing Paul's message, or possibly regard as a slightly different nuance, is presented by the apostle as a major error and deviation.

In the *peroratio* the author usually writes openly, without unduly complicated strategies.[91] In Gal, we find too obvious a contradiction. Previously Paul claimed unconditionally and emphatically: "If you receive circumcision, Christ will do you no good at all... every man who receives circumcision is obligated to keep the entire law" (5,2–3). As a symbol of deviation from Paul's version of Christianity circumcision can ruin everything. But in the peroratio he rephrases a slogan:[92] "Neither circumcision or uncircumcision means anything (οὔτε τί ἐστίν)" (6,15): A minor surgical operation as such means nothing.

---

[89] The commentators tend to be so excited about the episode itself that they miss this stylistic feature: Rohde 1989, 100–105; Fung 1988, 106–109. Longenecker (1990, 62–72) even undermines the expression. The exceptions include Mussner (1974, 137 n. 15) who, referring *inter alia* to Polybios, translates "rückhaltslos, in aller Öffentlichkeit" and Betz 1979, 106 n. 443. But even they do not dwell on the message of the exceptional expression.

[90] Fung observes the absolutist role of the expression (Fung 1988, 94), whereas usually the scholars preoccupied with theology neglect the powerful signal given thereby.

[91] See Thurén 1995a, 273.

[92] Longenecker 1990, 295–96.

Taken at their face value, the verses reveal an enormous inconsistency and logical break. However, their rhetorical nature is too obvious to be misunderstood. It sounds as if Paul admitted that he has overreacted to the question about circumcision. What is really important is not this question but a new creation. Yet he has tried to show that this little "yeast" can be fatal for the Galatians.

δ) *In conclusion* we may say that the text does not indicate that Paul saw any dramatic difference in the practical life between the two versions of Christianity in Galatia. He attempts to arouse his addressees' awareness of the theoretical, theological difference, and does so by dramatizing rhetoric.

The emotional, exaggerating and dramatizing style befits the dissuasive goal of the Epistle. The disturbing, impassioned ambience is intended to enable the addressees to perceive the imminent danger beneath a calm surface. By creating an urgent, black-and-white situation the apostle exhorts the addressees to take a stand. Thus the style simply meets the rhetorical exigency of the text.

We cannot know, whether Paul's ultimate motives were purely theological or whether they pertained at least to some degree to his personal authority.[93] But the immediate aim of Galatians is clear: to dramatize the situation. The apostle sought thereby to regain his absolute theological authority over the congregations, which in turn was needed for renewing the addressees' "allegiance to the one and only true gospel". In this difficult task Paul hardly acted without thought. The Letter is a stylistic and rhetorical masterpiece, and there is no reason to doubt that the same applies to its theology.

But simultaneously: Here the very rhetorical techniques enable us to see Paul's theology. Paul attempts to display as vividly as possible the different religious, principal structures of thought behind the practical life. This kind of rhetorical polarization of the actual, in practice similar alternatives – Paul or the local "Judaizing" Christians as authority – *is theology*. The multiple variations of religious expressions, opinions and feelings are simplified into clear ideas in order to be more perceptible, intelligible, communicable and persuasive. The analogous reality is digitalized for better functionality. In this sense all theology is rhetorical; ideological thinking and persuasion are apposed.

Yet the question from the last chapter remains: Was Paul as a theologian sincere? Was the theology presented in Galatians too purposeful and tailor-made? Can it be compared to his other letters?

---

[93] Against du Toit (1992, 279–80), who only makes emphatic claims, and adduces no arguments. We can never reach the possible, unspoken, intentions of the author.

# B. Theology behind Rhetoric?

If the goal of the letter is to dissociate, this presumably affects the issue discussed, too. Thus, after characterizing the rhetorical nature and purpose of Galatians, we can turn to our main question, Paul's teaching about the law. We have assessed as plausible, that Paul did not dictate in a perplexed, furious state, but must be held wholly responsible for his words. He was not forced to do anything but operates on his own initiative.

But how does the rhetorical consciousness and the dissociative, dramatizing purpose of the letter affect his theology? Is he ready to compromise his view of the law for the sake of persuasion? Although Paul does not present any "doctrine" in Galatians, his expressions concerning the law reflect a system of ideas, and we can ask what is the role of the rhetorical aim of the letter, viz. dramatization, and some possible minor persuasive devices.

In the survey, the rhetoric of the text calls us to bear one thing in mind: When sketching theology based on a short, consciously one-sided text like Galatians, *argumentum e silentio* cannot be used. What Paul does not say about the law is here irrelevant; in the prevailing rhetorical situation a comprehensive presentation is not to be expected.

## a. Semantic Observations

A closer study requires first a semantic analysis of the word *nomos* in Galatians. It is obvious, that the word can have different connotations in Paul, as it did in contemporary Judaism. Insofar as this does not confuse the implied addressees, it indicates no obscurity.

In Galatians, as also elsewhere in the *Corpus Paulinum*, there are but a few semantically diverse meanings of *nomos*. In most cases it simply denotes to the Mosaic law, viz. the Sinaitic legislation, expressed in the OT.[94]

Although Gal 3,21b could also be seen as referring to any law (including the law of Moses),[95] such an addition is not necessary for understanding the sentence. Further, Westerholm rightly rejects attempts to interpret the law in Gal 3,12.15–21 as meaning something more or less than the Sinaitic legislation.[96]

Although Paul's antagonists hardly demanded obedience to the whole law, but just discussed mainly ritual matters like circumcision, Paul does not clearly

---

[94] Westerholm 1988, 108–109; Hong 1993, 122–23.
[95] Guthrie 1973, 107.
[96] Westerholm 1988, 110–11.

distinguish between ritual and ethical commandments in Gal.[97] Räisänen however claims, that Paul *unconsciously* makes this distinction. The apostle is unaware of "this looseness of speech", yet simultaneously uses this oscillation as a means of "impress[ing] his readers on emotional level", viz. as a rhetorical tool creating *pathos*.

Two arguments are presented:[98] a) Mainly the cultic side (circumcision, food ordinances and the calendar) is discussed in Galatians; b) In 5,14 the whole law is reduced to the love commandment, viz. a moral requirement (which is to be fulfilled even by the Christians): ὁ γὰρ πᾶς νόμος ἐν ἑνὶ λόγῳ πεπλήρωται, ἐν τῷ· ἀγαπήσεις τὸν πλησίον σου ὡς σεαυτόν.

I find these arguments difficult to follow. a) If the opponents discussed cultic rules, it is natural for Paul as well to concentrate on these issues. Yet he explicitly claims that such rules cannot be separated from the totality of the law (3,10 γέγραπται γὰρ ὅτι ἐπικατάρατος πᾶς ὃς οὐκ ἐμμένει πᾶσιν τοῖς γεγραμμένοις ἐν τῷ βιβλίῳ τοῦ νόμου τοῦ ποιῆσαι αὐτά). On the contrary, a central goal in throughout the letter is to argue that a demand to follow some cultic instructions unavoidably leads to a necessity to obey the whole law.

b) It is correct to say that the maxim in 5,14, as well as many other expressions in Gal, is a mode of emotional influence, and thereby used as a rhetorical device. But does it mean that some commandments of the law are excluded? The idea of expressing the core of the law with one commandment, especially the love commandment, was not invented by Paul, but has Jewish parallels: Hillel, Eleazar the Modite, Aqiba, and Simlai could express the whole law in a single commandment – without any oscillation. Such a concentration needs to be derhetorized, too: it arouse from the situation and was never intended as a theoretical definition of the Torah. I find it hard to conclude from this device, that the rabbis thereby meant that the law was divided into two parts.[99] Nor did Paul. Yet his view probably differed from that of the rabbis. What then did he mean?

Let us see 5,14 in its context. The sentence belongs to the paraenesis, which is not aimed at theological discussion but at modifying the addressees'

---

[97]In accordance with Räisänen (1987, 25–26), insofar as he states that Paul makes no conscious distinction, although mainly the cultic side is discussed; against van Spanje 1999.

[98] Räisänen 1987, 25.28, referring to Gardner 1913, 162.

[99] For examples and discussion see Nissen 1974, 389–415. Self-evidently the rabbis thereby did not reject or "water down" any part of the law (in agreement with Räisänen 1987, 33–34). But this only demonstrates that they could express the whole law with one commandment without compromising the concept in any respect.

behaviour. The addressees are said to be free from the law (5,1–13); yet their freedom ought to be controlled by mutual love, since one fulfills the *whole* law (be it cultic or moral) by loving.[100] Similarly in the correspondingly paraenetical Romans 13,8–10, Paul refers not only to moral rules or the Decalogue, but to any ordinance in the law. Although the addressees are free from the law, they ought to fulfil it, or its "just demand" (τὸ δικαίωμα τοῦ νόμου, Rom 8,4).[101]

In each case Paul clearly speaks of the whole law. He is not "tacitly reducing the Torah", but loudly and explicitly (πᾶς νόμος, τις ἑτέρα ἐντολή) keeping all its parts together. Räisänen claims that Paul thereby ignores "the ritual part of the Torah" and maintains: "If the 'just requirement *of the law*' is fulfilled in the life of the Christians, *nomos* cannot really mean the Torah *in its totality*."[102] But how do we know, what was the one "just requirement" of the ritual prescriptions or any other commandment according to Paul?

Unable to provide a precise answer here,[103] we can still study, to what does "fulfilling the law" (or its just demand) by the addressees refer, inasmuch as they are earlier claimed to be free from the law? To see here a paradox[104] or contradiction[105] is not necessary. The simple logical solution is that the law or its 'demand' is fulfilled without complying with its particular commandments as such, but in some other way. It is most natural to see that behind many rules, be they cultic or moral, a common basic intention, purpose, or 'demand' was envisaged. The addressees are free from the law, but not from the principle, of which its exhortations were but an expression. The law as such no longer concerns the addressees, yet its one single demand is justifiable.

The emphasis on a great principle behind, and even beyond the particular commands, is a recurrent theme in the OT. The prophetic ideologies often contain the idea of a single demand behind, particularly, cultic regulations. Actually the great principle overrides them when formal obedience is harshly

---

[100] So also Thurén 1986, 168–69; against Hübner 1978, 37–39.

[101] Paul may distinguish between "doing" and "fulfilling" the law (Hong 1993, 177–79; criticized by Thielman 1994, 140), the latter indicating "satisfying the true intention". Nevertheless, this distinction is not necessary for understanding the sentence.

[102] Räisänen 1987, 27–28; his emphasis.

[103] Hong presents a three-phased "logic" behind 5,14: In the OT, the observance of the law was Israel's response to God's saving grace in the Exodus, in the NT it is a response to the Christ event; therefore loving one's neighbour is the eschatological fulfilment of the law as a whole (Hong 1993, 182). For me it is somewhat obscure, how this train of thought is rooted in the actual text.

[104] Westerholm 1988, 205.

[105] Räisänen 1987, 26–28.

criticized.[106] Thus the idea is not ideosyncratically Pauline. Whatever the great principle may be according to Paul, it will be fulfilled in "love" or by "walking in the spirit" (5,13–14.16).

J. Thurén takes circumcision as an example of the difference between the commandments and the demand. The one demand for the prophets was circumcision of the heart (Deut 10,16; 30,6; Jer 4,4), viz. love toward God. According to Paul, this demand concerns even the Christians, who actually in this sense are circumcised (Rom 2,25–29; Phil 3,3; cf. Col 2,11). Therefore the practical circumcision has lost its importance (Gal 6,15).[107] Such conclusions were radical, but they were not without Biblical roots.

When Paul speaks of the law in Gal 3–4, an interesting variation between the pronouns "you" and "we" can be found. Is Paul here speaking of a general law, which concerns the Gentiles, and of the Torah, concerning the Jews? Or is the concept even more obscure? Two explanations have been offered.

According to Hartman, the shifting of the person is caused by Paul's persuasive purpose. According to him, "the shift to 'we' language has the rhetorical effect of engaging the listeners, and of bringing speaker and hearer on the same footing. - - - Thus, I suggest that there is much less theology than rhetorics behind the 'we' of v 23."[108] Hartman concludes that instead of "much theologizing" one ought to concentrate on what Paul is doing.[109]

Räisänen, instead, argues that we actually have a series of four cases, which indicate a "double concept" of the law.[110]

First, the law of Moses ought naturally to concern only the Jews. However, in Gal 3,13–14 Paul states that Christ redeemed "us", viz. all nations, from the curse of the law.[111] This statement does not however blur the concept of the law: The *curse* of the law may well rest even upon those ignorant of it.[112] To claim

---

[106] See Micha 6,6–8; Hosea 6,6; Amos 5,21–27; Isa 1,10–17; Jer 6,19–21, Mal 1,10; 2,13.

[107] Thurén 1986, 173.

[108] Hartman 1993, 142–43.

[109] Hartman 1993, 146.

[110] Räisänen 1987, 19–23.

[111] Hong (1993, 78–79) argues that the mention of τὰ ἔθνη in 3,14a signifies a shift in the meaning of the word "we". I find this explanation difficult to follow.

[112] Thurén (1986, 167) claims that according to Romans (2,15; 3,19), the judgement of the law concerns also people without the law, since they have its demand in their hearts.

the opposite would require additional knowledge of the function of "curse" in Pauline theology.[113]

Second, from 3,23–25 to v. 26–27 the pronoun changes from "we" to "you". It can be suggested, that even the Gentiles were under the law,[114] which thus must be a universal concept. This, in turn, cannot be temporal, but is qualificatory: People are no longer judged on the basis of the law. But how were they then judged at the time of Abraham? Does not the concept vary so as to bewilder?

Third, the style continues in chapter four, where "we" and "you" seem to be almost interchangeable, so that it is impossible to determine who are the Jews and who the Gentiles. There is even an obscure, implicit, suggestion that the Torah is included in the elements of the world. The worst example is yet to come: According to 5,1, Galatians ought not to be bound again, since Christ has set *us* free.

Räisänen rightly claims that this oscillation cannot be accidental. But I have difficulties in following the conclusion, according to which the concept of the law oscillates. For the 'pendulum' in the text is not the law but the *person*.

Thus we may turn to the first explanation. To understand the text, we must not start with an assumption, according to which the primary function of "we" is to indicate nationality or religion. If such an hypothesis does not fit the facts, it must not be accepted. The natural function of personal pronouns in a letter concerns primarily the relation between the sender and the addressees. If the author or speaker sometimes identifies with his audience, the alteration of the pronouns serves a particular purpose: To establish a close contact between the partners in communication. This in turn builds up his *ethos,* thereby increasing the acceptability of his message.[115] This is the 'preset value' of the pronoun even in Galatians, unless the context clearly indicates otherwise.[116]

But does not the choice of the person however suggest some ambiguity concerning the *nomos*, for sometimes "we" obviously means the Jews? Is the concept solid in this section? The idea of Gal 3,23–29 is clear as such: The law governed "us" (probably Paul actually thinks of himself as a Jew) until Christ and faith came. Now "we" are no more under the law. Since everyone of "you"

---

[113] Such information is not provided by the dictionaries; see Hübner (1981) or Büchsel (1933), who referring to Rom 3,23 argues that even in Gal 3,13 nobody is excluded from the curse.

[114] Unless an attempt is made to involve the metaphor in ch. 4, as Räisänen surprisingly does (1987, 20).

[115] Cf. Martin 1974, 158–60.

[116] Cf. also Hartman 1993, 148 n. 51 on the shift of person in Gal 4,6.

(mostly Gentiles?) who believes in Christ is an heir of Abraham, the ethnic background is no longer relevant. Here *nomos* clearly indicates the law of Moses, no additions are needed to understand the text.

In Gal 4 there is a second metaphor, which is not to be mixed with the previous one. In 4,1–5 Paul does not give the law another meaning: According to 5 "we" (the Jews) lived under the law. He also states that "we" were enslaved by *stoikheia*, probably cosmic powers, presumably just because we lived "under the law". Yet the two are *not* identified in the text. Thus we must ask, how does life under the law result in slavery to the elements.

According to 4,8–11, "you", viz. the addressees (mostly Gentiles?), formerly worshipped the *stoikheia* as gods, and now run the risk of falling into the same idolatry, while wanting to obey the law. In practice this means that they "observe days and months and seasons and years".

The Gentiles closely followed these "basic principles"[117] because of their ignorance (of God), whereas the Jews acted similarly on the basis of the law. How is that possible? The most natural explanation refers to Gen 1,14, according to which the lights were set in the sky to mark "seasons and days and years". Observing the Jewish cultic calendar means thus in practice observing these *stoikheia*.[118] Irrespective of the origin of such worship, it means slavery, into which the addressees as free Christians should not fall.

But how can this negative result be combined with ch. 3, where the law served as a "positive" guardian, fulfilling God's purpose?[119] Or were the Gentiles too guarded by the law? The answer is simple: They are not to be combined – they are two different metaphors emphasizing different truths. The Jews being kept under the law in ch. 3 is indeed seen as a positive phenomenon, but the Jewish life under the *stoikheia*, to which the Gentiles' worship of *stoikheia* is compared in the text, is presented as negative.

But is not Paul now criticizing a Jewish misuse of the law? The same can be suspected in ch. 4, where the "minority" or slavery of the Jews is compared with the ignorance of the Gentiles. All these are negative words. Contrary to ch. 3, Paul here refers to a perverse result of following the law. However, as Hartman notes about Gal 4,10, "the line is best understood as irony." A specific

---

[117] For the obscure meaning of the concept, see Hartman 1993, 147.

[118] See Mussner 1974, 297–303; Betz 1979, 215–18, Thurén 1986,167.

[119] Räisänen (1987, 20) wonders: "How could namely the Galatians' pre-Christian past under control of heathen idols... in anyway be conceived as a preparatory stage which was all right until the coming of Christ?"

definition about the "dark past of both Jewish and Gentile Christians" is not provided.[120]

But as to the semantics, when the metaphors are not mixed and the text is read as it stands, the concept of the law remains the same in both sections. Only neglect of the message of the text will cause logical and linguistic problems – in this section such are not created by Paul.

There are in Galatians, however, some exceptions, where *nomos* does not refer to the Mosaic law. Yet the specific use of the word in these cases is semantically too distinct to be confused with the general meaning. Play with different meanings of a word is a natural and common device in communication.[121]

In Gal 4,21b *nomos* refers to Genesis or the entire Pentateuch, since the *nomos* here pertains to a story about Abraham: "Tell me, you who desire to be subject to the law, will you not listen to the law? (4,22) For it is written that Abraham had two sons..."[122] This was the other standard meaning of the word in Judaism; its use was hardly seen by anyone as perplexing.

Here Paul actually utilizes this semantic ambivalence: He apposes the *nomos* as Pentateuch to *nomos* as law. This play on words is not merely a rhetorical device, but also signifies that Paul has found a tension within the same book: the law simultaneously makes demands and claims that they cannot be met.[123]

In Gal 6,2 Paul speaks of the "law of Christ". The relationship between the "law of Christ" and the Torah will be discussed below; here it suffices to say that they are not identical, but *nomos* is here used metaphorically. The expression hardly refers to the legislation in the OT, or even an explicit ethical code established by Jesus as a new Moses.[124] It remains unclear, to what degree Paul refers to the historical Jesus, or if he only means "prescriptive principles stemming from the heart of the gospel".[125] At least in the context, the expression

---

[120] Hartman 1993, 148.

[121] Lausberg 1998, §§ 657–64.

[122] Cf. Rom 3,31b. Hong (1993, 123) argues that Gal 5,23b does not belong to this category.

[123] Thus Thurén 1986, 166: Torah as law implies that it can be obeyed, yet like story of Abraham's sons it says that the heritage belongs to the son who could not rely on his background or ability to fulfill the law (cf. Phil 3,4–6).

[124] Räisänen 1987, 16: "patently metaphorical"; 77–81; Longenecker 1990, 275–76. I find Martyn's (1995, 37) and Stanton's (1996, 111) idea of the law as commandment, but with a sudden "evangelistic witness" difficult to follow. For further discussion, see below chapter c.

[125] Longenecker 1990, 275–76.

belongs to the Pauline paraenesis and is aimed at supporting his own ethical
teaching.

Summing up, it can be stated that in Galatians the concept of *nomos* is
semantically stable and clear. Paul's ideas cannot be explained by referring to
oscillation of this word. Excluding the common standard Jewish alternative
meaning in 4,21b, and the transparently metaphorical 6,2, the word simply
refers to the Mosaic law in the epistle. Difficulties emerge only if we, as
modern exegetes, overlook the natural rhetoric and create semantic obscurity
in order to avoid *contentual*, theological difficulties with Paul's view on the
law.

### b. The Law and God – is Paul Blasphemous?

Paul's obvious aim with Gal is to persuade his addressees, that the law has been
superseded by the Gospel. To this end he utilizes several ideas, some of which
have given rise to suspicion. Does the apostle go too far? Is he contrary or even
blasphemous? Such problems ensue from Paul's statements about the origin
and purpose of the law in Gal 3.

Schweitzer and Hübner argue, that the law in Gal 3 represents evil demons,[126]
whereas most scholars dare not claim that Paul denied its divine origin.
Räisänen maintains that Paul is ambiguous, giving two signals simultaneously.
On the one hand, God was not involved in the law-giving process; it was given
by angels. This is called "the natural literal understanding of 3.19–20". On the
other, God was not excluded, since the law had simultaneously a positive
purpose in God's plan.[127]

We have seen above that this "internal contradiction" cannot be due to
Paul's anger, his emotional overreaction, in which he happened to reveal his
deepest feelings.[128] Therefore we must look for a different solution. If, as it
seems, the letter is – both rhetorically and ideologically – carefully constructed,
how can Paul give such an equivocal message? For ambiguity was usually seen
as a problem, at least in juridical rhetoric.[129]

α) *The Exigency of Gal 3,15–29.* At this point it is important to examine the
argumentative situation of the section 3,15–29. What kind of exigency does
Paul envisage here? What are the addressees' convictions which he is

---

[126] Schweitzer 1930, 70–75; Hübner 1986, 70–78.
[127] Räisänen 1987, 130.132.
[128] See above section II 2Aa.
[129] Martin 1974, 44.50–51.

attempting to modify, and what arguments does he choose for this purpose? I find two intertwined targets.

The first goal is self-evident: Paul argues the inferiority of the law, presenting different grounds. This suits well his general goal. But he also poses two interrelated questions: "What is the purpose of the law (in the first place)?" (19) and "Does the law contradict God's promises?" (21). We might invert these questions and ask: What is the function of these topics, and do they contradict Paul's attack on the law?

The addressees are expected to respect and honour the law, and they are even supposed to be willing to practice at least some of its prescriptions. Especially in the beginning of the chapter however, Paul makes some very adverse claims about the law. In accordance with his general stance, Paul as a true Christian has become free from the law (2,19). God has provided a better means to justification: the promise (3,6–18).

Now a natural response by the addressees[130] is to think that Paul regards the law as evil, or a divine error, or that God's own action was contradictory, as He gave both the law and the promise. Such an idea, however, is blasphemous and therefore hard to accept. Paul thus runs the risk of losing his ethos and credibility. He needs to guard himself. What is needed in this situation is an explanation: How does dethroning the law not imply criticism of God?

The argumentative situation is thereby twofold. Paul must continue to disparage the law, otherwise he would compromise rhetorical effectivity.[131] The same danger threatens, however, from the opposite side, if he goes too far in his criticism. Paul seems not only to attack, but also to be on the defensive. In a good rhetorical manner, *refutatio*,[132] he anticipates a possible counterattack and guards himself against covert accusations.

β) *The Origins of the Law.* Our first task is look for the "natural literal" meaning of the origins of the law in the section 3,15–20. In these verses Paul does not directly discuss the issue of who gave the law. His subject, beside the *purpose* of the law, is *when* and *how* the law was given. It was "added" 430 years later (than the promise), and it was ordained by or through angels, and by means of a mediator. Thus the answer to the question about the originator requires that implicit information be extracted from the material.

---

[130] Here no accusations by the antagonists are implied.

[131] Longenecker sees Paul's negative mention of law-giving angels as an *ad hominem* argument against his opponents, who attempted to add the glory of the law by referring to the angels (1990, 140).

[132] Martin 1974, 124–33.

If the angels used a mediator, did they act on their own? Who actually compiled the law? In other Pauline texts, as well as in Judaism in general, the law is associated with God, representing His will.[133] In the context, in 3,16 (ἐρρέθησαν) and 19 (διαταγείς, προσετέθη), the promise is spoken by a *passivum divinum*, so also presumably the law in 3,22 (δοθῇ). Thus, the natural "preset value" for the logical subject behind the passive forms is God.[134] Moreover the law is said to serve God's purpose.[135] Therefore the *onus probandi* lies upon the opposite thesis, that there is another participant behind these passive forms.[136]

Assuming this burden, Räisänen puts forward the following arguments:[137] 1) The preceding context: a) Paul creates distance between the law and God by personifying the law in v. 17; b) The law cannot be made by the testator himself, as it is emphasized that it is an addition 430 years later. 2) The succeeding verse 20 is to be understood: "God, being One, needs no mediator... a mediator was needed, because God was not involved." When speaking of a "mediator", Paul actually means "originators". From these arguments, Räisänen arrives at a solution, which according to himself is not only "certainly strange", but also contradicts many features even in the immediate context, let alone the average Pauline theology.

Is this contradictory, abrupt theory really the "natural literal" interpretation of the passive forms? Let us scrutinize the arguments.

1a) The personification of the law in v. 17 corresponds to the personification of faith in v. 23.25, and likewise the personification of the law in Romans (5,20). Such a method, *prosopopoiia*, is a normal rhetorical device.[138] It is fair to say that it serves to create *some* distance, as does the use of mediator in v. 19. The effect of the device is however seriously overestimated, if it is seen as indicating a total separation.[139]

---

[133] Räisänen 1987, 128.131.

[134] Mussner 1974, 247 n. 17; Räisänen 1987, 130; Hong 1993, 153–54, who also recalls that the law is part of a contract between God and Israel (154). Eckstein (1996, 187) claims that the whole argumentation in 3,15–18 and 3,19–4,7 is based on the idea of the law's divine origin.

[135] Westerholm 1988, 178.

[136] Hong also argues that 3,21 implies that the law originated from God.

[137] Räisänen 1987, 30–32.

[138] Bühlmann and Scherer 1973, 70. Cf. Paul's use of *prosopopoiia* in Rom 7 (below section II 3Cb).

[139] Cf. the personification of God's qualities, e.g. *pneuma*, *sofia*, and *logos* in the OT and in the Gospel of John.

1b) It is a cardinal mistake to press too much information from a metaphor, simile or parable.[140] Likewise we could wonder, whether Paul implies that God is now dead, or why the testament is not executed until several hundred years later. Such fancies are due to unnatural rationalization of the metaphor.

2) The remaining argument is the puzzling v. 20, which has prompted the symbolic estimation of 430 different interpretations among scholars.[141] Räisänen ascribes the difficulty of interpretation to the scholars' unwillingness to "swallow Paul's message", but this rhetorical device can also be turned against Räisänen's own solution: Maybe the bad taste of a demonic origin of the law is not due to the apostle.

A simple reading of verses 19–20 postulates that the many angels speaking to the people of Israel, needed a mediator, Moses, whereas one God, speaking directly to Abraham had no such need.[142] Although other interpretations are possible, nothing in the verse indicates, that Paul would here present a novel idea of a demonic origin of the law. It is unlikely that the verse contradicted the traditional Jewish idea, that God sent the angels to give the law – notwithstanding that the use of the tradition for undermining the law is radical.[143] In accordance with Jewish tradition, different figures – angels and probably also Moses – were involved in the process of communication, but to claim on the basis of v. 19 that the use of a mediator indicates that God was not involved at all, is a *non sequitur*.

We can conclude, that distance between God and the law is established by many rhetorical means, and that the law and the promise are even further apart. This serves the main goal of the text: to polarize the situation and emphasize the superiority of Paul's own theological position. It also defends Paul against implicit accusations of criticizing God when rejecting the law. Paul's main thesis, according to which the law is no longer valid, is radical and exaggerated – a modern hyperradicalization suggesting a demonic origin of the law would have been rhetorically unwise and cannot be supported by the actual document.

γ) *The Purpose of the Law.* In 3,15–29 – beside postulating an inferior means and time of publication of the law (although not an inferior origin) – Paul emphasizes that the law had its purpose, a certain function, and presumably

---

[140] Who has not heard parables of Jesus being wildly interpreted by violation of this rule?

[141] Oepke 1973,117.

[142] Thurén 1986, 178–79.

[143] Westerholm 1988, 177; cf. also Hong (1993, 155) and Hartman (1993, 140), according to whom "it... must have appeared horrendous".

served it well. Now, however, its mission is accomplished, since Christ has come.

The Galatians were assumed to respect the law as divine. Now Paul solves the tension between the two exclusive entities, the divine law and his Gospel, in a way which was for the addressees easier to accept and therefore rhetorically more effective than claiming a demonic origin for the law. Paul claims not only that the law, although being divine, reflects plurality whereas the Gospel means oneness;[144] the main argument is that the law has served a good purpose, which now however has been fulfilled. Therefore it is a mistake to continue to follow its obsolete prescriptions.

What then was the purpose of the law according to Paul? To what does τῶν παραβάσεων χάριν (Gal 3,19) refer? It hardly pertains to the prevention of crime.[145] Instead, cognitive and causative interpretations are possible.[146] In the context, the former makes more sense, viz. is the more natural solution: The law identifies sin as transgression.[147] As Longenecker points out, the causative alternative contradicts the rest of the sentence: How would increasing the amount of the sin build up the coming of Christ?

The purpose is unfolded with another metaphor in 22–25: The law is presented as a guardian slave, who took care of the people until the promise was fulfilled and Christ came. This is not presented as an "indirect purpose in God's plan".[148] On the contrary: The law is portrayed as a preliminary step toward faith in Christ. Paul's protest against continuing obedience of the law is not based on its originally negative role.

Thus the question about the function of the law is to be seen in its context in view of its purpose, in the rhetorical situation. Paul is both diminishing the authority of the law and defending himself against possible charges. When speaking of the purpose of the law he attempts to explain why God gave it in the first place: it performed a necessary task. Now, however, its goal has been achieved.

δ) *Conclusions.* Gal 3,15–29 resolves the exigency implied. Paul's ethos and the acceptability of his solution remain intact, since he avoids any criticism of God and His law. Yet Paul's defence does not compromise the rhetorical

---

[144] Thurén 1986, 179.

[145] In accordance with Räisänen 1987, 140.

[146] Hong (1993, 150–51), supporting the causative interpretation, ignores the cognitive alternative. Westerholm (1988, 179–89) holds both as possible.

[147] Longenecker 1990, 138.

[148] Räisänen 1987, 151.

effectivity of his main point. He does not give a puzzling, ineffectual *sic et non* signal, but a persuasive, clear message.

The law had its good purpose, which did not contradict the promise. Now, however, the purpose is fulfilled. In the new situation the law belongs to the past. According to Paul, there is nothing wrong with the law as such; the fault is in the Galatians who think that it, or some parts of it, still ought to be obeyed. For all who have been baptized into Christ are free from the law – in this sense the law's dominion ceased when Christ came. The claim that a Christian is free from the law does not imply that the law was a mistake. It was a necessary means for preparing the coming of the faith or Christ.

The devices creating distance between the law and God (angels, mediator, temporality, and plurality) have a double function. First, they underline the superiority of the new situation, the promise and the Gospel, which are marked by a direct contact with God and Oneness. Second, the distance protects Paul from sounding blasphemous. Since God's traditional role as the good establisher of the law is not actually questioned, Paul can expect to avoid possible counterarguments and assume that his message is persuasive.

## c. The Law as Moral Guidance

One of the most controversial topics in the interpretation of Galatians is: Do the moral prescriptions of the law still govern the Christians' behaviour according to Paul? Many scholars think they do,[149] whereas some think they do not.[150] Or is the man again inconsistent?[151] This problem is not to be confused with the question about Paul's possibly *negative attitude* to the law.[152]

According to Westerholm, the phrase "died for the law" (Gal 2,19; Rom 7,4) cannot be restricted to some parts of the law or to its misunderstanding. The expression is absolute. Similarly, Paul states that "he cannot be said to transgress a law to which he is no longer subject";[153] the whole law is obsolete (Gal 3,19–4,6), and Gal 5,3 implies that the Christians are no longer bound by

---

[149] E.g Hong 1993, 170–83; Thielman 1994, 139–43; Dunn 1996b, 3; 1996c, 333–34; Wright 1996, 137; Stanton 1996, 116.

[150] E.g. Thurén 1986, 172–74; Westerholm 1988, 205–209; Becker 1989, 416–23. Chrysostom is even more outspoken (PG 61.668-69), see Thurén 2000a.

[151] Räisänen, of course (1987, 63).

[152] See below section II 2C.

[153] Gal 2,17–18 according to Westerholm 1988, 206.

it.[154] Yet other scholars argue that the law after all "serves as an expression of God's will",[155] and the Spirit "enables the people of God to fulfil the law".[156]

α) _The New Moses?_ The expression ὁ νόμος τοῦ Χριστοῦ in 6,2 is crucial for the argumentation. While the law in 5,14 refers incontrovertibly to the law of Moses,[157] the "law of Christ" in 6,2 "must be taken as _another reference to the Mosaic law_".[158] Although the addressees are not told to "do" the law, the law still "serves as a norm and standard of Christian conduct _if it is rightly interpreted_".[159]

The expression in Gal 6,2 is certainly short and therefore open to different interpretations. Above I argued that the expression is most naturally understood as metaphorical and hardly refers to the Torah.[160] Now a rhetorical argument can be added: a new role of the law, contradicting the previous message, would be very unwise regarding the persuasion.

In the first chapters Paul is arguing against applying any part of the law to the Christians' life. To invalidate the law, he has even used stark expressions, running the risk of blasphemy. Since in Galatians he makes a trifling practical matter a huge, decisive issue, he needs to articulate his message as clearly as possible. There is no room for explanations or second thoughts: The law has been superseded once and for all. Whereas the Galatians may have just been searching for a mature application of something in the law of Moses, Paul goes into battle with a plain message: Even the slightest acceptance of the law is fatal for the addressees' religion. Indeed this exaggerated view in Galatians has caused problems, when compared with Paul's utterances in other letters.

Now Paul would hardly compromise the message in the latter part of the letter. Therefore his sharp rhetoric has its consequences: The apostle is compelled to abolish the law even in practical matters. It is not persuasive first to regard the law as an abomination and then recommend it for another purpose. Thus it seems unlikely, that Paul would suddenly give the law a positive role

---

[154] Westerholm 1988, 206–208.

[155] Instead of complying only with external demands, more is required: "... a much deeper commitment, the _total submission of his whole life_ to the sovereign control of the Spirit... The Christian is impelled and enabled to love his neighbour in response to God's grace unfolded in the cross."(Hong 1993, 188). A mighty sermon by Hong, yet its _pathos_-effect does not suffice as a scholarly argument.

[156] Thielman 1994, 142. Cf. also Brooten 1990.

[157] See above section II 2Ba and Hong 1993, 171–72, against Hübner 1986, 36ff.

[158] Hong 1993, 176 (his emphasis); Sanders 1983, 97–98; Stanton 1996, 115–16.

[159] Hong 1993, 178.182; my emphasis.

[160] See above section II Ba; Räisänen 1987, 16; Longenecker 1990, 275–76.

in the addressees' life, with one obscure expression. I find it difficult to believe that the addressees were expected to produce Hong's sophisticated "right" interpretation of the "extremely baffling phrase" in 6,2,[161] so that they were able to distinguish notwithstanding a positive application of the law to their life. To quote Hays (in another context): "The law is not so easily domesticated..."[162] For me it seems more probable, that to force such a "positive" role into Gal is due to the scholars' own, more balanced view of the concept.[163]

How then is the relationship between 5,14 and 6,2 to be understood? I have argued above, that if the addressees are told in 5,14 to fulfil the (true intention of the) law, this does not mean that they are obliged to obey the particular commandments.[164] The addressees are free from the law, but not from the main principle behind it. Similarly, in 6,2 the short mention of the "law" of Christ cannot suddenly contradict the letter's main tendency. Christ is not a new Moses, but his counterpart, and his "law" rather serves as a diametrical opposite concept to the "law of Moses".[165] Although the precise meaning of the metaphorical 6,2 remains unknown, combined with 5,14 it indicates that the one requirement of "the whole law" is fulfilled by obedience to the "law" of Christ.

β) *Enabling Exhortation?* Closer to the existing text than Hong's too "mature" view of the law, is Räisänen's suggestion, according to which Paul maintained his new theology throughout Gal. However, he could not fully refute the traditional Jewish attitude either, so ended with contradictions. Although I am not entirely happy with this thesis, it offers a good point of departure. Thus I turn to particular questions connected with it.

Without claiming it as a standard, one can still wonder, whether the Galatians are expected to be *able* to live in accordance with the actual prescriptions of the law. The answer seems to be negative. In principle Paul clearly states that all who seek to be justified through the law are under a curse, since it ought to be fulfilled in its totality. A missing, implicit element in this argumentation is that such a fulfilment is impossible.[166] Gal 3,10 and 5,3 imply that none can fulfil the whole law. But is Paul inconsistent? Is a life according to the law sometimes possible?

---

[161] Hong 1993, 173.
[162] Hays 1996, 157.
[163] See below section II 2C.
[164] See above section II 2Ba.
[165] Cf. Westerholm 1988, 198–218, esp. 214, n. 38; Longenecker 1990, 275.
[166] Räisänen 1987, 95.

At least Gal 5,14ff does not contradict the pessimistic view, since – as seen above – the verse rather refers to a way of keeping the main principle or requirement of, or behind the law, without necessarily following its specific ordinances.[167]

But compare Gal 5,16 "Live by the Spirit and you will not carry out the desires of the flesh". Does it give an over-optimistic picture of the Christian's life while maintaining that she/he can live without "fulfilling the desire of the flesh"? In that case, Paul's argument would go astray: "He compares Christian life at its best (if not an ideal picture of it) with Jewish life at its worst (if not a pure caricature)."[168]

These observations are on the right lines, but not taken far enough. Paul is indeed operating with radical images instead of well-balanced, neutral descriptions of reality, but for the sake of rhetoric. Paul is not informing or describing, but persuading, for the sentence belongs to the paraenesis. To make his point clear, Paul contrasts an ideal model with a caricature. The addressees are invited to follow an ideal picture, instead of choosing its opposite, which is painted in dark colours. An *exhortation*, however, is not to be identified with a direct *description* of its target.[169] If the persuasive exhortation in 5,16 is converted into a dull statement, it could read as follows: "As far as you live by the Spirit, you will not..." Complete success is not guaranteed.

γ) *The Exigency of Gal 5,13–6,10.* In order to grasp the full meaning of the exhortation in 5,16 we must first turn to a larger question within Galatians, the function of the *paraenesis* in 5,13–6,10.[170]

It is common to see chapters 5–6 as an addition to the main text, or as dealing with another problem in the congregation.[171] Many modern scholars associate it with discussing a second problem in Galatia, libertinism.[172] This is

---

[167] Above section II 2Ba.

[168] According to Räisänen (1987, 117–18), Paul saw at least himself as a sin-free person, although his addressees were not necessarily such.

[169] We must be careful in the exegesis: Paul is by no means characterizing his actual readers nor does the caricature claim to describe actual Jews. See above section II 2Ac.

[170] The strategic function of the paraenesis in Gal has been emphasized by Kraftchick 1985, 209–72.

[171] Maybe the sharpest representative of this view is O'Neill 1972, 67.

[172] For discussion regarding this "two-front" hypothesis, see Lategan 1992, 260–61. According to his own position, only one front is needed, since the letter discusses "two modes of existence – one of slavery under the Law and one of freedom in Christ".

seen as an alternative way of falling from grace.[173] Bradley assesses the section as a random, traditional paraenesis,[174] and even Betz in his rhetorical analysis fails to see any proper function therein; the chapters are characterized as an addition to the judicial speech.[175]

However, the discussion of the rhetorical *genus* proves useful here. Contrary to Betz' judicial assessment, the letter is currently most often seen as deliberative, viz. advising the addressees to make a decision on some matter.[176] In this genus, the section 5,13–6,10 fits precisely into the text. For in the deliberative speech, the discussion of a matter is followed by *exhortatio*, where the audience, the *ekklesia*, is told to make up its mind, to draw the practical conclusions.[177] As an *ekklesia* the Galatians ought to retain their position as free men, not to become slaves of the law, viz. the Judaizing teachers (5,1–12), *or* under the power of the flesh (5,13f).[178]

This does not, however, prove that we should imagine libertinism as another, prominent or acute difficulty among the Galatians, beside the first problem, the "Judaizers".[179] The right behaviour was always an important issue in the first Christian congregations, as we can see from most of the NT epistles. In Galatians, nothing indicates a specific urgency in this question. Instead, the paraenesis can more naturally be seen as belonging to the prior discussion with the opponents. It not only serves as a final exhortation, but as such carries a message to the antagonists. Just as in 3,15–29, Paul uses *refutatio*, viz. defends his Gospel against possible counterarguments.[180]

Above Paul proclaimed that the law has served its purpose for those who believe in Christ. This exclusivity is important for rhetorical and theological reasons. But this message immediately prompts a question: What then happens to the ethics, to the daily life and morals of the Christians? Will not the

---

[173] E.g. Lütgert (1919) finds here antinomian pneumatists. Longenecker explains that the chapters discuss the second danger in Galatia: He sees the exhortations as an attack on libertine tendencies within the congregation, which have little to do with the first problem (1990, 235–38).

[174] Bradley (1953, 238) identifies Gal 5,13–6,10 as the paraenesis of Galatians in the Dibelian sense of the word: general rules of behaviour without any specific target or structure.

[175] Betz 1979, 271ff.

[176] See above section II 2A.

[177] Martin 1974, 167–76.

[178] J. Thurén (1993j, 80) even argues that the first part of the letter aims at regaining the apostle's authority, which is essential to solve the question of freedom, and to persuade the addressees to obey the paraenesis.

[179] In agreement with Hong 1993, 100–101.

[180] Cf. above section II 2Bbα.

abolition of the law lead to libertinism or negligence of ethics? This question may well be presupposed by Paul.[181] A corresponding, more theologically explicit line of thought can be found in e.g. Rom 6.

Kraftchick has put forward the thesis, that in Gal 5–6 Paul is counteracting charges of antinomy, which ensue from his theology.[182] In order to substantiate the thesis it ought to be explained, how the paraenesis actually yields such a result. According to Kraftchick, chapters 5–6 serve as an *ethos* and *pathos* appeal. The goal is to affirm that by accepting Paul's exclusive Gospel the addressees do not lose the concrete rules of behaviour as a way of structuring the world.

Although there may be some truth in Kraftchick's theory, it seems more natural that the paraenesis in chapters 5–6 belongs also – and perhaps mostly – to the *logos* appeal. This means that they belong to the theological argumentation of the epistle. The paraenesis too aims to show the inadequacy of the law. Its "theological" function is to indicate, that abolition of the law will not lead to libertinism, on the contrary. Just as the law was unable to give life and salvation, it cannot produce good behaviour. But the Gospel of Paul, including the Spirit, is likely to produce good conduct among the addressees.

For Paul does not identify the paraenesis with the law. The goal of the paraenesis is to make the addressees obey the holy will of God, something which the Mosaic law could not achieve. The paraenesis and the Christians' new life are necessary in order to prove empirically the superiority of Paul's gospel over the message of his antagonists. Although the main principle of Paul's paraenesis or the 'law of Christ' is identical with that of Moses – to love God and one another – the are two major differences.

The first one concerns the practical contents. The paraenetic exhortation in Gal, as in Early Christianity in general, is not identical with the Mosaic law, although e.g. the Decalogue is presented (Rom 13,9–10). But the paraenesis is not genuine and originally Pauline either. It rather reflects various contemporary Jewish and Hellenistic ethical ideals. Recent studies have demonstrated, that Early Christian paraenesis was strongly influenced by contemporary Hellenistic ethical ideals, popular philosophy, and the Halakha, even

---

[181] E.g. the letter of James seems to criticize Paulinism at this point (James 2,14–26).

[182] Kraftchick 1985, 265–71.

if they were chosen at random.[183] These rules, together with some references to the sayings of Jesus,[184] have in large measure displaced the Mosaic legislation.[185]

The foundation of the paraenesis, however, is original, despite some external correspondence.[186] The distinctive component is the motivation.[187] In Gal (contrary even to 1 Peter), the motivation is simple and idealistic: The Spirit enables the Christian to live according to the exhortation. This does not imply that the Spirit "automatically ensures that the believers produce the virtues".[188] But it gives motivation, and the paraenesis is aimed at showing the goal, or what it means to "walk in the Spirit".

Thereby Gal 5–6 prove that, despite rejecting the law, the Pauline Gospel has capability of creating a new way of life. However, Gal 5–6 is not a theoretical treatise. Despite the theoretical function, the section also has a corresponding practical aim: To make the addressees actually live in such a way that they prove the viability of Paul's theological solution with the law. The will of God, the one requirement behind all the commandments, is done by obeying the paraenesis, not the law. Therefore the practical function of the paraenesis is so vital: Only by being obedient to the paraenesis will the addressees prove the validity of Paul's teaching, even regarding the justification.

Now it is possible to discern a simple "systematic" connection between Gal 3 and 5–6: Nobody can fulfil the whole law, which thus does not lead to justification or salvation (Gal 3). The Christians are now set free from the law, and have another way to justification before God – Christ – and another way to ethical life: the Spirit and the paraenesis (Gal 5–6). Paul does not distinguish between two roles of the law so that a social function remains even when a cultic function is abolished. For a Christian, the law as such does not serve even the practical goal, viz. a proper way of life.

Paul's answer to implied charges of libertinism thus functions at both the theoretical and the practical level. The proclamation of the guiding Spirit and the paraenesis is aimed, both theologically and empirically, at rejecting the charge of libertinism as an inevitable consequence of Paul's Gospel. The paraenesis is necessary to make the eschatological "new creation" (Gal

---

[183] See Piper 1979, 101–102; Tomson 1990, 260–64; Thurén 1995b, 11–12.

[184] Piper 1979, 63–65.

[185] Cf. Becker's (1989, 417–18) discussion of the differences between Pauline paraenesis and the Torah.

[186] Against Brooten 1990, 72–73.

[187] Cf. Thurén 1995b, 11–12.

[188] Hong 1993, 185.

6,9–10.15) a visible reality. This is also the goal of Gal 5,16, perhaps of the whole letter, for obedience of the Mosaic law prevents the new life in Spirit. They are mutually exclusive (Gal 5,18). Thus also 5,16 calls for high ethical standards, and reveals an uncommon theological foundation and motivation thereof.[189] Yet nothing in the text indicates that it describes an already achieved strong moral status among the addressees.

# C. Conclusions

Summing up the results concerning Paul's view of the law in Galatians, we can state that:

1) The use of the word is simple: *nomos* denotes the Sinaitic legislation, with two exceptions: the reference to the Pentateuch in 4,21b and the metaphorical use in 6,2.

2) Nobody can fulfil the law – Paul's exhortation to fulfil the demand of the law does not describe his addressees.

3) The new substitute for the law (promise, faith, Spirit) is superior in many respects, concerning how and when these blessings are given. Yet God's role as the source behind each is never even implicitly denied.

4) The law once had a proper purpose, yet its mission is now accomplished – it no longer binds the Christian.

5) The law does not suffice even for moral guidance, and does not deliver the new eschatological creation. In this sense it is replaced (or in practice modified and completed) by the Pauline paraenesis. The new life is provided by the Spirit (5,18).

When Paul conveys these ideas to the reader, he is not (at least unduly) influenced by emotion. There are no excuses – he is completely in charge when dictating. Unless the apostle is deliberately deceiving his addressees, the letter to Galatians reflects his genuine theology at the time.[190]

Yet the deliberative goal of the letter affects the presentation of the ideas. Paul's expressions reflect one simple, bare perspective on the question, for the objective is not theoretical, to educate the addressees, but pragmatic: to persuade them to make a decision to follow Paul, not the other teachers.

The explicit theology in Gal is therefore simplistic and polarized. Paul hardly records all his thoughts on the topic. In order to achieve rhetorical effectivity his presentation is one-sided. Regarding a possible theology beyond

---

[189] This motivation is not shared e.g. by 1 Peter (see Thurén 1995b).

[190] Provided that the letter was not strongly edited later.

the text, such a technique is of course viable and acceptable, insofar as the expressions do not explicitly contradict what he says elsewhere. Our view of his set of ideas can thus be complemented by examination of his other production, since our task is to construct a system of ideas beyond the text. Such a structure can contain more than the ideas presented in Galatians, provided that additional components do not contradict those already in place.

Finally we must ask: If the Pauline presentation is even too clear, as I claim, why has it confused so many interpreters? I suggest that the confusion is at least partly due to the way of reading Paul. The scholars may have sought a balanced, normative, or practical truth instead of giving a neutral account of Paul's arguments, which are indeed biassed.

Sanders argues that the Jewish-Christian theology in Galatia was understandable, Biblical and reasonable.[191] And indeed, a combination of salvation through God's grace with respect for His law in Holy Scripture was widespread before and after Galatians. Beside faith in God's good will (and in Christ), most Christian communities often present some rituals and rules to be obeyed.

A theology, in which the believer is proclaimed totally free from the law, is often pejoratively called "antinomism", and such ideas have won little support among the great Churches. Let us consider only the Calvinist interpretation[192] or the orthodox Lutheran Christianity, hailing the *tertius usus legis*, which guides the believer.

Galatians is in sharp contrast to this view.[193] It represents one-sided antinomianism in the *etymological* sense of the term, as Paul writes against obedience of the Mosaic law, and if this was Paul's only letter, one could imagine it promoting spiritual movements so labelled.[194] References to separate commands in the Torah do not indicate any validation of the whole law. Law and faith definitely exclude each other. Even the slightest demand for obedience to the law ruins the whole Christian system of salvation. In Gal, the Christian is totally free from the law. The word is accepted in a metaphorical sense only (Gal 6,2), and its main principle is fulfilled by new means (Gal 5,14–18).

No wonder Paul's radical view in Gal has gained little support in the later Christianity. Theologians still wanting to quote Paul have been forced to

---

[191]  Sanders 1983, 18–20.

[192]  See Thielman 1994, 244.

[193]  Thus also Eckstein (1996, 257) argues against any *tertius usus legis* in Gal.

[194]  Hengel's distinction between Paul's message in Gal and the actual antinomism implied in 1 Cor is useful (Hengel 1996, 29). Perhaps the ethical turmoil in Corinth was partly caused by a disrupted understanding of Paul's proclamation. See below, section II 3Ab.

confuse his statements. The problems of these interpretations are easy to perceive, but this does not imply corresponding problems in Paul. As far as Galatians is concerned, there is no obscurity; the problems begin when people simultaneously honour Paul as a great teacher, but reject his central theological views, for hermeneutical reasons.

Paul's one-sided treatment of the law in Gal has also led many scholars to characterize the apostle's *attitude* to the law as negative.[195] This is certainly the feeling provoked by reading the letter. But can it actually be substantiated in the text? Paul states that the law does not obligate the Christians, it has been superseded, and its continued obedience is not advisable. Even from the outset the law was inferior to the promise. We cannot however deduce *e silentio* a disapproving attitude. The one-sided treatment is necessitated by the rhetorical situation, but does not *per se* indicate difficulties compared with other, more balanced letters.

---

[195] E.g. Hong 1993, 170, referring to Hübner 1986, 15–50 and Drane 1975, 3–59.

Chapter 3

# The Law Strikes Back: Romans and 1 Cor

In Romans Paul speaks of the law in a starkly positive manner:

> "We uphold the law" (Rom 3,31); "The law is holy and the commandment holy, just and good" (Rom 7,12); "...in order that the righteous requirement of the law might be fully met in us" (Rom 8,4)

How does this relate to Galatians? Of course we could refer to the results above and say that in Gal Paul merely discussed the law from a narrow angle, excluding many issues, in order to convey a persuasive message. This theology is solid *per se*, although immoderate and excessive. By adding matters omitted in Gal, but explicit in other epistles, we can reach a thorough, balanced picture of Paul's theology concerning the law. Unfortunately, the task is not so simple.

Hübner, who assesses the picture of the law in Galatians as extreme but consistent, argues that Romans represents a clearly different, developed view of the same questions. Räisänen goes even further, claiming that, whereas Paul may have altered his views on some points, the new theology remains contradictory, including opposite opinions about the law.[1] Yet even these claims cannot be fully accepted. While it can be taken for granted that Paul's thinking must have undergone *some* development, and that some logical difficulties are to be expected, not *all* the anomalies we find in Paul's texts can be explained with such phenomena.

I reiterate that we as modern, theologically oriented readers may easily disregard a fundamental aspect: the exigency at hand, argumentative tactics and strategies, even the character of persuasive devices in which each expression occurs – all these impinge on how Paul presents his ideas to each audience. Only a dynamic view of Paul's texts enables us to assess the effect of these phenomena on his statements.

But even if we could recognize and filter out most of this influence, it is not certain, whether any solid view can be achieved. In other words, it is unclear, how stable and consistent an ideological structure can be delineated behind the persuasive language, when the expressions concerning the law in Romans, 1 Corinthians and other Pauline letters are "derhetorized" and compared with

---

[1] For discussion, see above.

those in Gal. The author can still be incoherent and/or opportunistic, either spontaneously, as some scholars sympathetically infer, or consciously, as some of Paul's contemporary critics claimed.[2]

In this chapter, Paul's view of the law will be studied especially in Romans and First Corinthians, and compared with that implicit in Galatians. I shall discuss first the conditions for communication in Rom and 1 Cor, and study their impact in utterances about the law. Then, after some semantic observations, I shall focus on issues where deviation, or incompatible theological ideas, can be assumed.

Finally, in chapter four, the roots of Paul's critical attitude to the law will be examined. Beside the sociological and strategic explanations, a theological explanation based on the OT will be presented. Even the now unpopular thesis about boasting as an important factor in Paul's view of the law will be re-examined, for the roots of this idea can be found in Galatians.

# A. Conditions for Communication

## a. Romans

Scholars have reached a consensus concerning Romans: the letter is not a dogmatic presentation of the Pauline theology, as was previously thought, but a real letter written for a specific purpose, which in its turn affects what Paul says.[3] This is, however, also where the unanimity ends. There are several rival explanations why the letter was written, and of its actual message; none is more convincing than the rest. The main problem is how to integrate the framework and the theological body of the letter.

An increasing number of scholars maintain that the exigency of the letter cannot be reduced to one single purpose.[4] Instead, many co-existing goals can be identified. We may take Dunn's proposal as an example. According to him, three main exigencies coincide: a) a missionary purpose: Paul needed a base for his mission in Spain (Rom 15,24.28);[5] b) an apologetic purpose: Paul needed acceptance in Rome, not least in view of the forthcoming talks in Jerusalem;[6] c) a pastoral purpose, viz. to deal with the Jewish-Christian dilemma in Rome.[7]

---

[2]  See above chapter I 4.
[3]  See above section I 2B.
[4]  Donfried 1991, lxx; Wedderburn 1987, 1–6.140.
[5]  For arguments and discussion, see Dunn 1988, lv–lvi.
[6]  Jervell 1991 (originally 1971).
[7]  Dunn 1988, lvi–lviii.

But could such a combination of goals be achieved simultaneously? Could even an attempt be rhetorically effective? While it seems evident, that several targets on different levels can be identified, it remains unclear, how they were combined in a single letter. For Romans was presumably intended to function as a distinct, persuasive entity. As a rhetorician Paul hardly sent random thoughts to Rome, or fired a sawn-off shotgun, hoping that at least some of the missiles would the target. Instead, it is reasonable to presuppose that most parts and themes in the text rather directly serve the (possibly complex) purpose of the author, creating one communicative, convincing unity.

This issue is taken seriously by two recent studies. Neil Elliott argues that the epistle must be seen as a real letter with a target in Rome. He uses rhetorical criticism in order to reveal the strategy of Romans.[8] Elliott rightly emphasizes, that the opening (1,1–17) and closing (15,14–32) sections are here of especial weight, as they perform the rhetorical functions of *exordium* and *peroratio*.[9] In these parts the author was supposed to deal with the main issue, first cautiously, then explicitly.[10]

Elliott finally claims, that the main purpose of the letter is to resolve internal problems, caused by Christian Jews returning to Rome.[11] The goal of Romans is thereby the *paraenesis*, which excludes a self-introduction, a theological essay, a plea to Jerusalem or any other explanation separating the text from the concrete situation.[12] L.A. Jervis, a student of R. Longenecker, starts from a corresponding methodological position, also emphasizing the situational and communicative character of Romans. Using the approach of epistolography, she concludes that the main goal is the opposite, to proclaim the Gospel.[13] Both explanations, however, disregard signals in the text, which point to other explanations.

Sharing the new emphasis on the communicative aspect of Romans, J.N. Vorster claims that we nevertheless have a deadlock. According to him, even rhetorical criticism, including Elliott, has yielded little more than a new terminology.[14] The point of departure for reconstructing the context of the letter has remained the same. Modern approaches accept the same basic assumptions

---

[8] Elliott 1990.

[9] Elliott 1990, 69–104.

[10] I discussed the importance of the speech/letter framework for amending the situation in Thurén 1995a, 269–74.

[11] Elliott 1990, 95–96.

[12] Elliott 1990, 290–92.

[13] Jervis 1991.

[14] Vorster 1994, 127.

as conventional scholarship. The text is seen as a direct route to the historical reality, as a reflection of its context.[15] The study of the context is based on an image of the omniscient Paul, who provides us with correct information about the situation. But what if Paul's knowledge was very limited – and possibly unreliable – and e.g. the greetings in chapter 16 are merely an attempt to conceal his ignorance?[16] Vorster claims that we have many axiomatic hypotheses, but little and accidental external information about the situation.

Concerning the 'rhetorical situation', Vorster argues that such reconstructions tend to be based on an uncritical acceptance of Bitzer's original definition, which was widely criticized and modified later.[17] The result is just another historical reconstruction under a different name. Vorster claims that a rhetorical situation should not be seen as consisting of factors, but "should be located within a wider context, that of culture, formed by the linguistic power of people".[18]

Against Vorster one could argue, that the scholarship simply has to devise theories about the specific context from the information available, even if this is haphazard. How else could we understand the message of Romans? But when a reconstruction of an historical construction is based upon meagre information, the gaps are filled with surmise, and rhetorical "clues" are misinterpreted, the message may be even more difficult to understand. When the wrong hypotheses become axiomatic, the results are disastrous for the message.[19]

The scholars disagree about the details of the situation in Rome,[20] and a precise definition of the historical identity of the addressees is hazardous. For example, we do not *know*, whether all the 50 000 Jews (or were they Jews?), or only some troublemakers among them, were expelled from Rome in 49 CE (or was it 41 CE), and what was the effect on the Christian congregations of their return in 54 CE.[21] Maybe the expulsion remained just a proclamation? Or what if only the meetings of the Jews were prohibited?[22] And what did Paul actually know about the current state of the constantly changing situations in the synagogues and churches in Rome? Of course accurate information would

---

[15] Vorster 1994, 128–29; 138–42.

[16] Vorster 1994, 137–38.

[17] Bitzer 1968; for criticism, see Stamps 1993, 193–210.

[18] Vorster 1994, 144.

[19] Cf. Thurén 1997, 451–53.464–65.

[20] For an overview, see Vorster 1994, 130–31; cf. also Wedderburn 1988, 44–65.

[21] Vorster 1994, 129–30.

[22] Voerster 1944, 33.

yield a better interpretation of the letter, but as far as the answers only remain wild guesses, they must be treated with suspicion.

Yet there is solution. The situation as envisioned by the author is more important for understanding the message, than are the "actual" historical circumstances. This implicit view can be perceived from the text. It is more specific than the general rhetorical situation of the text,[23] which is also necessary for the understanding. In creating such a view, reliable historical information is of importance, but far-flung guesses are not as necessary as in conventional scholarship. Since the goal is different, the text-internal indication assumes greater importance.

What practical consequences does this modification of perspective have for the study of Romans? At least the interest is directed to the *type* of situation which Paul faces, not only to the concrete facts. The communicative character of Romans can be taken into account with full force. Although the letter is particularly interesting for later Christians because of its theological content, it has actually been studied in order to learn about the theology of Paul himself. But before they can use Romans as a source, the exegetes must recognize that the text was primarily a means of persuasion, not neutral presentation, and that it was aimed at the congregation(s) in Rome. Thereby we can hope to limit the effect of its genre to the theological content. Only then can the theology be generalized.

The situational character of Romans implies, that the questions most discussed – the relationship of Jews and Gentiles in God's plan, but also the paraenesis at the end – must have been, according to Paul, crucial for the Christians of Rome. This accords with the "wide-ranging agreement" that the chapters dealing with Israel (9–11) are an integral part of the main argument of the letter, not a secondary afterthought.[24]

We can sketch a rough overall target for Romans:[25] On one level, Paul seeks to sort out the relationship between Gentile and Jewish Christians in Rome. Since neither group, nor its position is to be rejected, the goal requires a decent theological treatment of the convictions of both.

Simultaneously, several underlying purposes can also be identified. They undoubtedly colour Paul's presentation, but no one of them can be declared the primary reason for writing. Thus the main discussion may also serve as a rehearsal for the imminent talks in Jerusalem. Maybe Rome was a convenient theological test-bed? The letter may also build up Paul's *ethos*, presenting him

---

[23] Cf. Wuellner 1987, 456; Thurén 1990, 70–75.

[24] Donfried 1991, lxx.

[25] Cf. Wedderburn 1988, 140–42, who also assesses the situation as complex.

as a trustworthy teacher for the congregation, as does the "name-dropping" in chapter 16.[26] Especially the framework of the text, viz. exordium and peroratio, indicate that Paul seeks to establish a good contact with Rome (1,11–13; 15,14–16.22–24.28.32). Did Paul just desire more power in a large congregation, which was an ecclesiastical no-mans land? At least he presumably expected to consolidate his position as the "apostle of Gentiles", and to support his future missions. Further purposes too can be imagined.

Actually we can never know whether one of these subsidiary reasons or something else actually was the ultimate trigger of the letter. It would be easy to pick up any of these themes and claim it as the real reason for Romans. However, to uncover such a psychological intention of the historical author is beyond scholarly methods.

It is important to note, that most of the suggested underlying purposes do not *rhetorically* obscure the search for the overall target on the surface of the letter. My point is, that even if we knew exactly what prompted Paul, this would not be crucial for studying the theology behind the text. Irrespective of whether Paul actually wrote Romans in order to gain more authority, or simply because he wanted to visit the famous city, or for any other imaginable reason, its interpretation requires identification of the *explicit* issue of the letter, insofar as it can be assessed from the signals in the text, and examination of how this message is communicated.

The rhetorical situation of Romans, with any historical or psychological modification, calls for an impartial presentation of ideas concerning the relationship between Jewish and Gentile Christianity. How does this characterization of the exigency of the letter impinge on the question of the law in Romans? Paul cannot undertake a unilateral attack as in Galatians. Instead, when settling a dispute Paul needs to show compassion and understanding for both sides. He is not instilling a simple principle into the minds of a rather homogeneous group, but treats the question as delicate and complex. Especially if the forthcoming negotiations in Jerusalem influence how Paul writes, we can suspect more reasonable and moderate argumentation than in Gal. Vilification of the villains is not feasible.[27]

The complexity of the goal, however, does not guarantee that Romans is a well-balanced presentation of Pauline theology. The letter is persuasive in nature, aimed at modifying the recipients' thoughts and behaviour. Thus it was

---

[26] Wedderburn 1988, 14.

[27] For instance, Rom 3,8 requires no particular adversaries to be understood (Dunn 1988, 136–37), and instead of proper argumentation and vilification, a stark reference to the Judgment suffices for Paul.

composed in order to reach its immediate goal by all means available. This can be inferred already from the hyperbolical expressions,[28] or the increasing number of rhetorical studies written on Romans.[29] Although he is more polite than in Galatians, Paul has by no means abandoned his target: persuasion. This means that he presents even theological matters in a way suited to his purposes.

Focussing on our specimen question we ask: Does Paul, in his search for a positive side to Jewish Christian theology, go too far in praising the law? Can his presentation be explained as merely a change of style, or does he contradict what he preached in Galatians? The latter question is commonly answered "yes": Paul has realized that the Jewish Christians in Rome or the apostles in Jerusalem would never accept the radicalized view of the law in Galatians. Thus he has adjusted not only his way of writing but the theology behind it towards greater "maturity".

However, I argued above, that also Galatians, despite the impression it first provokes, is a well-prepared document. Therefore it is interesting to see, what ideas remain contradictory after some derhetorization of the text. If Gal seeks to create a sharp distinction and Romans to diminish it, how do the ideas behind these tendencies finally coalesce?

### b. 1 Cor and Other Pauline Epistles

One of the reasons for writing 1 Cor seems to be factionalism. But the integration of this opening theme with the particular questions discussed later in the letter has proven difficult, as chapters 5–16 lack direct reference to factionalism.[30] Margaret Mitchell's rhetorical analysis attempts to overcome this standard objection. She focusses on formal rhetorical features and finds terminology referring to factionalism throughout the text. Furthermore, 1 Cor 1,10 is the *propositio* for the whole letter.[31] Paul does not challenge any one group, but the general phenomenon, which is then demonstrated in numerous ways by the particular questions discussed later.[32]

Without any specific rhetorical method, Fee penetrates the rhetoric of 1 Cor deeper. He wonders, why the language and style of the letter are so "rhetorical and combative", if the goal is to reconcile the different parties and make peace. Thus the real problem concerns the authority of the apostle. He has to regain it, but he also needs to modify the addressees' theology, which tends to lose the

---

[28] See 1,8–11; 2,21–23; 14,9 and 15,18.
[29] For literature, see Watson and Hauser 1994, 184–88; Porter 1997, 558–61.
[30] See Mitchell 1991, 67.
[31] Mitchell 1991, 182.
[32] Mitchell 1991, 67.68.

real gospel "every bit as much as the Judaizers in Galatia were doing it in another direction".[33]

A rhetorical perspective requires us to be cautious in commenting on the historical situation.[34] But it seems that whereas an overemphasis of either of the two goals leads to problems, they can easily be combined. Social tensions in some form inevitably existed,[35] and Paul needed all the *ethos* available to overcome them. It is difficult to say which problem he adjudged the "real" one. Perhaps Paul e.g. discusses and exaggerates the problems concerning the Eucharist in order to condemn the addressees. By using this heavy example he puts the shame on the Corinthians, in a good *epideictic* manner: irreverent, impious and disgraceful behaviour in a holy setting demonstrates the fruits of factionalism, rejection of Paul's authority, and independence of the tradition transmitted by him.[36]

Knowledge of the source of the "heresies" in 1 Cor is essential for understanding the nature of 1 Cor and for studying the question of the law, for this question has specific relevance to the way in which Paul operates. Modern scholarship has begun to doubt the validity of theories of direct external influence, such as Gnosticism, Stoic philosophy, Philo, Qumran, imperial eschatology etc.[37] Although some links with most of them can be demonstrated, it remains uncertain whether there was any direct historical influence. Occam's razor is a good (albeit hazardous) tool in Biblical scholarship.[38] Fee therefore argues that the most natural source of the "heresies" was the addressees' former paganism.[39]

But the "edges of the beard" (Lev 19,27) of one man escape the Razor. Paul himself is another natural source of the Corinthian "heresies". As seen above, the apostle's teaching did sometimes lead to misunderstanding. The cultural background of the addressees inevitably gave rise to the wrong interpretation,

---

[33] Fee 1987, 6–10.

[34] Eriksson (1998, 237) reminds us that the opponents' opinions were generally represented in a distorted way. Maybe Paul creates theological "straw men" in 1 Cor, just as he does in Gal.

[35] Although the thesis of rival house-churches (Theissen 1988) may not be necessary.

[36] That the words of institution are used as an *ethos* appeal is stressed by Eriksson 1998, 94–95.

[37] Fee 1987, 13–15; For discussion concerning 1 Cor 15, see Witherington 1995, 292–98.300; Tuckett 1996 and Eriksson 1998, 234–35.239.

[38] Actually, the Razor applies only in science, for in history fortuitous and unpredictable factors often occur.

[39] Fee 1987, 14.

but the rhetoric of the apostle is guilty as well. We may examine some examples.

Above we focussed on the question of immoral people in 1 Cor 5,9–13, which reflects a Corinthian misunderstanding of Paul's proclamation.[40] 1 Cor 8 and the question of food sacrificed to idols can be mentioned as another example. Perhaps the monotheism proclaimed by Paul was re-interpreted by the addressees as atheism (οἴδαμεν ὅτι οὐδὲν εἴδωλον ἐν κόσμῳ, καὶ ὅτι οὐδεὶς θεός) with one exception (εἰ μὴ εἷς),[41] or it gave support to inherent atheistic ideas in Corinth. This in turn allowed a negligent attitude to the gods and their cults. Such an interpretation of monotheism was not refuted in Paul's earlier teaching – maybe he as a Jew did not envisage such a possibility. Now he has to correct the situation. Since the Corinthian radical monotheistic "knowledge" can be derived directly from the Jewish (-Christian) monotheism proclaimed by Paul, one is tempted to use Occam's razor and cut off all theories of Gnostic or Hellenistic Jewish influence.[42] Such an influence is possible, but not necessary. However, it remains difficult reliably to estimate how great the effect of such factors actually was. Similarly, the spiritual gifts (1 Cor 12–14), which were a natural part of the Pauline teaching[43] had developed in an unwanted direction. The question of the resurrection (1 Cor 15) may also reflect a misunderstanding of the Pauline proclamation,[44] and will be discussed below.

However, for our purposes it is unnecessary to arrive at a precise estimation of the grade of external influence on the Corinthians' problems. As we are looking for situational factors, which affected Paul's approach, it suffices to say that the previous Pauline education was at least partly responsible for the difficulties. It provided good soil for the radical monotheism and many other problems in Corinth. Thus he cannot plead innocence.

Such an inconvenient background inevitably influences his way of proceeding. Paul does not blame external influences and he is more careful and cautious than in Gal. He cannot reject his own former teaching but has to

---

[40] Section I 3.

[41] Cf. Hurd 1965, 278–80. See also below section II 4Db.

[42] Against Schrage 1995, 219. For discussion, see Eriksson 1998, 138–44, who believes in some external influence.

[43] Cf. e.g. Gal 3,2: "The only thing I want to learn from you is this: Did you receive the Spirit ἐξ (the word may be causal, but a temporal meaning is even more concrete) doing the works of the law or ἐξ believing what you heard?" By this often overlooked argument Paul refers to clear manifestations of the Spirit (cf. Longenecker 1990, 101–102), probably spiritual gifts of some sort.

[44] See above section I 3.

modify the addressees' interpretation thereof and provide additional material.[45] In every question Paul first seems to agree with the addressees, but then highlights the problems and arrives at a view different from the Corinthians'. This tactic is well suited to the rhetorical situation, which must be borne in mind when reading the text.

Closest to our topic comes the Corinthian "libertinism". It is mentioned in 1 Cor 6,12;10,23, where Paul may rephrase the slogan: "Everything is permissible".[46] Like the examples above, this idea too may originate from Pauline proclamation. His rhetoric was misinterpreted and led to heavy libertinism.

Even now Paul is unable to reject his earlier teaching. But it has been argued, that he in fact needs to be more "positive" toward the law. Due to obvious spiritual and ethical turmoil in the congregation, he has to moderate the addressees' enthusiasm concerning their conduct, their attitude toward spiritual gifts etc. The Spirit, which in Gal allowed of a proper way of life even without the law, has given rise to disorder. Moral instruction is required. According to Drane, this means a return to the law, or at least, some form of legalism.[47] He is right in emphasizing that 1 Cor indicates a need for moral instruction in the congregation. But does Paul rely on the law?

It surprises that despite the obvious request, Paul leaves the topos "law" almost unutilized. Forensic language is not directly discussed.[48] But he does not avoid the word either: the law is briefly mentioned on several occasions, especially in 1 Cor (9,8–9.20; 14,21.34; 15,56; cf. also Phil 3,5–9). It seems that although there were serious ethical problems, the question of the law was not as inflamed and controversial as in Gal or Rom. Paul's explicit utterances about the law are remarkably negligent, e.g. 1 Cor 9,20. There is, however, the obscure, but extremely negative reference in 1 Cor 15,56, which associates the law with sin and death.[49] But questions concerning behaviour are discussed

---

[45] Even the Corinthians' behaviour at the Eucharist (1 Cor 11) may reflect insufficiency in Paul's original teaching. As a Jew who had so often attended the Passover meal, Paul had hardly envisioned that unseemly behaviour was conceivable at the holy meal. Obviously lacking any direct support in the Christian tradition, he has to appeal to the *pathos* effect created by the Words of Institution (see Eriksson 1998, 194–95).

[46] Another explanation too is possible: Whereas the Corinthians assessed many things as permissible, Paul wants to be even more radical in order to show that he has not rejected his theological principles to which the Corinthians refer. Only then can he proceed with reservations, without sounding like a legalist.

[47] Drane 1975, 64–65.

[48] Conzelmann 1975, 110; Fee 1987, 252.

[49] See below.

without relying on the law.[50] Instead, e.g. the Early Christian tradition is a major source of arguments.[51]

Drane admits that Paul does not discuss the Old Testament law, but adds that the apostle nevertheless introduces a series of his own ethical commands as a new moral code. This code replaces the Spirit as a source of proper behaviour. Thereby he is said to revert to the doctrine he had rejected in Gal.[52] Drane refers to several verses, the contents of which will be studied below. He argues that the main difference between Gal and 1 Cor is that only the latter contains specific ethical instruction in particular circumstances.

However, the effect of the rhetorical situations must also be observed. Gal is sent to a number of congregations, whereas 1 Cor is aimed at one, specific group. Thus it is only natural, that the later is more precise – Paul can use a precision weapon because of the limited audience.

But the relationship between the law and the Pauline paraenesis in 1 Cor is interesting, and will be examined below in section D. It suffices to say now, that this relationship does not differ radically from that present in Gal. But 1 Cor cannot be interpreted as an especially sharp attack on the law.[53] The opposite could rather have been expected. Paul's failure to choose this option could indicate that the law is so contaminated by negative soteriological and social connotations, that it is of little use in ethics.[54] All he can do is refer to it as an additional source (1 Cor 9,8; 14,34),[55] Otherwise Paul has to cope with the paraenesis. In order to reject charges of *anomia*,[56] he can call it the law of God or Christ (1 Cor 9,21), which however is essentially different from the law as such, viz. the law of Moses.

In general, compared especially with Gal, we can expect more neutral information about Paul's thoughts concerning the law. Although 1 Cor is rhetorically conscious,[57] and some rhetorical insinuation is required, its general communicative conditions do not affect the expressions dealing with the law to the same degree as in Gal and Rom. The immediate context and the narrow rhetorical function of those expressions may be more important. While the law

---

[50] Surprisingly, in 1 Cor 14,34 the law seems to have some *cultic* importance.

[51] See Eriksson 1998.

[52] Drane 1975, 64–65.

[53] Against Sandelin (1976, 84.97.130), who too explicitly equates the law with wisdom.

[54] Cf. above section II Bc. Or perhaps the Gentile background of the addressees influenced Paul's vocabulary.

[55] For the function here, see below section II 3Cb and Da.

[56] Which is not identical with antinomism: cf. the words apathy and antipathy.

[57] For some recent rhetorical studies of 1 Cor, see Mitchell 1991; Pogoloff 1992; Litfin 1994; Witherington 1995; Bullmore 1995; Porter 1997, 551–54.

is not discussed as a theological topos, we may assume that occasional references at least to some extent reflect Paul's unbiased view thereof. They can also enable us to visualize his ordinary teaching concerning the law.

Moreover, it is feasible, that short references to the law tell us something about the addressees' prior Christian education. When the issue is not clarified, Paul must count on what he has previously taught. He would hardly introduce new theology without a reason and a proper explanation. However, in practice it can be difficult to deduce much from those short expressions, as it cannot be taken for granted that we share the information referred to, irrespective of reading Gal and Rom.

1 Cor and Paul's other letters are thus valuable, when their "main stream" theology concerning the law is compared with the biassed Galatians and Romans. Are the expressions compatible or not, and can we find roots of short sayings in the two major treatments of the issue?

## B. Semantic Observations

Before penetrating the intricate theological issues, we must ask whether terminological and semantic clarity and integrity are present. In Gal the word *nomos* was found to be used consistently, meaning mainly the Mosaic legislation, with two obvious exceptions, one typically Jewish reference to the Pentateuch as a whole, and one clearly metaphorical usage. Does such a clarity exist in Romans and other letters as well?

Traditionally, the answer has been negative. The semantic field of *nomos* appears to be vague and broad; the use of the word has blurred the understanding of Paul's thoughts in many ways. Attempts to devise formal principles for delimiting the meaning of the word have not been convincing.[58]

It would, however, be too easy a solution to suggest that Paul does not *know* precisely what the word means in each case, or that the addressees were not supposed to understand Paul's semantics. A more humble point of departure is to refer to our own difficulties of interpretation. Different ways of playing with the meaning of a word were common in both Jewish and Greek literature, and this type of rhetoric must be taken into account. Such contemporary "humour" may be annoying for scholars in search of precise language, since it requires specific interpretation.

---

[58] See Räisänen 1987, 16–17.

Mapping of the semantic field of the word *nomos* in Paul, and a correct evaluation of each case, is crucial for the forthcoming ideological or theological discussion. I suggest that many of the arguments used in the exegetical discussion are based on a careless interpretation of Paul's semantics.

a) The typical Jewish reference to the Pentateuch or Mosaic legislation can be found in e.g. in 1 Cor 14,34 (if it pertains to Gen 3,16); whereas 1 Cor 14,21 and Rom 3,10–18 can allude to all of Holy Scripture.[59] Yet sometimes the two meanings – the legislation and the writings as an history – occur in the same sentence, as was the case in Gal 4,21.[60] This is a simple semantic trick, wordplay, and does not call for any deep theological consideration. Unfortunately it has not functioned well among later interpreters.

In Rom 3,21 we read: "A righteousness from God, apart from law (the legislation), has been made known, to which the law (the Pentateuch) and the prophets testify."[61] A corresponding wordplay occurs also ten verses later, Rom 3,31: "Do we then nullify the law (the legislation) by this faith? Not at all! Rather, we uphold the law (the Abraham story in the Pentateuch)."[62] The faith of the Christians proves that the faith of the Abraham history in the law (the Pentateuch), discussed further in Rom 4, was correct.[63]

b) The metaphorical use can likewise be detected: "The law of faith" (Rom 3,27), "another law" (Rom 7,20–25), "The law of Christ" (1 Cor 9,21), "The law of the spirit of life" (Rom 8,2).[64]

c) Other enigmatic passages too resemble Galatians and have been discussed above. Thus Rom 13,8–10 and 8,4 correspond to Gal 5,14.[65] It has been claimed

---

[59] Cf. Thurén 1986, 165; Räisänen 1987, 16; Westerholm 1988, 106–107.

[60] See above section II 2Ba.

[61] Westerholm (1988, 107) argues: "The wordplay is no doubt deliberate." See also above section II 1.

[62] Cf. Gal 4,21. See also Westerholm 1988, 108. The separate opinions of the commentators indicate the ambiguity in the verse. From Erasmus (according to Althaus 1966, 29) to Schmidt (1972, 75) many scholars see *nomos* as referring to the OT history, whereas Dunn (1988, 193–94) and many others interpret the word as meaning legislation only. For a detailed survey of the problem, see Rhyne 1981 and Hübner 1978, 122–24. Cf. also Käsemann 1980, 101–104, criticized by Dahl 1977, 178.

[63] Thurén 1986, 165–66.

[64] See Räisänen 1987, 16 n. 1; 50–52; 77–82.

[65] Rom 13,8–10: "Owe no one anything, except to love one another; for the one who loves another has fulfilled the law. The commandments, 'You shall not commit adultery; You shall not murder; You shall not steal; You shall not covet'; and any other commandment, are

that Paul in Rom 13,8–10 ignores ritual ordinances, reducing the law to a moral code, as if reading *nomos* as meaning here the whole law would be unnatural.[66] However, as was the case in Gal 5,14, Paul here explicitly emphasizes that love fulfills the *whole* law, viz. its just requirement. It has not been shown that the ritual codes of the OT would somehow fall outside the requirement of the law. On the contrary, the requirement can be found behind especially ritual codes.[67] To express the whole law with a single commandment is typical Jewish rhetoric.[68]

d) A similar condensation of the law can be found in Rom 2,14–15, where Paul speaks of τὸ ἔργον τοῦ νόμου as denoting a single requirement representing the whole law.[69] To be sure, *nomos* in these verses is metaphorically used, for the Gentiles are said to be the law, or that the law is written in their hearts.

This condensation has sometimes been interpreted as a reduction of the concept *nomos* to moral law. Here the Gentiles are said to fulfil the requirements of the law by their nature, which can only mean the moral requirements – how could Paul claim that they fulfil the Jewish rituals? At least they are not circumcised. Thus at least here Paul would glide – consciously or not – from one meaning to another.[70]

But how then does Paul, against the overall tendency in Rom 2,13–29, claim that the thoughts of the Gentiles also accuse them of *not* following the law? It is hardly plausible that they fulfil all the moral requirements according to him. However, in verses 26–27 such a total fulfilment reappears.[71] Then again, in the next chapter, all are presented as sinners!

In order to understand the reasoning, we must again focus on what Paul is doing. The aim is not to present dogmatics, but to decrease the self-confidence of the Jews in the audience. Thereby they can be brought onto the same level with the Gentiles. To this end, Paul must minimize the significance of the distinctive Jewish symbol, circumcision. The *propositio* can be found in verse

---

summed up in this word, 'Love your neighbor as yourself.' Love does no wrong to a neighbor; therefore, love is the fulfilling of the law."; Rom 8,4: "...so that the just requirement of the law might be fulfilled in us." Cf. Gal 5,14: "For the whole law is summed up in a single commandment, 'You shall love your neighbor as yourself.'"

[66] Räisänen 1987, 26–28.

[67] See above section II 2Ba.

[68] Above section II 2Ba.

[69] Michel (1978, 124). According to Wilckens the verse refers to the basic contents of the law (Wilckens 1978, 134 n. 315).

[70] Thurén 1986, 168; Räisänen 1987, 25–26.

[71] Therefore Räisänen (1987, 103–104) argues that total fulfilment must be meant.

13, which could be restated: neither the knowledge nor possessing of the law, nor circumcision as a sign thereof is crucial, but doing what is required. The same idea can be found in the Gospels as well.[72]

As an argument, Paul presents in v. 26 a theoretical case, *quaestio infinita*,[73] with ἐάν οὖν + subjunctive, of an hypothetical Gentile fulfilling the law. His obedience must pass as circumcision, if the implied Jewish Christian audience thinks that their circumcision is counted to them as obedience. In addition, disobedience must be a sign of uncircumcision.

Thereby such a Gentile will "doom" a Jew, just as the people of Nineveh and the Queen of the South in Matt 12,41–42 condemn the hearers of Jesus. In all these cases, obedience in an actual situation was decisive; the rhetoric did not require actual fulfilment of all moral and/or ritual commandments. But is the law divided? It is worth noticing, that if obedience is counted as circumcision, then the ritual requirements of the law are met *expressis verbis*.[74]

Instead of assuming that the law is divided into two parts, something which Paul never does elsewhere, or suspecting a novel theory of sinless Gentiles, which does not fit the context, it is more natural to characterize Paul's presentation as purposeful rhetoric.[75] The clarity of the underlying theology is not compromised if only the context and the natural dynamics of the persuasion are considered.

In Rom 13,9 Paul cites four ethical commandments of the Decalogue as examples of the law. They were "less distinctively Jewish" than e.g. the Sabbath law, but reference to them hardly means a distinction between ritual and moral ordinances, as Paul in the next phrase remarks that he could mention "any other commandment" as well.

To conclude: The semantic field of *nomos* in Romans and in other Pauline letters corresponds roughly to that of Galatians. The primary meaning is the Mosaic legislation, but the alternative meaning "Holy Writings", be it the Pentateuch or the whole OT, can be found. Further, *nomos* is sometimes used as a metaphor. These three meanings are sometimes utilized in a play on words, but the distinction is always so clear that the original readers were hardly misled.

It is important to notice that Paul does not distinguish between the cultic and the moral law, although he mostly discusses the latter. "Had Paul really taught

---

[72] E.g. the parable of the two sons in Matt 21,28–31; or Matt 3,8–9.

[73] For the term, see Eriksson 1998, 45.

[74] Cf. also Rom 9,4, where the cultic meaning of the law is emphasized.

[75] Eskola 1998, 133–36 correctly suggests a rhetorical understanding of the passage, although his assessment of the "rhetorical power" of the section remains obscure.

his converts that the 'ritual' law and that alone had been replaced, his task would indeed have been much easier."[76]

## C. The Functions of the Law

Despite the semantic correspondence between Galatians and other Pauline letters, there are difficulties in combining the contents of the sayings about the law. The main problem is that the narrow, extreme, and reprehensible position of Galatians is replaced by a wider and more favourable stance in the other letters. Sometimes they seem to be in direct opposition to each other. One can ask, whether Paul outside Galatians is too much a Jew for the Jews to have a coherent view of the law.

However, since this difficulty can be partly attributed to the different rhetorical situations discussed above, and some of the perplexity is caused by the techniques of communication, our first task is to filter out such variables. Only then can the real problem-areas be identified.

One basic misunderstanding is to claim that according to Paul the law is abolished to the degree that it has ceased to *exist* regarding the Christians. This view is easy to grasp, since many of his comments point in this direction. In Gal 3,19 he declared that the sway of the law was ended: The law was imposed until Jesus came. It served a purpose as a guardian, but now its task has been terminated (Gal 3,25). Many cases in Paul's other letters confirm this basic message: "Christ is the end of the law" (Rom 10,4).[77]

However, this idea by no means excludes the continuing existence of the law. Although its proper task as a guardian has ended, the law still remains a strong power, even according to Gal. Paul repeatedly needs to warn his addressees against becoming its slaves once more. He can proclaim that the Christians have become free of the law through the death of Christ (Gal 2,19; Rom 7,1–6), which also resulted in their own (symbolic) death in baptism (Gal 2,19; 3,13; Rom 2,19). But this implies that without participation in the death of Christ, people are still subject to the law. And vice versa – a resumed

---

[76] Räisänen 1987, 25.

[77] The expression τέλος νόμου is ambiguous. It has been interpreted not only as the end, but also as the goal or even the "summary" of the law (Barth 1948, 269) or the "climax of the Covenant" (Wright 1992, 241; for discussion, see also Fitzmyer 1993, 584–85). There may be some deliberate ambivalence in the expression, but as Räisänen observes, the immediate context is negative toward the law (1987, 53–56), which makes a positive interpretation unsuitable.

obedience to the law would nullify the liberating effect of the death of Christ (Gal 5,2–4).

Another unnecessary problem consists in *single positive statements* such as "Is the law sin? Certainly not!" (Rom 7,7) or "the law is holy and the commandment holy, just and good" (Rom 7,12).[78] First, when read carefully, they do not contradict the message of Galatians. Although they would hardly appear as such in Gal, both the structure and the content of these sayings resemble the more cautious Gal 3,21: "Is the law against God's promises? Certainly not!" In view of the rhetorical situation of Romans, it is natural that Paul rephrases the "positive" idea about the essence of the law in more emphatic terms.[79] This, however, indicates *per se* no theological difference.

Dunn rightly remarks, that Paul's rhetorical question in Rom 7,7 is very sharp[80] – it is intended to exclude completely the idea that Paul would have a negative attitude to the law. Neither in Gal nor in other epistles does Paul attack the law *per se*,[81] just as "an angel from heaven" (Gal 1,8) is not cursed as such. As stated above, a negative attitude to the law cannot be demonstrated even in Galatians.

Dunn further explains the positive expressions about the law by claiming that they are only possible because of Paul's bifurcation thereof: they concern the law itself, whereas the negative statements are directed against its abuse by the Jews.[82] But as afore said (section II 1), such a division is difficult to document in Paul's texts.

It is just as imprudent to reconstruct theology from the negative statements without a regard for their dynamic nature. Correspondingly, when in Luke 14,26 Jesus says, that whoever does not hate his father and mother cannot be His disciple,[83] this should not be taken as evidence of Jesus' generally negative attitude toward his parents or to the "fourth" commandment.

---

[78] According to Räisänen these expressions contradict not only Paul's negative references to the law (1987, 128.152), but also his positive comments thereon (1987, 68).

[79] Schweitzer (1930, 198.209) shows remarkable insight into the dynamic nature of the expressions. According to him, these positive evaluations are necessary, since Paul is addressing an unknown congregation. However, this does not mean that the content of the expressions contradicts the message of Galatians on the ideological level – on this point the Apostle is not to be suspected of insincerity.

[80] Dunn 1988, 378.

[81] Cf. Michel 1978, 229; Fitzmyer 1993, 469 on Rom 7,12.

[82] See above section II 1 and Dunn 1988, 385.

[83] Nolland (1993, 762–63) sees this expression as a "typical Semitic hyperbole", referring to Prov 13,24 and 2 Sam 19,6. He rightly dismisses the suggestion, that the strong verb originally meant "love less than", and that it was toned down by Matthew.

Thus the single positive or negative statements cannot be played against each other. Behind both we discern a simple structure: The positive sayings indicate, that the law as such is holy and good in Paul's eyes. On the other hand, the negative utterances in both Gal and Rom, emphasize that continued obedience to the ordinances of the law, which is now obsolete, is perilous, or at least inadvisable.

Were the situation so simple, the problem would be easy to solve. However, the issue of the law is not restricted to isolated statements or to the relationship between Galatians and other epistles. It is particularly difficult to understand Paul's view of the law's *continuing functions*. According to Galatians the law ceased to be valid after Christ came. Only a negative side-effect has remained for people who slide back into obeying the law. Yet in 1 Cor and Romans it seems most of the time be well nigh fully operative, and even worse, in contradictory ways. Three roles can be discerned.

### a. Producing Life

It has been suggested, that in Romans Paul presents the law as being able to produce life. It thereby performs a completely different function than in Galatians. Such a goal is sometimes found in Rom 7,10,[84] where Paul speaks of "the commandment for life", ἡ ἐντολὴ ἡ εἰς ζωήν. In that case the law proved to lead to death, yet it was originally intended to do the opposite.[85]

In the opinion of many scholars, the positive purpose contradicts the more common negative view of the law,[86] articulated in the hypothetical sentence of Gal 3,21: "If a law had been given that could give life..." The law has never been able to give life. We have to ask, which of the mutually exclusive ideas represents Paul's position, or is he ambiguous on this point.

Yet one thing is common to both verses: there is a positive purpose for the law, which however it cannot fulfill. This purpose is presented either as completely abstract and hypothetical (Gal 3,21) or as feasible, but still only theoretical one (Rom 7,10). I have difficulty in distinguishing between the two,[87] for the message for the addressees remains rhetorically the same: One cannot rely on the law, since it cannot produce life. There are only two different

---

[84] Sanders claims to find a positive, life-giving purpose for the law even in Rom 3,23f, but does so by emphasizing words invented by himself: "*First* all men sinned... *then* God provided the free gift" (Sanders 1978, 105).

[85] For the Jewish idea of the law giving life, see Dunn 1988, 384.

[86] Räisänen 1987, 152; and footnote 119.

[87] To find a "logical" controversy here reflects a rigid attitude to a dynamic text, viz. too simple a jump from the text level to its ideological background. Instead of looking for dogmatics, we should first ask, what Paul wants to *accomplish* with these verses.

ways of delivering this message. Whether however, there is an ideological difference, will be examined below.

A sharper contrast is found, when the "positive" law in Rom 7,10 is seen as an "ineffective medicine", and compared with cases like 2 Cor 3,6–7, according to which the law (the "letter") kills.[88] Has Paul had forgotten or neglected what he wrote in another letter?

The problem is even more serious. There is as sharp a conflict between Rom 7,10 and the preceding verses 7–9: "...Once, without the law, I was alive. But when the commandment came, sin became alive, and I died." These two previous verses also present the law as a negative, lethal poison, not only as a weak medicine. Then again, not only in verse 10 but soon after in Rom 8,3 the good but ineffective medicine reappears. However, even now the law cannot produce life, since it is "weak through the flesh".

Thus the contrast between the effective negative and ineffective positive law emerges already within Rom 7,7–11; 8,3. How was it possible, that the essentially life-giving law suddenly turned not only into a weak medicine but a poison? Paul's theological development or bad memory provides no solution. It is difficult to believe, that the difference between juxtaposed sentences is simply due to negligence. Therefore, before condemning the section Rom 7,7–8,3 as nonsensical, a second look is called for.

I begin by asking, is this interpretation of the "positive" Rom 7,10 correct? How should ἡ ἐντολὴ ἡ εἰς ζωὴν really be understood? The expression resembles Rom 10,5 and Gal 3,12, which fortunately are more verbose: "The man who has done [what is written in the law] shall live". This principle in turn is based on Lev 18,5.[89] Surprisingly there is no allusion to *intention* or purpose here. Paul is merely stating a rule or a fact: The law brings life to a man who abides by its ordinances. Most commentators see in Rom 7,10 an allusion to Adam: "if Adam had lived according to the commandment (Gen 2:16–17) he would have enjoyed free access to the tree of life (cf. Gen 3:22)."[90] Nowhere in the Corpus Paulinum is this idea contradicted or even questioned..[91]

---

[88] Räisänen 1987, 152–53.

[89] For discussion, see Dunn 1988, 601.

[90] Quotation from Dunn 1988, 384; for the commentators on Adam in Rom 7, see Laato 1991, 169 n. 5; Dunn 1988, 378.

[91] Against Betz (1979, 174), according to whom Paul argues against Jewish tradition, that the law was never given for the purpose of giving life. For where does Paul say so? Similarly Dunn (1988, 384) claims that in Rom 7,10 a "sharp reverse to and rebuttal of the traditional Jewish assumption that the law/commandment promoted life" is implied. In my view, both Betz and Dunn rush to their conclusions. For in Gal 3,12 Paul asserts that the man who fulfills the law will live by it. The problem is not the law but the man, who cannot comply with it.

Thus the law can give life in principle in all three cases (Rom 7,10; 10,5; Gal 3,21) – to whoever fulfills its requirements. What the law cannot do (Rom 8,3; Gal 3,21; 2 Cor 3,6–7) is to *enable* man to fulfil it.[92] In practice the law never gives life.

On the rhetorical level, the idea can be expressed in many ways depending on what kind of response is sought. Usually the unhappy consequence of the law is presented not as inevitable, but as the due of a man who does not share of the work. But when a sharper contrast is desired, as in Gal, the law itself can be presented in a bad light. Thus Gal 3,21 is a *breviloquium*, and could read as well, when combined with 3,12: "If a law had been given, that could be fulfilled by somebody, so that it could impart life..."

On the ideological level, however, the law's ability to give life to the man who obeys it is not challenged. Theoretically this idea fits well into all the Pauline letters, even Galatians, and can be found behind the explicit rhetoric. Both the seemingly contradictory sayings "the law cannot give life" and "the law can give life to anybody who follows it" are based on the same syllogism, by adding a premise: The law has in itself ability to give life, but since nobody complies with the law, the ability is never realized. The positive function of giving life thus remains abstract and speculative.

## b. Explaining the Death of Christians

Had Paul stood by the simple theme of Galatians, whereby the Christian is free from the law, his theology would be easier to comprehend. However, his other texts contain expressions, which suggest that the law not only remains valid, and not merely in the abstract, viz. in theory, but also concerns even the Christians.

As we have seen, some of these putative indications arise from modern interpreters' inability to interpret Pauline communication. The confirmation of an OT history (Rom 3,31) is not to be confused with the legislation; satisfaction of the one requirement behind the law (Rom 8,4; 13,8–10) is presented as different from observance of its many ordinances,[93] and when Paul claims to find additional support therein for his own ethics, this rather emphasizes the superiority of the latter (e.g. 1 Cor 14,34).[94]

---

[92] Cf. Dunn 1988, 419–20.

[93] Above section II 3B.

[94] See further below section II 3Da. The authenticity of this passage in 1 Cor has been challenged, but on weak grounds. For discussion, see Eriksson 1998, 202–203. E.g. Fee (1987, 707–708) claims that since the commandment quoted is not to be found in the Torah, the section must be an interpolation.

α) *1 Cor 15,56 – the Mother of All Contradictions?* The real problem arises in 1 Cor 15,56, where the law actually retains its hold on the Christians: "The sting of death is sin, and the power of the sin is the law." In the context (1 Cor 15,50–57), the physical death of the Corinthian Christians is presented as a result of sin, and consequently of the law, and these forces are not conquered until the parousia of Christ, when Paul and the Corinthians are transformed (52–54).[95]

In this section it is unmistakably implied, that even as Christians Paul and the Corinthians still live under the power of the law. Without the law, sin would have no means of causing death. That the cry of triumph over death will one day resound has no meaning, unless the law concerns the Corinthian Christians at the time when the letter was written. This however, is in diametrical opposition to Galatians, not only rhetorically but also ideologically. For in Gal the Christians are proclaimed free from the law, even in the paraenetical section (Gal 5,18).

The context of 1 Cor 15,56 provides us with additional information about the law's implicit jurisdiction over the Christians. The victory over death is said to be gained when "the perishable has been clothed with the imperishable" (54). A few verses earlier the concept "perishable" is presented as equivalent to "flesh and blood" (50), which in the context (36–49) means the physical body,[96] but generally has wider connotations.[97] Accordingly, the reign of death, sin, and the law is based on the perishable flesh of the Christians. Only when the flesh is transformed, will the three powers lose their control over the Christians.

Such an implication is certainly at odds with the rhetoric of Galatians. For the most concrete aim thereof is prevent the law from affecting the *flesh* of the audience!

On the theological level, further scrutiny is required. It would be too easy a solution to proclaim 1 Cor 15,56 a gloss,[98] or an *ad hoc* rhetorical figure without deeper significance. The annoying metaphor, and the surprising theology therein, have often been overlooked or (deliberately?) misrepresented by

---

[95] Beker (1980, 229) rightly argues, that death cannot be merely a consequence of sin, since then it could not be "the last enemy" to be defeated until the final triumph of God.

[96] Fee 1988, 798 "the body in its present physical expression".

[97] It seems to mean "all that resists what is Spirit" (Westerholm 1988, 56). See also Leeste 1980, 79–92.

[98] The idea is promoted e.g. by Weiss 1910, 380. For discussion, see Laato 1991, 179 n. 2.

scholars.[99] In the verse sin is the sting of a scorpion,[100] and the power of this sting, viz. the poison injected thereby, is the *law*.

Disregarding the crucial role of the law Beker postulates "a theological problem, that [Paul] does not resolve consistently", viz. a "fundamental inconsistency": sin has been overcome by Christ, yet its result, death remains the last enemy. The only viable solution found by Beker is the old "last resort" viz. no solution at all: the apostle contradicts himself.[101]

To be sure, in this context Paul is not discussing the law but only mentions it *en passant* when speaking of death, resurrection, and transformation. But for this very reason his comment on the law cannot be explained by a rhetorical scenario, where the apostle needs to emphasize the role of the law in order to bring the congregation to order.[102] For the law is here presented as harmful, as a real poison administered by death through sin. As such it cannot serve as a useful tool for keeping order. Yet the law appears as a natural, undisputed element in the train of thought; its role is implied to be easily accepted, maybe even self-evident for the addressees.

For a modern reader of 1 Cor or Paul's other epistles the whole metaphor of death using a poisonous sting is novel and peculiar. That the law's dominion over the Christians would be taken for granted by Paul seems odd. In the light of our previous observations, the teaching about the Christians' freedom from the law seems strongly to contradict this idea. *Is this after all what Paul normally taught about the law?*

Since no explanation is offered, it seems reasonable to assume, that Paul is here briefly referring to his previous teaching about the law and its role. Moreover, it is likely that he expects this teaching to be accepted by the addressees. Otherwise he would either provide further information or leave the controversial topic aside when discussing resurrection. Why cloud the sensitive issue of resurrection with a provocative statement about the law?

Of course we know very little about the probably oral teaching about the law, on which Paul counts in 1 Cor 15. But it is reasonable to infer that since the law is so frequently discussed in the Corpus Paulinum, corresponding ideas could be found elsewhere. Thus there is reason both to search Paul's texts for

---

[99] Commenting on 1 Cor 15,56 Fee (1987, 805) explains: "In Pauline theology sin is the deadly poison." According to Dunn (1998, 126) "sin is the poison which gives death its final effect". Can a metaphor be more gravely distorted?

[100] Liddell and Scott, s.v.

[101] Beker 1980, 222.228. To give Paul some credit he notes that the problematic relation of suffering and evil to sin and death, dependent on this inconsistency, has "haunted Christians throughout the ages" (Beker 1980, 232).

[102] See above section II 3Ab.

material including analogous, but more profound ideas about the continued hold of the law, and to assume such evidence will be found.[103] Romans in particular may be expected to provide us with good material, since it can hardly lay claim to much exclusively Pauline teaching.

β) *Rom 7,14–25 Revisited*[104] The only passage where we may find, in an explicit form, the same exceptional idea that the law and sin have power over the Christian is Rom 7,14–25[105] – provided that ἐγώ in this disputed section is interpreted so that Paul speaks of himself or a Christian in general. After W.G. Kümmel's critical dissertation in 1929,[106] Bultmann hastened to declare such an interpretation as passé,[107] and this still seems to be true among German scholars.[108] Currently, however, the problem seems to be far from solved.[109]

A major argument against the interpretation, according to which the Christian is still a sinner and under the law, has been that the idea contradicts Paul's theology elsewhere.[110] But since our intention is to clarify the law's jurisdiction over a Christian in 1 Cor 15,56, the use of such an argument would

---

[103]  Of course, our limited, scanty sources of Pauline theology mean that there probably were many issues which he does not happen to raise in his remaining epistles. But this issue is so crucial, that it would seem strange if he left such a second opinion of the law untouched in the whole Corpus.

[104]  For a more thorough and somewhat different discussion on ἐγώ in Rom 7, see my forthcoming article (Thurén 2000).

[105]  Concerning 1 Cor 15,56 Wolff (1982, 209) states that the idea is "durchaus paulinisch formuliert", and explicit in Rom 7,7f. Fee (1987, 805) goes even further, suggesting that the idea was essential in Pauline theology already before Gal, and that it is articulated in Rom 7. Correspondingly Wright (1992, 8–9) states that the "bold claim" of 1 Cor 15,56 is argued fully in Rom 6–8.

[106]  Kümmel 1974.

[107]  Bultmann 1932, 53.

[108]  See Hübner 1987, 2668; cf. Laato 1991,1 38–39.

[109]  According to Dunn (1998,472) "the function of Rom 7.7–25 is one of the most disputed topics in NT studies." Laato refers to fourteen critical scholars and provides a detailed discussion of Paul's anthropology (1991, especially p. 137–84). The exegesis of Rom 7 seems to be closely connected with the psychological development of the young Martin Luther – many scholars abhor the "Lutheran" interpretation, whereas Westerholm recommends "a career in metallurgy" to a scholar unwilling to learn exegetics from the Master (1988, 173). With all respect to the great reformer, emotions raised by him seem only to blur academic argumentation.

[110]  Kümmel 1974, 97–106; for current discussion, and other arguments, see Laato 1991, 137–84 and Thurén 2000. Concerning the postulated contradiction caused by Phil 3, see below section II 4Db.

be a *petitio principii*. The "Christian" interpretation of ἐγώ corresponds to 1 Cor 15 insofar as it should not be harmonized with e.g. Gal, or explained away.

But for Kümmel, there was an even stronger argument,[111] on which, by and large, his thesis is based: ἐγώ is used in Rom 7,7–25 as a standard rhetorical, stylistic figure.[112] Otherwise it would be difficult to explain, how the addressees were supposed to understand that the "I" did not mean Paul himself. All the theological explanations would be in doubt. Thus Kümmel's whole interpretation is sometimes called "the rhetorical interpretation".[113]

But did such a generally known stylistic device exist? Earlier scholars even knew its name: it was either *metaskhematismos*, *koinosis*, or *idiosis*. However, Kümmel admits that such technical terms are not found in ancient literature,[114] and states: "In der Rhetorik scheint diese Stilform nicht vorzukommen."[115] Instead, Kümmel refers to the general flexible use of the first person in the Pauline literature, as well as among ancient Greek, Latin, and Jewish authors.[116]

Stowers attempted to revitalise Kümmel's thesis by claiming that Paul uses the ancient technique of *prosopopoiia*.[117] He argues that Paul was aware of the uses of this device and thus could have employed it in Rom 7. The applicability of *prosopopoiia* here is however problematic. It usually meant personification of inanimate objects or abstract concepts; sometimes it was used of people who had died or had never lived, but were presented as living.[118] Thus the use of the device suggested by Stowers seems somewhat odd in ancient rhetoric.

To be sure, the ancient specialists could discuss, how an actor should present the *prosopopoiia* in Homer, and whether an orator should modulate his voice to indicate the device.[119] But Paul was hardly a well-trained actor or orator.[120] Porter states that rhetorical training "required years of work and included much theoretizing... and practice... it is difficult to believe that Paul through

---

[111]   Neglected by Laato 1991.

[112]   Kümmel 1974, 119–32.

[113]   E.g. Leeste 1979, 50; Westerholm 1988, 53.

[114]   Kümmel 1974, 120.

[115]   Kümmel 1974, 132 n. 2. Similarly Michel (1978, 224–25 n. 5): "Es ist aber nicht möglich, diesen 'Ichstil' dem hellenistisch-rhetorischen Material ein- bzw. unterzuordnen."

[116]   Kümmel 1974, 121–32. For additional examples from Qumran, see Braun 1959, 4–5.

[117]   Stowers 1995, 180–202. Already Kümmel considered *prosopopoiia* as a possibility (Kümmel 1974, 132 n. 2).

[118]   Bühlmann and Scherer 1973, 70; Martin 1974, 292–93. For a modern definition see Nida, Louw, Snyman, and Cronje 1983, 186–87.

[119]   Stowers 1995, 183–84.

[120]   Although 2 Cor 11,6 may be "mere rhetoric" (see Martin 1986, 342–43), serious questions concerning Paul's rhetorical education are raised by Porter 1997, 535–38.562–67.

haphazard means could have acquired a working knowledge of these categories, much less mastery of them, even if they were 'in the air'".[121] The same applies even more to the readers Paul envisages in Rome. Even if he knew some peculiar techniques, it is even less plausible that he used them when writing to the complex Roman audience with its various educational abilities. If however Paul knew *prosopopoiia*, he must also have been aware of the difficulty of identifying the person discussed in the training.[122] If the device was used in a peculiar way which could cause problems, why did he not so indicate?

But some Early Church Fathers had high rhetorical education and could therefore proclaim *ego* in Rom 7 as mere rhetoric. Thus the Greek fathers could interpret *ego* as referring to a non-Christian more easily than their Latin counterparts, yet even among them it could mean man in general including the Christians, "we", Paul himself, every Christian etc.[123]

Their tendency to explain away offensive passages in the Pauline texts is easy to understand, as the apostle became a saint in the first Christian centuries, and his image had to be polished as brightly as possible.[124] However, the readers, whom Paul envisaged in front of him when dictating Romans, hardly saw him as especially venerable. On the contrary, according to a common opinion, one of the purposes of the letter was to introduce Paul to the congregation(s) and perhaps defend his reputation against different rumors.[125] Thus the original readers were unlikely to share the Church Fathers' specific frame of reference for their interpretation.

Summing up: If Paul spoke in first person singular excluding himself, but without giving any sign thereof, he must have assumed that his audience was well aware of such a technique. But evidence from ancient rhetoric shows that no such commonly known device existed. References to the Fathers may be anachronistic: their interpretation was obviously suitable for the Church, but it is problematic for historical exegesis.[126] Modern exegetes decided to exclude Paul from Rom 7 only after much theological scrutiny. The first listeners did not have that option.

---

[121] Porter 1997, 563–64.

[122] As presented by Stowers 1995, 181ff.

[123] See Schelkle 1959, 242–48; more thoroughly Leeste 1980, 15–22.

[124] Thus Nilus of Ancyra denies, with a μὴ γένοιτο, that the θεῖος ἀποστολος could regard himself as a sinner in Rom 7,23 (Epist. I,152–53).

[125] For discussion, see Donfried 1991.

[126] According to Stowers (1995, 196) "Origen shows us how and why an ancient reader would have understood Rom 7.7–25 as προσωποποιία." I disagree: most ancient readers did not share his Christian tendencies.

Yet it can be demonstrated that in antiquity "I" did not always indicate the first person singular only, but could have wider connotations. This is certainly true even concerning Rom 7, which would be incomprehensible if the word was every time replaced by "Paul". Beside the annoying theological message, the flexible use of *ego* explains the many ancient and modern interpretations of Rom 7. Obviously Paul uses the first person as a rhetorical device. Different suggestions can be made.

a) Perelman's "Modern Rhetoric" too mentions *prosopopoiia*. His view resembles the ancient one: the device means personification of an object or a group. It gives coherence to the group discussed and stabilizes its boundaries.[127] Both modern and ancient general definitions of the device are well suited to the interpretation of many Fathers: In Rom 7 *ego* stands for all Christians, Paul included. It is indeed a rhetorical device, but the general use thereof, which can be grasped even without rhetorical training, does not allow the exclusion of the speaker himself from the first person singular.

The interpretation of the chapter becomes somewhat easier, if Paul's personal experience is not at stake. Instead of inferring "Western" introspective ideas, which could see Paul as a modern philosopher wrestling with his personal existential anxiety, the collective understanding of *ego* in Rom 7 sees him as an example, just as he claims to be in other cases.[128] Paul's goal is not to present the dark side of himself for the Roman Christians, but to discuss the role of the law and sin in the Christians' life. For such a theoretical treatise, personification could bring life and coherence.

b) Perhaps Paul builds up his *ethos*. Insofar as *identification* is a basic means of persuasion,[129] the use of first person makes it easy to identify with the author. Such a use of the first person plural is found in Rom 1,11–12 and in 5,1–7,6.[130] According to Holland, this involves subversion of "the philosophical *topos* of the teacher as a moral example". In the rhetorical situation of Romans, it would be unwise merely to discuss the sins of the addressees. Instead of claiming apostolic authority, Paul attempts to appear as a sympathetic figure, who shares the past troubles of the addressees, and hopes to be "mutually encouraged by

---

[127] "By means of *prosopopoeia*, the thing personified is turned into a speaking and acting subject", Perelman 1969, 330–31.294

[128] 1 Thess 1,6; 1 Cor 4,16; 11,1; Phil 3,17; 4,9.

[129] Burke 1962, 548.597–80.

[130] Thus both Stowers (1994, 269–70.292) and Holland 1999, 263.

each other's faith, both yours and mine" (Rom 1,12).[131] Paul is making his own character sympathetic by *not* being a superman. This technique is typical of him: not only the negative boasting in 2 Cor 11,23–12,10, but already the beginning of Rom, where Paul presents himself to the addressees as παῦλος δοῦλος, a little slave, may serve as examples. Some Church Fathers of course had difficulties in understanding this tactic.

But these two rhetorical explanations still assume Paul's past or present wretchedness, which is a classical problem of interpreting Rom 7. Lacking clear ancient references, or rules for its use, its function must be assessed by other means. Although Kümmel emphatically rejects the use of "Gefühlsurteil", an emotional evaluation is unavoidable in order to determine why Paul used the first person in this chapter. We must ask, how does the section operate with the *pathos* aspect; what kind of emotions were the verses designed to provoke?

In 7,7–13 the "I" is clearly universal and may refer to Adam.[132] Yet Dunn rightly states, that the addressees "could scarcely miss the intensified note of existential anguish and frustration which at once becomes the dominant feature" – the impression conveyed is that of a personal testimony.[133] Although "the universal 'I' of Adam" in 7,7–13 should be borne in mind, the tone from verse 14 onwards becomes very personal.[134] The verses appear to reflect a struggle by the author himself – at least if the desire to integrate the section with Paul's statements about the Christian's freedom elsewhere is not the predominant principle of interpretation.

With regard to Paul's theology, the same problem emerges as in 1 Cor 15. Beker calls it the "continuing dilemma" in Paul: despite his rhetorical proclamation about freedom from the law, sin, and death, they still retain their

---

[131] Holland 1999, 269–71.

[132] For the discussion, see Dunn 1988, 378.399–402; Laato 1991, 130–32.168–72, and Fitzmyer (1993, 463–64), who however is critical of the "Adam-interpretation". He cannot see, why Adam would be called *ego*, and claims that v. 9 does need Adam. However, *ego* is here a good literary device: it identifies the apostle with Adam, the addressees and all humanity. It also allows the rhetorical merger with a more personal, emotionally affective *ego* at the end of the chapter. – For the "death" of Adam, see Laato 1991, 29 n. 1.

[133] Dunn 1988, 405. However, Dunn is somewhat misleading in stating that "the expressions... are too sharply poignant and intensely personal to be regarded as simply a figure of style, an *artist*'s model decked out in *artific*ially contrived emotions" (my italics). Irrespective of the interpretation, and the degree of Paul's self-commitment, the use of the first person here is a stylistic device whereby Paul works with emotions. Even when referring to genuine feelings, the orator Paul works as an artist indeed, communicating an impression of existential anguish – of himself.

[134] Dunn 1988, 405: "so long as the resurrection is not yet, the 'I' of the old epoch is still alive, still a factor..."

hold on the Christian. But what if this unavoidable dilemma is exactly the topic with which Paul is dealing in Rom 7? There are three factors in the syllogism, which do not fit together: Death results from breaking the law, the Christians are free from the law – and yet they die.

In modern analysis of argumentation, such rigid syllogisms of formal logic are no longer considered adequate to describe human reasoning. One problem is that different factors, which are crucial for the persuasiveness of the argumentation, are not explicit.[135] In our case, the reasoning is problematic only insofar as we imply an underlying axiom, that the Christian is a monolithic entity.

For Paul all the statements were true, and his solution was based on the different dimensions in the Christian, viz. flesh and soul. But he implies addressees, who are supposed to understand both the problem and the solution. I shall return to this question below. Here it suffices to say that Paul probably wanted to convey his difficult theological message to his audience by presenting himself as an example, not discussing only Adam, or man in general. The tension thereby became more emotional and intimate, and the addressees could perhaps find similar experiences within themselves.

It remains unclear, how Paul's somewhat peculiar use of *ego* in Rom 7,14–25 functioned in the original setting. Although in ancient texts *ego* was used in a flexible way, Paul perhaps went too far in his play with Adam in Gen, every man, Christians, the addressees, and himself. At least later interpretations indicate that Paul's rhetoric here has not proved unconvincing.

We can conclude that although *ego* in Rom 7 is used as a literary device, it cannot be forced into a role, which would solve the theological tension in the section. In the light of ancient rhetoric, it is difficult to believe that the original readers would understand *ego* as not referring also to the Christian Paul. Such a self-exclusive use of "I", which would have enabled them to do so, was not then a conventional rhetorical device. Therefore Kümmel's rhetorical explanation cannot stand. His solution is rather an unnatural artifice, created for secondary theological harmonization. Furthermore, although providing an immediate solution of a theological problem, it results in claims of contradictions and inconsistency in the actual text.[136]

But how does the interpretation of *ego* as including Paul or any Christian accord with 1 Cor 15,56? Both sections describe the law's hold on the flesh of the Christians, and end with a rather similar thanksgiving: (cf. Rom 7,25a and

---

[135] For a brief introduction to this vast discipline, see Thurén 1993.

[136] E.g. Beker (1980, 216) and Räisänen (1987, 109 n. 84) depend on Kümmel's rhetorical explanation in their interpretation of Rom 7.

1 Cor 15,57). Rom 7 is longer and goes into greater detail. The Christian is dual: verse 18 implies that *ego* has two sides, when saying "In me, that is, in my flesh". Dunn is right to argue, that the "I" should not be separated from the flesh – instead, there is a split in the I.[137] However, since the "I" can specify "my flesh", he must be more than mere flesh.[138] One part of this split "I" is simply called "flesh", and ; v 18 explains that in this context Paul calls this part himself.[139] In other words, the verse distinguishes between the "I" who *has* flesh, and the "I" who *is* flesh.[140]

Now the *ego* as flesh is presented as living under the power of sin and the law, doing what he does not want to do (7,15.19). As such the idea has a parallel in the obscure Gal 5,17, where the flesh and the spirit "are in conflict with each other, so that you do not do what you want".[141] Speaking of a conflict means that both sides exist. Yet as far as the spirit is in control, the man as a whole is not under the law. Whereas even this sentence is a *breviloquium*, Rom 7–8 is more explicit.

The decisive point, according to Paul, is, which side is in the control (cf. Gal 5,21). When the man is under the control of the flesh, and consequently of sin, he "bears fruit to death" (Rom 7,5) viz. "will certainly die" (8,13); his "way of thinking is death" (8,6) and he is unable to please God (8,8). Before the final transformation the flesh cannot submit to God's will (Rom 8,7).

Correspondingly, participation in Christ (8,1–3) and the death from the power of flesh and the law, which has already taken place (7,4.6), means that the other side, the spirit, is in control: The Christians bear fruit to God (7,4) and serve him (7,5), their "way of thinking is life" (8,5–6). As long as God's spirit lives in the Christian, the spirit stays in control, and the Christian is "dead" and released from the law (7,4.6.9). Yet the law has not vanished, but exercises lordship over a man and his flesh as long as he lives (7,1). Notwithstanding, his

---

[137] Dunn 1988, 388.408.

[138] Thurén 1986, 171.

[139] As Dunn rightly observes (1988, 408), Paul does not here imply a separate spiritual *ego* who would be "incarcerated within the lower world of matter".

[140] Thurén 1986, 171.

[141] Cf. Laato 1991, 81–82. Kümmel (1974, 105–106) claims that the formal correspondence between Gal 5,17 and Rom 7 is only "scheinbar", since the imperative indicates that the Christians can master the flesh, and thus not commit sin. However, as stated above (section II 2Bcβ) it is a serious mistake to think that commanding something implies the possibility of compliance with the command.

spirit is free from it. He can serve the law viz. the will of God (7,25b)[142] viz. συνήδεσθαι with the good intention of the law (7,22).[143]

Rom 8,10–11 concludes the discussion: The body of the Christian is dead (viz. mortal)[144] due to sin. This implies that the law still has power over the body; therefore the consequences of wrong-doing persist. But the Spirit of Christ, living in them (viz. ensuring that the spirit stays in control) will bring them, even their bodies (in the *parousia*) to life.[145] Even here body and soul are not separated: the resurrection applies to the whole man.

This discussion fits well to 1 Cor 15,56, where the law is said to lose its final hold on the flesh only in the physical death. So long as the Christian is flesh, he is still under the law, and cannot "inherit the kingdom of God" (1 Cor 15,50). Only the transformed body will do that (1 Cor 15,51–57). Since however the flesh is an inseparable part of a man, the whole Christian must physically die – thus far he is still under the dominion of the law. But the two previous deaths – the death of Christ and the death of the Christian in baptism – ensure that the controlling part, the spirit, is free from the law and consequently free from the punishment. This principle will then materialize in the resurrection, where the whole man is renewed, and the triumphal cry of 1 Cor 15,56 is finally relevant both spiritually and physically.

Rom 7–8 is thereby Paul's solution of the "continuing dilemma", which the scholars have correctly recognized in his theology. The chapters provide us with a fuller explanation of the loaded, somewhat surprising idea that the law still has power over the Christian. In 1 Cor 15 the train of thought is taken for granted, whereas in Rom 7 the idea is discussed – probably because the addressees are not expected to know the specific Pauline teaching.

If this explanation is valid, we may ask why and how Paul arrived at so complex a theory – especially when the law in 1 Cor 15 is not utilized for a positive educational purpose. Would not it have been simpler to abide by the clear message of Galatians: the Christian is totally free from the law?

Above we saw that in 1 Cor Paul is often fighting against the outcome of his own rhetorically exaggerated teaching. This provides a specific challenge: a unilateral powerful attack à la Gal cannot be attempted; the apostle has to

---

[142] 7,25b is hardly an interpolation; for discussion see Dunn 1988, 398–99.

[143] Heitsch1989, 46–47: "Das Verbum meint... die freudige Übereistimmung mit jemandem und kann in diesem Zusammenhang nur die Übereinstimmung mit der Intention des Gesetzes, mir das Leben zu eröffnen, bezeichnen."

[144] Many commentators see here a reference to symbolic death in baptism, failing to recognize the typical Pauline hyperbolic expression. The verse alludes merely to the duality of the Christian.

[145] Cf. Fitzmyer 1993, 490–91.

explain that the situation is more complicated than the addressees realise.[146] Is this the case with 1 Cor 15, too?

According to many scholars the Corinthians believed in a "realized eschatology". They had already risen with Christ in baptism. Therefore there was no death or resurrection to be expected, and there was no sin anymore.[147] But in support of this thesis, no reference to influence by "Roman Imperial Eschatology"[148] or by mystery religions is required, not to mention an imaginary phenomenon called "Gnostic libertinism".[149] More likely, the source of the addressees' error is again the apostle himself.[150] As claimed above in section I 3, his baptismal theology could easily lead to misunderstanding.[151]

The problem was hardly only ethical. The contrast between Pauline rhetoric and harsh reality was probably intensified when some Christians in Corinth had died (cf. 1 Cor 15,12). This was probably a problem for the addressees who believed in the eventual resurrection and final victory over Death in baptism, which they had learnt from Paul. Despite the enthusiastic Pauline gospel – freedom from the law, from sin, and therefore from death – death remained a fact. This violated Paul's earlier proclamation; an explanation was essential.[152] Paul has to tell the addressees why the Christians were not actually immortal, despite his theological rhetoric. The least he could do was to explain death as a temporary consequence of the unfortunately remaining power of sin and the law, which however was about to vanish.

Thus Paul needed the idea of the law's continuing hold on the flesh of the Christian in order to explain why the Christians still die and await the resurrection despite their overall freedom from the law and its punishment. But the reference to the residual power of the law in 1 Cor 15,56 is so short, that the

---

[146] Cf. section II 3A above.

[147] For discussion, see Eriksson 1998, 239–41; cf. also Wilson 1968, 90–107; Thieselton 1978, 523–25 and Tuckett 1996.

[148] Witherington 1995, 292–98.

[149] Cf. Wedderburn 1987, 296–359. The Christian sources reiterate the same stereotypical charges of libertinism which may simply be attributable to standard vilification.

[150] See above chapter I 3. Cf. Thieselton 1978, 515: "We may assume that the Corinthians either took up Paul's own words about freedom from law, or more probably that they felt drawn towards a more radical application of Paul's own eschatological dualism than he himself had seemed to allow."

[151] As claimed in chapter I 3, Romans 6,3–4 display an unbalanced, unnatural, and ethically corrected version of the baptismal structure present later (again) in Col 2,12 and Eph 2,6. In Rom the resurrection is downplayed. Perhaps Paul had learned something from the Corinthian experience?

[152] Fee (1987, 716) states generally: "...it seems unlikely that an articulated doctrine of resurrection belonged to the earliest Christian preaching, especially among Gentiles."

idea cannot be an *ad hoc* solution of the question of death. Instead, Paul reminds the addressees of his previous oral teaching. Thus Romans 7–8 is crucial as these chapters explain this theology to an audience unaware of Pauline standard teaching.

Now how is this related to Galatians? In Rom and 1 Cor the law is still assessed chiefly as negative, and not to be followed by the Christians. But whereas Gal only hints (Gal 5,17), Rom and 1 Cor demonstrate that the total freedom from the law propagated in Gal (and in Rom 8) is a *rhetorically biassed phenomenon* – it is the truth, but not the whole truth – like the idea of the Christian's freedom from death. The Corinthians had misunderstood Paul's rhetoric in both cases by taking his expressions at their face value.

The same pattern can thus be found behind Paul's teaching concerning ethics and the resurrection: An overstated message had resulted in misunderstanding. Freedom from the law and from death was a major topic in the Pauline gospel, and Gal demonstrates how far he can go in emphasizing this freedom. But in Corinth he experiences the counter-effect: his rhetoric is taken too literally. The issue is particularly delicate, since Paul cannot blame external influences or foreign teachers as in Gal, and runs the risk of compromising his basic message of freedom. Or at least its persuasive force.[153] Thus in Rom 7–8, both sides are presented – but in an exaggerated, hyperbolical way, which has caused further problems for modern interpreters.

However, the somewhat unfortunate technique of rhetorical simplification is not a Pauline idiosyncrasy. The statement of the Johannine Jesus is a good parallel: "Whoever lives and believes in me will never die" (John 11,26). This sentence is usually interpreted as containing an important idea, although at the time of the final editing of the Gospel, many Christians had passed away.[154] For some reason, the rhetorical devices used in the Gospels seem to be much easier than those of Paul for modern scholars to comprehend. Maybe the latter provokes much higher theological expectations and a demand for straight-forward doctrinal presentation.

---

[153] Although (or simply because) any comparison between Paul and Luther is almost an *anathema* in current exegetical discussion, I should like to try: the Reformer too had to fight against people who had taken his rhetorically overstated proclamation too literalily and turned into antinomists. Both preachers faced a difficult rhetorical situation, as they could not deny their own proclamation to which the antagonists referred.

[154] Explanations of the verse are sometimes too precious. Thus Morris (1971, 550–51) explains that "Jesus does not of course mean that the believer will not die physically", since "millions of Jesus' followers have died since". Bultmann (1950, 307–308) similarly informs us that "der Glaubende mag den irdischen Tod Sterben".

## c. Identifying and Provoking Sin

The law concerns the Christian insofar as it lays claim to the body, thereby causing death. But even other continuing negative functions may be perceived. In Gal the law had a cognitive purpose: sin is identified by the law as transgression; thereby it also become more reprehensible.[155] Rom 3,20 ("through the law we become conscious of sin") reflects well this idea, as does Rom 7,13 ("In order that sin might be recognized as sin...").

In Rom 5,20a Paul claims that the function of the law is to increase sin. Paul does not speak of the law's psychological effect on a single individual, but, as in 19 and 20b, on the whole world.[156] But to what does this increasing, πλεονάζειν actually refer? Dunn offers three possible interpretations: a) the law turns sin into transgression, as in 13–14, viz. identifies it as a violation. Offenders become guilty, and consequently the problem can be resolved. Thereby the law makes the sin a visible, acute problem. b) It can add sin quantitatively, provoke to sin, as it provoked Adam. c) The Jews become too dependent on their own customs and the law, which obscures their relationship to God and the deeper righteousness.[157]

Dunn chooses the third interpretation, which to me seems the least likely. πλεονάζειν is a strong, hyperbolic term, meaning not just "to add" or "to increase", but "to excess", "to make too abundant",[158] so that to beat that word in 20b Paul needs a real overkill ὑπερπερισσεύειν. Thus according to the third interpretation, there was some sin before, but the real, overabundant sin was committed only by the Jews as they followed the law. However, although the Jews were strongly condemned in Rom 2–3 (e.g. "robbing temples"), they were not charged for misuse of the law. Paul never claimed that they were far worse sinners than the Gentiles, although their sins were "counted" unlike those of the Gentiles.[159]

The first two interpretations are more plausible. But if according to Rom 5,20 the sin is a reality already before the intervention of the law, how about Rom 7,7–11? Does not this passage imply that the law alone gives rise to actual sin?[160]

According to "most commentators" Rom 7,7–11, particularly the expressions "it deceived me" and "it killed me", refer to the case of Adam and Eve in

---

[155] See above section II 2Bbγ.
[156] Räisänen 1987, 143–44.
[157] Dunn 1988, 299–300.
[158] Liddell and Scott, s.v.
[159] Cf. the interpretation of Rom 5,13 below.
[160] Räisänen 1987, 144.

Gen 3;[161] indeed verse 10 is only relevant to Adam and Eve. The whole section describes Adam and his relation to the commandment which he had received.[162] Whereas Adam is presented as a prototype for man, the commandment is presented as a prototype for the Torah. In both cases, the sin is a reality before the actual law. The idea resembles closely Rom 5,13f:

> Sin was indeed in the world before the law, but sin is not reckoned when there is no law. Yet death exercised dominion from Adam to Moses, even over those whose sins were not like the transgression of Adam, who is a type of the one who was to come.

The death "exercised dominion" ever since Adam: thus sin and death existed already before the law. It may be odd that according to Rom 7,7–8 sin was "dead" before the coming of the law, and that 1 Cor 15,56 describes the law as a poison needful to inflict death. But if both Rom 5,12–14 and 7,7–11 refer to Adam, this gives us a coherent view behind the two sections. Adam and the commandment are seen as prototypes. We hardly have two different ideas about the origin of the sin. This enables us to comprehend why Paul adds 5,13b, which has been described as "completely unintelligible",[163] or at least aesthetically odd or awkward.[164]

What does it mean that before the law came, sin was not "counted"? If people lacking the law will still perish (Rom 2,12–16), to what does this "counting" refer? Does this contradict Rom 7,7–8? In the Rom 5,12–19 Paul uses Adam to highlight Christ. Adam's case shows how one man can affect the whole world. Whereas he inflicted sin and death to all men, Christ can likewise produce life. Now in v 13 Paul meets a rebuttal: How could Adam be guilty without the law, and if he could, what is then the difference between those lacking the law, viz. the Gentiles, and those possessing the law, viz. the Jews? Paul is forced to answer these questions, lest his theological system prove inconsistent indeed, which would have an adverse effect on his message – at least in Jerusalem, if not already in Rome.

As stated above, Paul's answer to the first question is positive: The culpability of Adam was possible because the commandment he received was a prototype of the law. The second one is more complex. After pointing out the similarities between the two Paul has to differentiate between the prototype law and the Mosaic law. He does so by referring to unaccounted and accounted sin.

---

[161] See above note 132.

[162] Thurén 1986, 180–81.

[163] Bultmann 1951/52, 252.

[164] Thurén (1986, 181) laments the literary awkwardness of 5,13ff, but sees it as theologically unavoidable. So also Dunn 1988, 274–75.

The first one ensued from the commandment to Adam. In another context, Rom 1–2, Paul speaks of the Gentiles' general knowledge of God, which suffices to victimize them.[165] The accounted sin was combined with the Torah.

The word "count" thus serves as a tool for differentiation. Whereas Adam was cursed for contravening the commandment, and the Gentiles provoke God's wrath already for their idolatry, the Jews are punished because they violated the law, which accordingly must be "counted".[166]

Thus in both Rom 5 and 7 Paul presents Adam as the prototype of sinful man, and the commandment he received as a prototype for the law. The law is used to identify the sin, to make it more serious, viz. a transgression. This identification does not *per se* affect the consequence of sinning – both Gentile and Jewish sinners will perish. The law can, however, provoke sin, as it did with Adam.[167] When the use of Adam as an example is correctly taken into account, Paul's train of thought is here manifest.

But his rhetoric is not. The sentences are too short, too compact for a modern reader to understand the message at first glance, and the emotional, persuasive effect may be lacking. How can this be explained? Is Paul using technical terms and referring to known topics, on which we can only speculate? Or does one of the possible rhetorical situations – a mental rehearsal and theological preparation for the talks in Jerusalem – blur his rhetorical aim?

Another unanswered question is, what was – according to Paul – God's *intention* in giving the law such a role. Is not God presented as cynical when imposing a law which in practice could not produce life? At least Paul was aware of the question.[168] His inability to offer us a satisfactory solution is another matter.[169]

---

[165] See Dunn 1988, 275.

[166] See Thurén 1986, 181. Cf. also Westerholm 1988, 179–81.183–84.

[167] There is no reason to speculate whether this provocation was quantitative or qualitative, or whether Paul assessed ancient Jews as worse sinners than others. Rom 1–3 clearly show his position on this question.

[168] According to Räisänen, to see God as cynical is the only logical conclusion of Paul's statements, although the apostle did not happen to perceive the problem (Räisänen 1987, 153–54). Thurén (1986, 181–82) points out that exactly this question is discussed in the following chapters, Rom 9–11: How could God reject his chosen people? Paul summarizes his "answer" in 11,32: "For God has confined all in disobedience in order that he might have mercy on all", followed by adoration.

[169] The question of God's possible cynicism resembles the classical problem of *theodicy*, which in turn is hardly specifically Pauline (see Eskola 1998). Our own possibility as scholars to assess God's nature is limited: the question is too religious to be treated with our methods.

*d. Conclusion*

The functions of the law are wider in Romans and 1 Corinthians than in Galatians. This is partly due to the different exigency: Paul is not propagating a single idea concerning the law, but refers to his standard teaching. Despite some seeming contradictions, there is no sharp contrast on the ideological level, when dynamic nature of the text is considered.

We find a simple derhetorized ideological structure, which fits Gal, 1 Cor, and Rom: As participant in the death of Christ, the Christian is wholly exempt from obedience to the law and should not even try to comply with its ordinances. Correspondingly, the Christian is free from death. However, the law continues to exist. In Gal it was only a threat to those who start again to observe it. In Rom and 1 Cor, it also has a hold on the flesh of the Christians, thereby causing their physical death. Their spiritual participation in Christ's death in baptism was in some sense only symbolic. The law continues to exert power over the Christian, who is flesh and blood.

According to Paul's letters death, sin, and the law are overcome by Christ – yet their dominion will not end until the Last Day. This "paradox" or inconsistency is more rhetorical than theoretical. Which side is presented depends on the exigency. Rhetorically Paul can claim that the death and sin were wholly overcome by Christ. For it would be less effective to explain the matter theoretically: "On one hand... but on the other..." Theologically Paul's idea is simple: Christ's victory over the law, sin, and death is not yet totally fulfilled inasmuch as the Christians are still flesh and blood. Thus they continue to sin and die. On the one hand death is won, on the other not. But in Paul's proclamation the aspects are presented in a more straightforward way in order to better influence the addressees.

As long as the Spirit retains control, viz. the Christian is dependent on the Pauline gospel and not on any legal ordinances, the power of the law is limited to the flesh and will eventually cease at the death of the body. These functions of the law are temporally limited and essentially negative. The law provokes to sin and identifies it as transgression. The Lutheran *usus elenchticus* or the "second use" of the law, as driving a man to Christ, viz. creating a need for the Gospel, is a logical consequence thereof, but it is emphasized by Paul only in Rom 3,19–20. The "third use" of the law, as a moral guidance for Christians would be a purely positive task, and contradict Galatians more sharply. Thus we turn to this question.

# D. Law and *Paraenesis*

The law was an impassable way to salvation for Paul. But in Galatians he also declined the law as an ethical guideline. Above I assumed that he did so for rhetorical reasons: It would have been unwise to encourage the Galatians in any positive use of the law, when the letter intended to turn the addressees away from it, in order avoid involvement in its Judaizing interpretation. As a source of motivation and advice on right behaviour Paul referred to the Spirit instead of the law (Gal 5,18). Moreover, the Spirit produces a new way of life according to Paul. In practice, he gave the addressees a set of moral rules and principles, which are commonly described as *paraenesis*.

In Romans the situation was different. It was important for the apostle to present himself as a mature, well-balanced teacher, to understand both sides, not to assume any extreme position. In a sense, he wanted to pass as a "conservative" theologian. Therefore it was advisable for him to speak well of the law.

A positive ethical usage of the law was prompted also by the situation in 1 Cor. Any weapon against libertinism was useful, and this time Paul's own character or the idea of justification was not at stake. Paul sought to restrain unduly exuberant charismatic phenomena and libertinistic behaviour, and to this end needed all the support available – even from the Torah. Thus a more positive view of the law on ethical matters, compared with that in Galatians, was required. However, the fact that Paul is not opposing foreign teachers but his own influence, restricts his approach.

It is natural, that in 1 Cor, Rom and other letters we find comments on the law, which would have been unwise in the situation and rhetoric of Galatians, just as the critical statements of Gal do not fit into Romans or 1 Cor. But once again: If the rhetorical effectivity and practical use are filtered out, do we find two conflicting lines of thought as regards the law as a norm for *behaviour*?

Before attempting to answer the question, one misleading interpretation must be refuted. Many scholars think that the Christians, in Paul's eyes, live according to the law. Thus Wright argues that in Rom 3,27; 10,4–11; 13,8; 1 Cor 7,19 Paul says – although "sometimes very cryptically" – that the Christians "do in fact fulfill the law".[170] However, as argued above,[171] it requires

---

[170] Wright 1996, 137–38.
[171] Section II Bc.

great imagination to read such an idea into the text, for Paul does not say there that the Christians keep the law. Scholars ought to clarify their implicit warrants and rules of argumentation, which are utilized when Paul's "cryptic" expressions are unfolded. Paul's negative message concerning his addressees' ability to fulfil the Mosaic law is explicit and rhetorically well emphasized. It would be odd and counterproductive, if he added an opposite message by utilizing the postulated cryptic expressions.

Yet two more difficult problems emerge: a) Has the law in Rom and 1 Cor regained its role as the authoritative source for moral instruction? b) If the paraenesis corresponds either formally or practically to the law, does not Paul's criticism thereof apply to the paraenesis as well?

### a. Should the Commands of the Law Still be Obeyed?

We start with a recondite sentence in Rom 8,4:

> "...in order that the righteous requirement of the law might be fully met in us, who do not live according to the flesh but to the Spirit."

Rom 13,8–10 contain the same idea: The Christians ought to fulfil the requirement of the law. Violence is done to the text, if we assume that the word "law" here changes its meaning, whether "abruptly" or "tacitly",[172] so that it would mean something other than the Torah, as in Rom 7. But how then does the sentence make sense, if not only according to Gal, but also in Rom 8,2, the Christians are set free from the law? If the law, despite some remaining negative functions, no longer has power to bind the free Christians, is Paul now contradicting himself? At least in Rom 8,4 he cannot have forgotten what he said in the previous sentence.

The parallel Gal 5,13–14 also argues that the just requirement of the law – the very essence of the whole law – must be fulfilled by the Christians.[173] I have claimed above, that Paul here follows the idea found in both the OT and contemporary Judaism: the one main requirement of the law expresses the goal of all the separate paragraphs, which are but manifestations thereof.[174] In Gal, this basic requirement is fulfilled only by "love" or by "walking in the Spirit".[175]

---

[172] Cf. Käsemann 1980, 217–18. Räisänen (1987, 66–67) rejects the first but supports the second alternative. However, since even according to him, "Paul's language does not reveal that shift", an imaginary source supporting such a change should not be invented.

[173] See above section II Ba.c.

[174] For OT references, see above section II 2Ba, footnote 105.

[175] See above section II Ba.c. Cf. also Becker 1989, 417–19.

The same idea can now be found in Romans. Paul states that, being set free from the law, the Christians possess a new power to fulfil this just requirement: the Spirit. Rom 2,25–29 provide an illustrative example: actual rules can be outdated, e.g. circumcision. Yet the basic requirement of the command, the change of the heart, still holds good.[176] "A man is a Jew if he is one inwardly, and circumcision is circumcision of the heart."

Thus, Rom 8,4 refers to the one requirement of or behind the law, but observance of the actual commands of the Mosaic law is not suggested as an appropriate means of its fulfilment. It should now be pursued without the law, by "walking in the Spirit". The great principle behind the law is stated more precisely in both Gal 5,14 and Rom 13,8–10: to love one's neighbour.

As for the rabbis, this command of love however encompassed all the particular rules of the law. Thus also Rom 13,9 rephrases some of the Decalogue. But does this mean, that at least some part of the law still serves as a moral guideline? Does e.g. the Decalogue function as a kernel of the law, which is still binding on the Christians?[177]

The same question can be raised when reading 1 Cor 7,19[178] (and Rom 2,25–29): Circumcision or uncircumcision is nothing, but keeping of God's commandments (τήρεσις ἐντολῶν θεοῦ). The idea differs interestingly from Gal 5,6 and 6,15. Instead of "faith active through love" or "the new creation" we now have *many* commands. Is there any essential difference between these "commandments of God", guidelines for "walking in the Spirit", or the Pauline paraenesis on the one hand, and the commandments of the Mosaic law on the other?

1 Cor 9,8–9 and 14,34 illustrate the relationship between the two. In both passages Paul supports his own commands by referring to the law in peculiar terms: ἦ καὶ ὁ νόμος ταῦτα οὐ λέγει (9,8); καθὼς καὶ ὁ νόμος λέγει (14,34). Paul is not adducing the law as an ultimate authority, but as an *auxiliary argument*. Correspondence to the law is used only as an additional source to support the Pauline paraenesis. A similarly supportive role is to be found in Rom 13,9, where some commands of the Decalogue are cited in the midst of the paraenesis. This indicates how Paul occasionally finds useful raw material in the law.

---

[176] This time, however, Paul speaks of δικαιώματα in the plural, following the standard phrase of Deuteronomy and Ezekiel (see Dunn 1988, 121–22).

[177] E.g. Brooten (1990, 72–73) argues that this was the case.

[178] Cf. also Rom 2,25–29, where Paul refers to the requirements of the law – however as something different from circumcision. I cannot see this as signifying a principal separation between cultic and moral law. Paul rather uses standard vocabulary; cf. above.

This use of the law as supplementary support to Paul's moral principles validates neither the whole law nor its kernel. Instead of proclaiming that the law as such possesses a continuing relevance for Christians, Paul only gives it an occasionally useful role. In Rom and 1 Cor nothing indicates, that Paul would identify "the commands of God" with the Mosaic law, which he distanced from God in Gal. His own paraenesis, "walking in the Spirit", and "the commands of God" (which are boldly identified), obligate the addressees, but are only occasionally said to correspond to the rules of the Torah.[179] To mention but one negative example: Paul's rule against divorce (1 Cor 7,10f) claims to follow Jesus' interpretation, but differs from the Torah itself.[180]

Thus in both Rom and 1 Cor we find a positive, supporting role for the law, which is different from that in Galatians. But although the approach is not as "anti-nomistic" as in Gal, it is questionable, whether this usage of the Torah can be called "conservative",[181] for it indicates a radical dethronement of the Torah. According to Becker, "er... beachtet sie einfach nicht mehr als Norm".[182] In fact the change is stunning and massive, as recent studies have demonstrated.[183]

To conclude, the dethroned law serves in Rom and 1 Cor as an additional source of moral guidelines. The law as such is presented as outdated, but as occasionally containing useful information even for the Christians. The variation between the mode of reference to the law in these epistles and Gal is due to different exigencies. In Gal it would have been rhetorically unwise to refer to the law as an additional source for right behaviour. It would only have impeded Paul's efforts to alienate his audience from people referring to the law on another question. Yet the law as a supplementary moral source does not contradict the theological thoughts presented in Gal. He may well have had a similar position even when writing Gal, for this could well be an extra component in the *ideology* behind Galatians. Nor can such a usage be attributed to development or maturation in Paul's thought. In this question, there are no substantial theological tensions between Gal, Rom, and 1 Cor.

---

[179] Cf. above the end of section II 3A, and the beginning of section II 3Cb.
[180] Thus Thurén 1986, 174.
[181] Räisänen 1987, 64.
[182] Becker 1989, 417.
[183] See above section II 2Bcγ.

## b. Has the Paraenesis Inherited the Negative Qualities of the Law?

If the law was superseded by the paraenesis as the main source for ethical guidelines, a new problem immediately arises: Does the paraenesis, as some kind of a *nova lex,* inherit also the negative properties previously attributed to the law? Or is the apostle simply unaware of the logical consequences of replacing Moses with paraenesis?

The questions become more intriguing, when we consider the content of the paraenesis. Much of the law still remains. Not only is the Torah cited, but one of its basic functions, to provoke a righteous way of life or obedience to God's will, is similar. Thus it is fair to ask: Does the paraenesis e.g. incite to transgressions, as the law does?[184]

Again it is important to expound the problem to its full extent, and add at least the following questions: If the law identifies sin as transgression, why does not the paraenesis? If the law enslaves people, why does not the paraenesis? If the law is the poison of sin, why is not the paraenesis? Or, if the slightest observance to the law[185] nullifies the work of Christ, why does not obedience to Paul's commands do likewise?

In Gal, Paul's ethos required, that he presents himself as a non-libertinistic teacher.[186] But would he first have cursed anyone requiring obedience to the law, and then nonchalantly or callously again demanded observance of essentially the same law, only in another guise? Did he simply first use all his theological and rhetorical capacity in order to dethrone the Mosaic law, or to be more precise, to recall people who, according to him, had "fallen from grace" to obedience of the law, and then replace the law with a basically similar paraenesis, disregarding the problems generated by such a solution?[187] Such tactics would seem rather peculiar. Therefore we at least have reason to

---

[184] Räisänen 1987, 148–49.

[185] I have argued above (esp. sections II 2Ba and 3B), that Paul does not explicitly or theoretically separate the cultic law from moral law, even though the original impetus to the discussion was circumcision.

[186] See above section II 2Bcγ. It was obvious that the gospel alone was not enough: Paul needed the paraenesis in order to defend himself theologically against possible charges of libertinism, and also for practical reasons, viz. to ensure that the lifestyle of the addressees actually does not defile his proclamation and mission.

[187] The phenomenon becomes very explicit in the heavily Pauline Colossians, irrespective of the identity of the author. The two first chapters argue strongly against observance of different rules and commands, but the second half of the letter consists of commands and admonitions. Yet this is done as if there were no tension between the two. Superficially the problem is so obvious that the author was hardly unaware of it. Thus we have to suspect that the author had somehow solved the problem for himself.

examine how Paul attempted to solve the relation between the law and the paraenesis on the theoretical level.

In Gal, the difference between the law and the paraenesis was marked by the Spirit (Gal 5,16–25).[188] People "driven" (ἄγεσθε) by the Spirit are not under the law. The life according to Paul's exhortation is described as a "fruit" of the Spirit, viz. a natural consequence of faith and loyalty to Jesus Christ (5,22–23). The Spirit enables the addressees to comply with the paraenesis. Besides that, they only need information about the right way of life.

Correspondingly in Rom 6, the reason for obedience to the paraenesis is presented as the addressees' baptismal death to sin (Rom 6,3–14). Their obedience can also be due to their status as God's servants who are free from sin (6,15–22). Sanctification is thereby a result, not just the purpose of God's act, or the addressees' adherence to the Pauline message. God's grace has replaced the law as their master (6,14) – therefore the sin ought not have power over them.

Now this idea may seem unrealistic, and on the basis of e.g. the Corinthian correspondence we have reason to doubt, whether it ever functioned in Pauline congregations, let alone later Christianity. Later writings in the New Testament have solved this issue in a more practical way. Thus 1 Peter includes clear suggestions for how the motivation should be created.[189] Such practical doubts should not, however, affect our view of what *Paul* thought about the issue. Whether his view has any practical value, or ever had, ought not to blur the study of the ideas in the text.

But obviously Paul's idea of the automatic fruits of Spirit is influenced by rhetoric; his purpose is not to describe the addressees' behaviour but to modify it. In 1 Peter, the technique of "alluring description" is used: The addressees are presented as good, perfect Christians, although the author knows their harsh reality. His aim is to make them what they are said to be.[190] Perhaps this is what Paul too is doing. But if this is "mere rhetoric", we have to doubt, what we really know about his theoretical view of the motivation for good works.

It can be somewhat confusing, that when speaking of these issues, Paul often uses hyperbolical language, viz. rhetorical exaggeration. He can, for instance, declare that the addressees' bodies are already dead (Rom 8,10). Correspondingly, he can say that he himself is wholly "sold" under sin (Rom 7,14). In such cases, a careful scrutiny of the immediate context is necessary.

---

[188] See above section II 2Bcγ.

[189] See Thurén 1995b. The letter of James may reflect the "Nachwirkung" of Pauline ethics, which does not seem to work: faith alone does not seem to produce good behaviour.

[190] Thurén 1990, 133.137–38; cf. e.g. 1 Pet 1,6 and 4,13.

As argued above, the crucial difference for Paul between law and paraenesis derives from the dichotomy of man, the distinction between flesh and spirit. In Rom 6–8 Paul attributes all the negative functions of the law to those, who are "in the flesh", viz. controlled by it (Rom 7,5). Adam is presented as the prototype (Rom 7,7–11) for the life in the flesh. He was unable to fulfil God's command. Christ, in turn, is the enabling prototype for the new life (ch. 8). Participation in the death of Christ not only leads to eternal life, but also enables obedience to exhortation.

Paul does not describe his addressees as purely spiritual beings. They consist of flesh and spirit, and both have their virtues. Only transformation of the flesh produces total liberation from sin (1 Cor 15,50–57 / Rom 8,17ff). The criterion is which side is in charge. The law still provokes sin, which means inability to do good, and it produces death due to its grip on the flesh. In that sense, the addressees are neither immortal or infallible. The paraenesis, in its turn, does not provoke sin, enslave, or bring death, since it is addressed to people "driven" by the Spirit, who are enabled thereby to lead a righteous way.[191] The same is true of the nullification of Christ's function. The Christians' good conduct is presented as a result of Christ and Spirit, which cannot be combined with obedience to the law.

Yet it remains somewhat unclear, why Paul even in Romans does not *in principle* accept the moral side of the law, as a guideline for the addressees' life – possibly with some modifications. For *in practice* this is roughly what he does. Why could not the Spirit serve as a new source of obedience to the law? The reason may be rhetorical, but one could assume also theoretical, viz. theological, grounds.

The profound connection between rhetoric and theology may well play a central role. It can be assumed that the rhetorically motivated total[192] rejection of the law in Gal, viz. failure to use it as a guideline, has resulted in a theological principle in Romans. While Paul never clearly separated the cultic and the moral law, the law remained an unbroken entity and an intact power. The law has in Pauline discussion become almost an independent person. The concept thereby became so loaded that it could not be used in a changed meaning. This positive use by the Christians would have jeopardized the simple rhetoric and its effect. Thus, when the exclusive Jewish ritual law is abandoned, even its ethically compelling role disappears.

Yet the issue calls for further study of the question: Why did Paul reject the law in the first place?

---

[191] Thurén 1986, 182–83; Westerholm 1988, 215–16.

[192] Only the basic requirement of the law (Gal 5,14) is preserved.

# Chapter 4

# What Was Wrong with the Law?

Why did Paul originally reject the law? Why could it not continue to serve as the basis of his relationship to God? Paul can admit that the law is in principle good, spiritual, and holy. It was given by God and served his purposes. Obviously Paul's view of the law differed from those of his fellow Jews, but how could this suffice for abandoning the law itself? Paul presents the law and God's grace as mutually exclusive alternatives for salvation, but was this really necessary? Could he not combine the law and grace in a co-operative system, as did contemporary Judaism, and later also many Christian churches?

Above we saw that in Gal rhetorical efficiency did not allow Paul to make any positive use of the law. But this is not yet theology: if deeper thinking is to be suspected, the criticism must concern the law itself, not merely tactical or rhetorical reasoning. When attempting to explain Paul's break with the law, part of the answer can be delineated in the current situation of research. There are certain characteristics, which are obviously connected with the solution(s), and these serve as guidelines for further surveys. I can find four principles, which will be briefly discussed below.

a) *Paul's rejection of the law must have theological foundations, too.* Recent exegetical studies have rightly emphasized that Paul's primary aim was not to write theology. Yet this trend to correct earlier, biased studies can backfire: Paul's overwhelming interest in theology, which is demonstrated by his habit of reacting theologically in different practical questions, must not be under-estimated. There is theology behind his rhetoric. Paul was a zealous, committed Pharisee, and his attack on the law was too arrogant and massive to be explained with practical reasons only.

b) *The rejection must have* something *to do with the contemporary Pharisaic view of the law.* Paul's target was not a perverted Jewish vision thereof. His heavy rhetoric has again confused the issue. However, there was also a theological difference between Paul and Pharisaism. The latter can hardly be accused of Paul's "faith alone" soteriology, which in a singular way rejects the role of good works, and seldom occurs even in Early Christianity.

c) *The explanation must connect criticism of the Mosaic law with the sociological dimension.* On the one hand, contemporary religious problems would hardly prompt a committed Pharisee to break with the core of his religion; the solution must pertain to the very essence of the Torah. On the other, however, the solution in practice was well suited to Paul's Gentile mission. Therefore the national dimension cannot be excluded either. The two dimensions ought to be seen together.

d) *The roots of Paul's rejection of the law must exceed specifically Jewish issues*. The reception history of Paul's letters and his examination of the law demonstrate how they have impressed religious people in different contexts. This is hardly fortuitous. The problem of the law has general human con- notations, which made Paul's texts a source for inspiration for later theologians, such as Augustine, Luther, and Bultmann. As their fascination for Paul is due more to the literary qualities of the texts than to the original situation, direct historical conclusions cannot be drawn. Yet it is plausible that such influential ideas also have their roots in Pauline thinking.

Let us now scrutinize the foundations and consequences of these four theses.

## A. Theology Must not be Disregarded

The surprisingly comprehensive rejection of the law is sometimes explained on strategical grounds only: Paul's poor success in the Jewish mission forced him to preach to others. This in turn required theological revision.[1] But if Paul thus reasoned, was he non-theological? Acts 13,46–47 refer to Isa 49, when presenting Paul's frustration in the Jewish mission as a background to his decision. There the Servant laments: "I have laboured to no purpose; I have spent my strength in vain and for nothing..." Then God gives him a new task: "I will make you a light for the Gentiles..." (Isa 49,4–6). Paul's move to the Gentile mission corresponds to an OT pattern, of which he must have been aware. However, the pattern includes no theological compromise, on the contrary.[2]

Dunn's sociological explanation is more moderate: The law had become a symbol of the division between Jews and Gentiles. Ethnic and religious issues were inseparable.[3] Therefore the law could not be re-defined into a positive

---

[1] Watson 1986, 28–40; see above section I 2B.

[2] For a finer analysis of the historical and ideological background of Isa 49,1–13 see A. Laato 1992,106–22.

[3] Dunn 1991, 230.

principle.[4] This idea suits the rhetoric of Galatians, where compliance with the law is of major symbolic significance. If this solution supersedes theological reasoning, it is plausible that Paul first changed his practice, and only as a result of conflict with the Judaizers attempted to produce an ideological, secondary explanation.[5]

The lack of theological dimension in Dunn's solution has often been criticized.[6] He bases his view partly on Neusner,[7] who however emphatically rejects Dunn's interpretation. According to Neusner, the law was only a theological, not a social, barrier for the Jews. He even argues that "the category *ethnic identity* bore no meaning whatsoever".[8] But even this extreme expression is difficult to accept. For instance Ezra 4,1–5 reflects a situation, where ethnic boundaries transcend religious aspects.[9] Furthermore methodologically, Neusner's thesis is not acceptable.[10] Thus both extreme solutions are unsatisfactory.

Westerholm rejects the mainly sociological solutions, wondering how Paul, who was usually so interested in theological questions, and who could raise "no practical issue without resolving its place in a theological framework",[11] would have waited so long after his conversion, before finding a suitable theory to match his behaviour. As a Pharisee Paul was preoccupied with the Torah – even before his conversion.[12]

Westerholm's theses are worth studying. I start from the latter claim. The Torah surely played a central role in Paul's life, even when he was a Pharisaic

---

[4] Dunn 1985, esp. 527; 1988, lxiv–lxxii; followed e.g. by Hays 1996, 152–54. This idea would justify the positive use of the OT law in modern Christianity, since the word no longer carries such sociological connotations.

[5] See Räisänen 1987, 253–63.

[6] See especially Eskola 1998, 209–12. For additional criticism of Dunn's thesis, see below section II 4Dd.

[7] Dunn 1985, 359 n. 16.

[8] Neusner 1995, 39, his emphasis; see also 3–4.37–39.

[9] Ezra 4,2–3: "They approached Zerubbabel and the heads of families and said to them, 'Let us build with you, for we worship your God as you do, and we have been sacrificing to him ever since the days of King Esar-haddon of Assyria who brought us here.' But Zerubbabel, Joshua, and the rest of the heads of families in Israel said to them, 'You shall have no part with us in building a house to our God; but we alone will build to Yhwh, the God of Israel, as King Cyrus of Persia has commanded us.'" Cf. also Ezra 9–10.

[10] The sociological function of the Jewish customs cannot be determined solely by the sayings of the rabbis, just as any sociological observation cannot rely only on a self-analysis of the group studied.

[11] Westerholm 1988, 222.

[12] Westerholm 1988, 217–18.

scribe. It is widely accepted, that the Damascus road encounter was decisive for his new attitude to the law.[13] But Hengel's description of that incident as *Vulkanausbruch* is telling:[14] the pressure must be tremendous before eruption ensues. This was probably true regarding Saul, too, even though his possible underlying problems with the law are difficult to study.[15]

When Saul was persecuting Christians, the impetus of his action (beside some imaginary psychological or sociological motivations) was the Torah: the Christians worshipped a man, who was cursed according to the law.[16] Thus they must be eradicated. The conversion meant an end to Saul's mission, and correspondingly a different interpretation of the law. Here theology and action can hardly be separated.

Agreeing also with Westerholm's first point I do not believe that Paul discarded one of the most precious components of his religion simply in order to achieve a practical goal. Although, as seen above, Paul had wide rhetorical flexibility in many pragmatic, and even in some theological, issues, this was not always the case.

According to Paul's own testimony he was a fanatic Pharisee prior to his conversion (Gal 1,14), and at the time of writing Philippians still proud of it. Thus in Phil 3,4–6 he emphasizes his pre-Christian ζῆλος, which exceeded the usual Jewish piety.[17] As a Christian Paul seems to be similarly extremist in his statements,[18] which confirms the description of his Jewish past. Another typical feature for Paul is that throughout his letters he seems to react theologically even in practical questions.[19] This is true also concerning the law. The lack of

---

[13]  Gal 1,1. See Dunn 1996c, 313; Hengel 1996, 51.

[14]  Hengel 1996, 34.

[15]  At least no "Lutheran" problems are plausible, see below. An alternative explanation of Saul's problem with the law will be offered below.

[16]  Cf. Gal 3,13, where Paul cites a form of Deut 21,23. For a Jewish understanding of this curse, see Betz 1979, 152 n. 136.

[17]  Cf. Phil 3,4–6: "If anyone else has reason to be confident in the flesh, I have more: circumcised on the eighth day, a member of the people of Israel, of the tribe of Benjamin, a Hebrew born of Hebrews; as to the law, a Pharisee; as to zeal, a persecutor of the church; as to righteousness under the law, blameless." For the Jewish "enthusiasm", see Hengel 1961; Michel 1978, 325 n. 4.

[18]  For Paul's current *zelos*, see 2 Cor 11,2.29. Against Dunn (1996c, 313), insofar as he argues that Paul converted from all *zelos*.

[19]  See above chapter I 2.

discussion of the law in 1 Thess does not prove its absence from Paul's theology at that time.[20]

These two features are particularly visible in Gal. Paul's fierce, theologized attack on the holy Torah indicates that it was not a matter of flexibility. For Paul not only criticized a different view thereof; he concluded by conditionally cursing everybody, including himself, an angel from heaven (and even more),[21] who had a view of the gospel, and therefore the Torah, deviating from his own. Thus, whether or not there are other reasons, a strong theological incentive, or at least an explanation of Paul's solution is to be expected.[22]

Considering these two characteristic features in Paul – an extreme way of thinking and a special interest in theology – it is difficult to believe that he would have rejected the law as an *adiaphoron* or for strategic reasons alone. Paul's arrogant move implies a huge theological step, and knowing his tendency to react theologically to even minor questions, sociological and psychological explanations are insufficient. The break with the law probably had profound reasons. But when seeking a theological explanation, we have to dig deep. Although Paul may have criticized any Jewish interpretation or practice of the law, or even had some thoughts on a general philosophical rejection of man's innate arrogance, it is difficult to regard these as a satisfactory basis for his theological insurrection.

To sum up: It seems unlikely that a practical goal or a religious laxity sufficed to dethrone the law, which Paul after all never ceased to honour as one of the most holy aspects in his religion. The stark antithesis between grace and law, and the similarly mutually exclusive alternatives – Christ or the law – indicate, that Paul's rejection of the law had ideological grounds, too. Although the current trend of research, to detheologize the Pauline texts, is in a sense correct, scholars tend to overreact and neglect their heavy ideological dimension.[23]

To be sure, in the last resort it is difficult to determine whether theoretical or practical reasons are original and profound, just as the event which actually triggered the writing of Romans remains a riddle for us.[24] Since we do not possess enough data about Paul's psychological development, and have but few

---

[20] Thus also Westerholm 1988, 217. *Argumentum e silentio* is particularly weak with regard to short documents aimed at specific situations (cf. also section II B, introduction; II C and II 4Dd.

[21] See above section I 4E.

[22] Thus also Westerholm 1988, 216–17.

[23] See above chapter I 2.

[24] See above section II 3A.

hints about his life as a Jew, it is mere guesswork to decide whether or not his ideas about the law were devised afterwards to justify his feelings and behaviour. The best we can do is to study the explicit documents in order to reconstruct the theological roots of his radical attitude to the law.

## B. Jewish Theology or Pauline Exaggeration?

*Motto*: καὶ συνυπεκρίθησαν αὐτῷ οἱ λοιποὶ Ἰουδαῖοι (Gal 2,13)

When Paul wanted to refute the contemporary Pharisaic religious system, and wholly reshape one of its central topics, the law, he probably thought that it was at fault. Thus it is important to ask, how did the apostle actually perceive the role of the law in Jewish theology and religion. This classical question is however rendered difficult to answer by the heavy rhetoric of Paul's epistles.

To what degree does Paul describe Jewish thinking and theology in his letters? The great shift in current Pauline research has demonstrated the inaccuracy of the earlier scholarship's negative reconstruction of Jewish soteriology and theology. Furthermore, it has shown that such a picture is based on a careless or biassed reading of Paul.[25] The case can be compared to the use of Romans 13 to justify the *Apartheid*: Although the apostle's texts were used for unfortunate purposes, this does not indicate that the South African Government read Paul aright. On the contrary, the official Afrikaner interpretation of Rom 13 was distorted and led to grotesque hermeneutics.[26] The same is true of many definitions of the apostle's attitude to other Jews. Paul should not be blamed for later misreading. This fact has not yet been sufficiently recognized.[27]

In Gal we saw, that Paul does not discuss Jewish soteriology or theology, but "Judaizing" tendencies among the Christians. And even such tendencies were not objectively *described*: Paul creates a caricature, viz. his own theological vision of what the antagonists' idea may or should lead to. His reasons were rhetorical: It is always easier to oppose a "straw man" or an adversary characterized by oneself than the real enemy.[28]

Turning to Romans, where the Jews and their fate are actually mentioned, we may ask again, whether Paul there attempts to characterize Jewish

---

[25] Cf. Sanders 1977, 549–52.
[26] See Botha 1994, esp. 1–9.219–27.
[27] An exception is Illman 1996, 50–54.
[28] See above section II 2A.

soteriology or their relationship to the law, and how far can his statements be attributed to a rhetorical technique as in Galatians. It is somewhat difficult to distinguish between Jewish and Jewish-Christian opinions in Rom. But it is questionable, whether Israel or Jews as such are discussed elsewhere than in Rom 9–11. Two problems are particularly interesting: Did the apostle charge Judaism with perverse morals, and/or perverse soteriology?

*First*, does Paul accuse the Jews of being especially immoral and guilty?

In Rom 2 he attempts to condemn the Jews or his Jewish-Christian readers. The serious charges, culminating in 2,21–22, are however not to be taken as a source of Paul's view of the Jewish lifestyle.[29] It is hardly plausible that any of Paul's original addressees would have interpreted the verses in such a way. Instead, these rhetorical questions constitute an hyperbolic persuasive device, comparable with Jesus' saying about a beam in the eye in Matt 7,3–5.

The exaggeration does not, however, indicate that there is no alleged truth in the accusation. On the contrary, just as in the case of the "beam" in Matthew, the addressee is supposed to understand the criticism inherent in the overstated charge and to accept it. The whole point of the accusation lies in this agreement: if the charge is wholly rejected by the addressee, it is null and void.

From Rom 2,19–3,20 we can assume that Paul judged the Jews to be as guilty as the Gentiles in the eyes of God. Their measure or grade of good behaviour is not discussed; Paul is only concerned to that the Jews (maybe even as Christians) cannot fulfill the law sufficiently to be saved thereby. In Rom 3, Paul tries to prove through the Law and Scriptures, that everybody is a sinner, even the Jews. Hard evidence of crimes committed by the Jews is not provided. The reason behind their condemnation is presented as God's plan to prove all men guilty before him and thereby create a need for his gift in Christ (Rom 3,4.19–25).

Summing up: Paul never even tries to prove that the Jews were especially guilty or immoral. They are but accused of sins comparable with those of the Gentiles. Both alleged transgressions are in the end seen as purposeful, inasmuch as they serve God's plan. Only a static attitude toward Paul's texts, viz. a total misunderstanding of his approach to his audience, can lead to the assessment that the apostle regarded the Jews as exceptionally sinful or blameworthy. But although they too were said to have failed to follow the law, such a reference did not suffice as a *theological* reason to reject the law.

---

[29] For the discussion of the rhetoric in the section, see above section I 3C n. 48.

*Second*, we can ask more generally: Does Paul impute to the Jews or Jewish-Christians a soteriology, whereby one tries to reach salvation by following the law, or by referring to his good deeds?

In Rom 3 and 4 Paul presents a model for justification by faith, using the Abraham narrative as foundation and example. The counterpart to this model, partly implicit, is justification by works and the law (especially Rom 3, 20.28; 4,2.4.14). This alternative model, however, is not attributed to anybody, not even Jews. Nor is the model said to comply with Jewish soteriology. On the contrary, it reflects the imaginary theology opposed already in Galatians. Justification by works serves here as a theoretical antithesis to Paul's own doctrine. It is necessary to highlight the specific character of the apostle's position. Just as the opinions contradicted in Gal are not ascribed to Paul's opponents, likewise it is in Rom 4 incorrect to say that this doctrine even "implicitly" refers to real Jewish or Jewish-Christian soteriology.

In a sense Paul is unfair when creating so soft an opponent. He can easily survive as a theological hero in a battle against a tailor-made antagonist. But simplification and exaggeration of problems enables their solution on the ideological level.[30]

It has also been alleged that Paul attacks a perverted Jewish understanding of the law, especially when contrasting the "letter" and the "spirit".[31] But at least this contrast does not reveal such an attitude: Westerholm correctly states that for Paul the "letter" as such never signifies a perversion, as it refers to several aspects of the law, such as possession of the written law (Rom 2,27) or obedience to the law (Rom 7,6; 2 Cor 3,6).[32] For the apostle, it was not wrong to keep the law literally, on the contrary: under the law every commandment must be obeyed. Problems begin when you do not obey.

The guilt of Israel is discussed in Rom 9,30–10,4. According to 9,31–32 the Jews have pursued the righteousness based on works; according to 10,3 they sought to establish their own righteousness. In both cases the accusation is supported by an explanation: own righteousness based on works is wrong because its pursuers are offended by Christ and not submissive to God's righteousness. Philippians 3,6.9 conveys a similar picture. This description means, that in Paul's polarized diagram of salvation the Jews are said to have chosen the wrong alternative, the works. But there is no sign that such a Jewish

---

[30] See above section II 2Adγ.

[31] Thus Cranfield 1982, 339–40, who in many questions represents the pre-Sanders era. See e.g. Cranfield 1983, 519–20.

[32] See Westerholm 1988, 210–13.

"righteousness by works" is ideologically distinguishable from the caricature of the antagonists in Galatia. For baking such a bread, a little yeast suffices.

However, it is too simple a solution to reiterate Sanders' thesis: "...this is what Paul finds wrong in Judaism: it is not Christianity."[33] For since Jews are discussed throughout Romans, the opposed doctrine must have *something* to do with the actual Jewish or Jewish Christian thinking, especially regarding the purposes of the letter. In Gal Paul's point was clear and practical: He tried to demonstrate, the kind of theology to which the antagonists' teaching may lead; he attempted to show the addressees the totally "leavened batch of dough", nullification of God's grace and the death of Christ.[34] In Rom 4, he may have a similar purpose, although the rhetorical function is less simple. In any case, the rhetoric presupposes that the Jews or Jewish Christians at least to some degree recognized the importance of good works for salvation, no matter how much the grace of God is emphasized. Otherwise Paul's message never reaches the audience and is doomed to remain ineffective. Notwithstanding that the rhetorical, antithetical, exaggerated position "good works vs. faith" as mutually exclusive alternatives, was not a neutral or even viable description of either Jewish or Christian faith, and was hardly even meant to be taken as such,[35] the good works and obedience to the law had according to Paul an important function in the Jewish religion.

Indeed, Pharisaism can hardly be charged with a "faith alone" soteriology, viz. as totally rejecting the role of good works for salvation. Such a religious attitude was condemned in the Epistle of James,[36] but *the author was hardly attacking Pharisaism.* Injustice is done to the Pharisees, if exclusively Pauline theological ideas are read into their religious attitude.

Sharing Sanders' basic idea of an homogeneous Judaism as a "pattern", T. Laato represents another absolute view.[37] According to him, the essential difference between Paul and Pharisaism, neglected by most scholars, was

---

[33] Sanders 1977, 552.

[34] Gal 2,21: "I do not nullify the grace of God; for if justification comes through the law, then Christ died for nothing."

[35] Rom 4,5 τῷ δὲ μὴ ἐργαζομένῳ πιστεύοντι δὲ belongs to the picture used, which cannot be taken literally, as if faith meant cessation of all work or that good behaviour was seen as generally irrelevant to God (cf. e.g. Gal 5,6). According to Dunn "the language used here... should not be taken as a description of the Judaism of Paul's day. - - - The wording is used simply as part of the analogy drawn from the world of contract and employment." (1988, 204).

[36] Even James presents it in an overstated form, if compared with the doctrine of Paul.

[37] Laato 1991.

anthropological. Building especially on H. Odeberg[38] Laato claims, that according to the Pharisees, man is capable of making right decisions before God, and this results in a co-operative soteriology.[39] Paul's anthropology, in turn, was pessimistic, and thus the salvation had to depend solely on God's grace. Although the Pharisees did not strive for salvation, relying exclusively on their good deeds, their own activity played such a decisive role that they were justified in boasting of it. This did not suit Paul's exclusive soteriology.[40] Laato has indicated how ideas opposed by Paul could exist in the contemporary Jewish thought, but his view of Judaism is too homogeneous and based on narrow material. For instance, Qumran and the Psalms of Solomon are not considered (with one exception).

In current Pauline scholarship, there are signs of a move from the one-sided amendment of Sanders' study of rabbinic theology to a more balanced post-Sanders era. Careful studies have shed new light on the complex, all-encompassing role of the law in the rabbinic texts.[41] The picture is also widened by the focus on Early Jewish sapiential and apocalyptic texts, and Paul is placed in this context.[42] These studies cannot be refuted on the ground that anything can be found in a vast material. Instead, they witness to the fact that ancient Judaism was a diverse phenomenon,[43] which does not easily fit into any modern ideological matrix. Concerning salvation, this diversity could be wide-ranging; both divine grace and human obedience could be emphasized. Yet the central role of the law was never challenged: it was the unifying factor of different "Judaisms".

A recurrent idea in Early Jewish texts is a "synergistic" view of salvation, where the human factor in salvation is emphasized side by side with the divine action.[44] People were divided into righteous and sinners. In IV Ezra the decisive

---

[38] Odeberg 1945.

[39] See also Maier 1971.

[40] See Westerholm 1988, 142–48; Laato 1991, 210–11; Seifrid 1992, 132–33. Thielman (1994, 240) finds two groups among the Jews: some had an optimistic anthropology, whereas others "understood the biblical witness to God's prevenient grace".

[41] See e.g. Avemarie 1996, 575–84 and the thorough study of the research on Pharisaism by Deines (1997).

[42] See e.g. Schnabel 1985; Schimanowski 1985 Westerholm 1988; Thielman 1989, 1994; Tomson 1990; Seifrid 1992; Garlington 1991; Winninge 1995; Avemarie 1996a and b; Lichtenberger 1996, esp. 10–11. For a brief presentation of this new trend in recent scholarship, see Eskola 1998, 20–26.

[43] See Dunn 1996c, 311–13.

[44] Eskola (1998, 27–94) reviews soteriological thoughts in sapiential and apocalyptic literature, and in Qumran, and speaks of soteriological dualism ever since Sirach (1998, 41–43).

importance of human obedience is prominent,[45] but such an idea can be found in e.g. Qumran and Philo as well.[46] Repentance and obedience to the law play an essential role in salvation. This is partly admitted even by Sanders: "...works are the condition of remaining "in", but they do not earn salvation."[47] Yet amid the diversity, Paul's extreme soteriology seems to be a singular phenomenon.

To conclude: When the bias of Paul's rhetoric is translated into neutral language, his view of Judaism roughly corresponds to, or befits, the pictures preserved in ancient texts. However, the only difference between them and Paul hardly identifies Jesus as the Christ; e.g. the radical view of man's universal guilt and explicit disregard of the human contribution to salvation seldom occur in Jewish texts.

Yet the discovery of divergent insights between Paul and Pharisaism hardly suffices to explain Paul's rejection of the law. For contemporary Judaism was a flexible religion containing many different theological concepts, which could exist without challenging the central role of the law. If the law is rejected, there must be something problematic in the law as such.

# C. Tensions within the Old Testament

*a. Introduction*

We have stated that strong theological reasons were required for Paul's break with the law. Practical drawbacks or criticism of the features of some form of contemporary Judaism would hardly suffice for him. Thus it is interesting to study, to what degree his most telling criticism concerned the Torah itself, rather than consequential issues. The problem with such an undertaking is that we must look beyond his rhetoric, which is, after all, closely connected with practical questions. Although a full scale analysis would exceed the scope of this study, our previous observations prompt some hypotheses, which need to be expounded in this chapter.

So what did Paul criticize in the law? In fact nothing, maintain most modern scholars, who allege that the only real difference for Paul was made by Christ.

---

[45] Thus Sanders sees IV Ezra as an exception in Judaism (Sanders 1977, 418.546). See further Longenecker 1991 and Eskola 1998, 71–73.78.

[46] E.g. according to 4QMMT C, good works will be counted as righteousness. For other references and a survey of soteriology in Qumran, see Eskola 1998, 79–93. About Philo, All III,77–78.83 see below.

[47] Sanders 1977, 543.

Sanders argues that the law was to be rejected only because Christ excluded it.[48] The current post-Sandersian trend sees the situation slightly differently, emphasizing the problems in Early Judaism, which are said to point to Christ as the new solution.[49] These scholars face the challenge of finding a theological explanation. Instead of only correcting mistakes in earlier scholarship, or psychologizing or sociologizing the question, Paul and his theology are set in the context of contemporary Jewish thought. The scholars try thereby to identify the ideological factors which provoked Paul's radical solution with the law. Since reference to human failure to obey the law hardly sufficed to dethrone the divine law, other reasons are sought.

Thus Westerholm puts the blame on the Torah and God's intention therein. The law had failed, but only because people had fallen short of its standards. This in turn served God's purpose or "ultimate design" to demonstrate human guilt. God's final goal thereby was to show mercy to all (Gal 3,19.22; Rom 11,32), and to this end, Christ was needed.[50] Thielman and Eskola continue on this path. They argue that among the Jews of Paul's time, Israel's wretched fate and sin constituted the major problem: God's help was long overdue.[51] According to Eskola, Early Judaism generally solved this problem of theodicy with "synergistic nomism", whereas Paul saw Christ as the new solution. Eskola too emphasizes that Paul found a divine plan behind the situation.[52] He proclaimed the sinfulness of all men, Gentiles and Jews alike, ever since Adam. Behind this there is not just an "ultimate design" but "predestination", which is "God's coercive act where the whole of humankind is imprisoned in disobedience". This act opened the way to God's salvation in Christ, which correspondingly must be granted to both Jews and Gentiles. Such a salvation, in turn, is possible only through justification by faith.[53]

The strength of this explanation compared with the solution of Sanders is that it avoids seeing Paul as a theological phantom appearing out of the blue. But the same does not apply to the role of Christ in the change in Paul's theology. According to Westerholm, "a heavenly vision changed [Paul's] commission completely".[54] Even if a vision did trigger the change in Paul's life,

---

[48] Sanders 1977, 551–52; 1983, 45–48.
[49] See above.
[50] Westerholm 1988, 195–97.221.
[51] E.g. Thielman 1994, 241–42.
[52] Eskola 1998, 293ff.
[53] Eskola 1998, 302–306.
[54] Westerholm 1988, 218.

as the eventual explanation of Paul's revolt against the law, it is a *deus ex machina* indeed.

The definition of the basic problem solved by Christ as a collective version of sinfulness is at least easier to justify than the earlier individual Bultmannian interpretation. Undoubtedly Paul as a Christian regarded both Jews and Gentiles as sinners who cannot fulfill the law.[55] However, this was not the case before his conversion, and thus cannot explain the *change* in his theology. As "secondary rationalization" after the Damascus incident, the explanation is of course viable.

A third problem is that even this explanation does not answer the question why the *law* was to be rejected. Indeed it could not save people, but how could this make compliance with its requirements theologically so dangerous as Paul claims in Gal? Why could not Christ be a new Moses, who does not drop one stroke of a letter from the law (Matt 5,17–18), but merely guides to a better understanding thereof, perhaps to a quantum leap in the theology of the law? Or why could not Christ be a new source of motivation and power to obey the law?

This is actually what many interpreters believe.[56] Thielman argues: the law was not really rejected, but only reinterpreted. This forces him to see a *paradox* in Paul's theological thinking.[57] But if notwithstanding we expect consistency in Paul's thinking, better explanations have to be pursued. Then it is necessary to focus on the law itself and seek something that could have irritated Saul, and justified the Paul's solution.

But does anything in the OT prompt a change in the theology of the law? Hofius discusses many passages, which refer to *iustificatio impii* – Israel is forgiven without, or even against, the prescriptions of the law.[58] Although such sovereign acts of the God in no way diminish the validity of the law, Hofius

---

[55] Rom 1–3. For discussion of the groups fulfilling the law, see above sections II 2Bcβ and II 3Da. Westerholm (1988, 218) favours an old "Lutheran" explanation: Paul struggled with his inability to fulfill the law and found Christ. This explanation is however generally rejected, since it is difficult to combine with the fact that in his letters Paul reviews positively his Jewish past (e.g. Gal 1,14; Phil 3,6). For the discussion, see Räisänen 1987, 229–36.

[56] See above section II 2 Bc; II 3Da. In this sense, Westerholm is an exception.

[57] Thielman 1994, 237.240–44. Eskola too refers to "paradoxical polarization" in Paul's theology (1998, 137–42). Räisänen, however, has already suggested a better name for a paradox as a theological solution: *contradiction* (1987, 4). Dunn avoids the theological contradiction by simply detheologizing the whole issue.

[58] Hofius 1989, 121–247. Thus Hosea speaks of Israel as an unfaithful wife (2,4) or a rebellious son (11,1) – both offenders deserve the death penalty according to the law (Deut 22,22; 21,18–21). Yet Israel is forgiven (Hos 14). Correspondingly passages of God's mercy without the law are found in Jeremiah (3,12–22) and Isaiah (43).

rightly sees them as implying its weakness: It could not help when people were totally dominated by sin.[59] Thus something new was needed.

More explicitly, there is the concept of a new covenant in Jer 31,31–34, which speaks of the law, and Ezek 11,19–20; 36,25–27,37, foreseeing a new spirit. Now Paul could see Christ as an eschatological sign of this new covenant, which could include even the Gentiles.[60] Yet, although Paul refers to Jer 31,[61] this alone does not suffice for such an interpretation: Jer explicitly speaks of a covenant with Israel and Judah, and the law is by no means outmoded thereby, on the contrary: "I will put my law within them, and I will write it on their hearts" (Jer 31,33). And as Lars Hartman notes, Paul nowhere indicates that the old covenant had been totally superseded.[62] Thus, although the idea of a new covenant plays a major role in Paul's theology,[63] it cannot be directly adduced as an explanation of why Christ was the end of the law.

To sum up: On one hand, we can expect the roots of Saul's/Paul's problem, and solution concerning the law to be found within the "law", viz. in the OT. On the other, we must bear in mind Dunn's thesis: "Any attempt to enter sympatheti-cally into the context of Paul's teaching on the law must take into account the social function of the law at that time."[64] The practical use of Paul's theology of the law must not be overlooked, as does Westerholm, simply referring to it with an italicized "*of course*".[65] For just as Paul recognized no practice without theology, nor was there a presentation of theology without a practical incentive. And was not Gentile mission *per se* a major theological issue for a good Pharisee, rather than simply a practical matter? An integration of the two may help us to understand the theology.

We thus have two tasks. First, the theological origins for Paul's criticism of the Torah should be sought, even if they were not clearly prompted by the result, the Gentile mission. Secondly, the indivisible practical, historical or sociological explanation ought to be more precise and gain theological support. In both cases, the best source is not Paul's contemporary issues, which were too petty theologically to disqualify the Torah. In addition, it must be borne in mind

---

[59] Hofius 1989, 145–46. According to him, Gen 3 labels all mankind in this way (Hofius 1989, 142–45).

[60] For discussion, see Räisänen 1987, 240–45.

[61] Rom 15,27.

[62] Hartman 1980, 116.

[63] See Hartman 1980.

[64] Dunn 1985, 538.

[65] Westerholm 1988, 222.

that our knowledge of First century Judaism is still meagre. Thus we ought to examine the "Torah" viz. the OT itself, too. For Paul it was holy and divine, and it is better preserved than Paul's contemporary Jewish sources.

### b. Contradicting the Promise

*Motto*: εἰ γὰρ ἐκ νόμου ἡ κληρονομία, οὐκέτι ἐξ ἐπαγγελίας (Gal 3,18a)

Again the complex of problem is mapped clearly by Räisänen: "Paul... makes a sharp distinction between two sets of concepts. On the one side stand the law and the works (of the law); on the other side Christ, grace, the Spirit, faith and promise."[66] The distinction is obvious in Gal 3, Rom 3 and 4. However, it hardly describes the actual difference between Paul's theology and that of his opponents.[67] According to Hays, Paul's novel statements about the law are "a direct theological consequence of reading Scripture freshly..."[68] For instance Gal 3,15–18 and Rom 4 discuss the case of Abraham's righteousness in the OT, which seems to be problematic for Paul, and which he interprets differently from his contemporaries.[69] With our methods it is difficult to determine, whether the exegesis of the Abraham-narrative was the primary problem for Paul or only "secondary rationalization". It may well be that for a committed Pharisee exegetical problems loomed "larger than life".

J. Thurén explains Paul's solution as a revolt against the Apostle's own previous interpretation of the Torah, not as direct criticism of his contemporary Pharisaism.[70] Paul had found in the OT two soteriological lines: The one based on the works of the law, the other on God's promises, faith, and Christ. Thurén presents the central verses of Gal discussed by Räisänen as antithetical and mutually exclusive:

| | |
|---|---|
| Law vs. Grace, Christ | Gal 2,21; 5,4 |
| The Works of Law vs. Faith (in Christ) | Gal 3,12; 3,11f; 2,16; 3,2 |
| Law vs. Promise | Gal 3,17.18 |
| Law vs. Promise, Faith, Christ | Gal 3,21f |

---

[66] Räisänen 1987, 162–64, against many scholars, who deny this contrast (p. 162 n. 5).

[67] I have suggested above (sections II 2Ac, 2Bb and 4B), that we there only meet caricatures, rhetorical devices used by Paul for identifiable tactical reasons.

[68] Hays 1996, 158. He however continues: "...through a new hermeneutical filter shaped by the cross and by the Gentile mission." Admittedly Paul agrees that a new radical perspective is required (2 Cor 3,13–15) before a Christian interpretation is possible. But could not *something* be observable even without the filter?

[69] Cf. below section II 4C.

[70] Thurén 1986, 183–91.

Correspondingly in Rom 4,1–5:[71]

| | | | |
|---|---|---|---|
| The Works (of the law) | Something due | Wages | (Righteousness) |
| Faith (on the promise) | Mercy | (Gift) | Righteousness |

Thurén further states that Paul does not here illustrate an existing Jewish soteriology or even the teaching of his own adversaries. The distinction between faith and the works was devised by Paul himself.[72] He constructs it from the Torah, and must "mobilize all his exegetical and rhetorical skill in order to demonstrate the incompatibility of these two ways".[73] Normally the two belonged together even for Paul (Rom 1,5; 16,26).

Thurén claims that according to Paul even other Jews ought to have recognized the exclusivity in order to be consistent.[74] Or, we could say: In Paul's letters we find rhetorical "straw men" who seek salvation solely by their own merits, without any need of God's mercy, and who act as Paul's opponents. They represent for him a result of an OT study – a result at which all who wish to obey the law should arrive. Thus, whereas different forms of Judaism as we know it could combine God's mercy and *zelos* for the law, at least the Christian Paul assessed the alternatives as mutually exclusive. But could such a reading of the Torah constitute a factor in Saul's theological frame of reference, and thereby partially explain the change in his theology?

The Pharisee Saul presented in the Pauline texts is presumably a rhetorically coloured figure, serving as a dark background for Paul. But an assessment of the historical reliability of this picture is not crucial for understanding Paul's thoughts. The Pharisee Paul, as he appears in the text, sheds light on Paul's thoughts. For Saul, as portrayed by Paul, there was no room for mercy. He was blameless regarding the law, and his driving principle was a fanatic *zelos* to obey the law, which exceeded the zeal of his contemporaries (Gal 1,13–14; Phil 3,6; cf. Rom 10,2). One of the consequences of this fervour was that Saul persecuted those who believed that Jesus is the Messiah.[75]

But to be blameless involves reliance on oneself. This, in turn, could be seen as contradicting many sayings in the OT, such as Jer 17,5:

---

[71] Thurén 1986, 185.

[72] Cf. above section II 2Ac. In a similar way, even Rom 6,14 is Paul's own thesis, and in Rom 10,5f the conflict exists within the Torah, not between Paul and Pharisaism.

[73] Thurén 1986, 184–85: "Han måste mobilisera hela sitt exegetiska och retoriska kunnande för att bevisa dessa vägars oförenlighet."

[74] Thurén 1986, 190–91.

[75] Cf. Hengel and Schwemer 1997, 100.

"Thus says Yhwh: Cursed are those who trust in mere mortals and make mere flesh their strength, whose hearts turn away from Yhwh."

Thurén claims that this was not realized by Saul until the divine revelation.[76] Yet such a psychological assessment is hard to validate – the tension between different OT sayings may have irritated Saul, who sought a consistent theology, to the degree that this contributed in his conversion. The conversion meant a radical change from one exclusive alternative to the other. But in contrast to the first choice, he simultaneously managed to solve (at least for himself) the tension within the two lines in the OT: instead of creating a new eschatological version of the law, he simply proclaimed that Christ is the end (termination) of the law – and thereby also the end of the tension caused by the co-existence of the law and the promise. This solution will be studied below.

In practice, the situation was far from clear. There were many Gentile "Godfearers", mixed marriages and proselytes.[77] But obviously this practical development was not based on any clear theological solution, which would have satisfied Paul.[78]

The idea of two exclusive lines in the OT, and Paul's solution thereof, illuminate a possible theological background for his criticism of the law. It also befits our previous observations about the hyperbolic nature of Paul's thinking. The tendency to present reality in polarized absolutes is a symptomatic feature in his rhetoric, but at the same time characterizes his entire theology. Paul was motivated by an eschatological vision: the end was present, and it radicalized everyday life (1 Cor 7,29–31). In this sense even the exaggerated sentences are "sincere".

However, this explanation is not yet theologically sufficient. To assess two lines of thought in the OT as incompatible alternatives, and to change from one to another, does not explain why the latter superseded the former. If we reiterate that Paul really was a theologian, or continue to look for theological reasoning, "a heavenly vision" (Westerholm) or "the Resurrected" (Thurén) alone are not satisfactory answers.

In addition, as stated above, the question about Jews and Gentiles must not be overlooked. Paul's solution precisely fits the goal for supporting the Gentile mission: if the law was not in force, it could no longer separate the Gentiles from the God of Israel, and the promise was a way to God which even they could follow. But was there anything in the law itself, which made this idea the

---

[76] Thurén 1986, 191.

[77] Hengel and Schwemer 1997, 50–54.61–76.

[78] For the question of the "godfearers" and Jewish proselytism, see below.

only viable possibility? What was wrong with the alternative, characterized by the special status of the Jews? We now turn to this question.

### c. Counteracting Monotheism?

*Motto*: ἢ Ἰουδαίων ὁ θεὸς μόνον; (Rom 3,29)

We saw above that the relationship between Israel and the Gentiles is the main issue of Romans on the ideological level. Irrespective of what Paul hopes to achieve in Rome, or in Jerusalem, this question has to be discussed. At this level, many practical matters, of which the law is but one, are related to this relationship.

But what exactly is the role of the law? Its replacement with faith and grace seems to put the two groups on a par. Paul claims that justification is now possible without the law – which opens salvation also to the Gentiles, and which is the only way even for the Jews. But further questions emerge: How is this equalization justified? And does this goal constitute a sufficient reason for overthrowing the law?

Dunn emphasizes the role of the law as a social "boundary marker", which separated the Jews from the Gentiles. For Paul, this landmark was then removed by the death of Jesus.[79] Nor can such a social role of the law be rejected, since it can be demonstrated ever since the Maccabean period.[80] However, we have already seen that this explanation is not unproblematic, because it takes too little account of the theological aspect, most critically argued by Neusner.[81] And although Dunn adds an important perspective, his thesis is questionable even as a partial solution, as it involves two further difficulties.

α) *Persistence of the Social Difference.* The social function creating the Jewish distinctiveness did *not* totally vanish according to Paul. For him the Jews still enjoyed a privileged status before God. For instance Rom 3, which indeed seeks to demonstrate the equality of Jews and Gentiles before God, however begins by emphasizing the peculiarity of the Jews (Rom 3,1–2). The whole of Rom 9–11 shows that Paul still regarded the Jews as a distinct social group

---

[79] Dunn 1985, 539. He believes that the law continued to have a positive role (538).
[80] Dunn 1985, 524–27.
[81] See above section 4A.

with a special status before God. He even enumerates some "boundary markers"[82] in Rom 9,4–5:

> They are Israelites, and to them belong the adoption, the glory, the covenants, the giving of the law, the worship, and the promises; to them belong the patriarchs, and from them, according to the flesh, comes the Messiah, who is over all, God blessed forever. Amen.

Dunn explains this passage by focussing on the word "Israelites". According to him Paul chose this word instead of "Jew", to emphasize that he is not speaking of his "fellow countrymen and blood relations as such", but of a scriptural entity, viz. all who inherit the promise of Abraham.[83] I find the explanation artificial, as if Paul was not referring to real Jews, his "kindred according to the flesh" (9,3) in these chapters. It is even possible, that in Gal 6,16 this Israel *kata sarka* is meant.[84]

Correspondingly, Gal 3,28 is not a general social, political, or sexual proclamation of equality or similarity, although modern commentators would see it as such.[85] The verse speaks of the addressees' homogenized *religious* position, especially toward the law. Using *repetitio* (three times οὐκ ἔνι) Paul specifies that in this sense (viz. concerning baptism and termination of the law) there is no difference between Jews and Gentiles. But the social wall between the Jews and Gentiles was never completely broken down. What Paul emphasizes instead is the new religious unity in Christ. Although some social consequences of this unity were desirable in Rome, the important change caused by Christ was theological. Correspondingly, it needs a thorough theological foundation: Why was such a theological unity good or necessary? Moreover, what in the OT could justify it?

Although the Torah, and observance thereof, functioned as an expression of Israel's social distinctiveness, the social role was, from an ideological point of view, but a visible consequence of the basic religious difference between the Chosen People and other nations.[86] Only Israel had the Covenant with the living

---

[82] Dunn (1988, 524–25) emphasizes rituals, but they were hardly the only social boundary markers for the Jews. Even modern Christian Jews can regard themselves as Jews.

[83] Dunn 1988, 533.

[84] Thus Hartman 1980, 117. For discussion of this unique expression, see Betz 1986, 321–23 and Longenecker 1990, 296–99, who present various interpretations. The message of Gal cannot be used as unequivocal support for the exclusion of non-Christian Jews from the semantic field of the expression, since they are not discussed as Paul's antagonists in the letter.

[85] Cf. Betz 1979, 189–201, who even finds abolition of biological differences; Longenecker (1990, 156–58) too perceives a general proclamation, which Paul however states "admittedly, not always as clearly as we might like".

[86] Cf. Neusner 1995, 39 and the discussion above, section II 4A.

God, and the law served as a theological boundary toward the nations. This is the difference of concern to Paul. His solution had its social consequences, too, as he probably wants to inform the Roman Jewish and Gentile Christians.[87] But neither the ethnic nor the social differences vanished in the Pauline congregations.

β) *Tension within Judaism.* Another difficulty with Dunn's thesis is that he gives an homogeneous picture of Jewish attitudes toward the Gentiles. In fact, the situation was ambivalent. "The tension between universalism and particularism was constant."[88] Jewish proselytism flourished, although there were negative attitudes toward the converts, too.[89] There were many "God-fearers", and many people were attracted by the Jewish religion.[90] And like particularism, also universalism resulting in Jewish missionary activity, had deep Biblical roots.

In the Psalms we find nationalistic propaganda, which however is so far-reaching as to include roots of universalism. The basic intention was to promote Israel's political and religious leadership, to emphasize their virtues vis-à-vis other peoples. But in the good style of the ancient Near East, the propaganda was exaggerated, maybe too much. Thus there were claims that Israel's God and King rule over all nations, which must submit to this sovereignty (e.g. Ps 2; 18,44–48; 72,8–11; 89,26). Such an imaginary common leadership, however, made the difference between Israel and other nations smaller! The political picture of the Messiah developed later toward a universal, religious direction,[91] but the basic tendencies remained. Thus there are vague prophecies of the coming golden age, when all nations will gather at Mount Zion, but also more theological solutions. For example, Gen 12,2; 17,1–7; 22,17f; 1 Kings 8,60; Isa 2,2f; 14,1; Jer 1,15; Zephaniah 3,9 and Zech

---

[87] Cf. above section II 3Aa.

[88] Rosenbloom 1978,45 Cf. also Nissen (1974, 52–98), who discusses especially the ethical aspect of this tension. In his recent book, Dunn recognizes the tension (1998, 43–46), however without making any weighty conclusions of it.

[89] Rosenbloom 1978, 35–46 (his presentation is biassed in the other direction compared with Dunn); see also Bamberger 1968.

[90] Hengel and Schwemer 1997, 61–80.

[91] For the ideological development of the universal and religious Messiah see especially the comprehensive study of A. Laato (1997).

9,9–10; 14,16–19 reflect this vision in different ways.[92] These ideas were prevalent in Paul's contemporary Judaism.

But universalism and particularism were not merely two different emphases. In fact, taken as such the function of the law as religious and social landmark was in obvious and diametrical contradiction to another principle of Judaism, the confession, Sh°ma (Deut 6,4). If God was one, the idolatry of the Gentiles could not be a good thing. However, the Gentiles were in practice forced into idolatry, since God had chosen only one people and made his covenant with it. And the law served as a "boundary marker" for this covenant. Dahl discusses several rabbinic passages and means of coping with this tension between the two impulses in the Scriptures,[93] but concludes: "Yet, at the time of Paul, the problem of God's relationship to mankind in general and to Israel in particular must have existed, even if the stereotyped forms for discussing it did not."[94]

Obviously many of Paul's fellow Pharisees could tolerate this tension. Gentile proselytes to the Jewish religion could be grafted[95] into the Chosen People. There were disputes as to whether the second generation converts already could be counted as true Jews or if only the third generation sufficed.[96] Current scholarship incorporates many opinions about the Jewish practices and attitudes toward the "Godfearers" and "mission", but obviously no general theological solution was achieved among the Jews.[97] For Paul the situation was different. As in the case of sin, or in many other questions, Paul required a theologically motivated solution, which in addition needed to be strictly consistent. His rhetorical-theological absolutism could not tolerate controversy on the ideological level.

The roots of a solution for the tension between universalism and particularism are to be found already in the OT. Typically, the explanation could be eschatological: at the end of time God will be the One Lord of all mankind.[98] This solution is prophesied in a radical and explicit form in Zech 14,9:

---

[92] Eg. for universalism and nationalism in Isaiah, see Laato 1992, 119–21. For additional discussion, see Nissen (1974, 55–60), according to whom no coherent view is to be found in the OT (1974, 57), and Rosenbloom 1978, 28–31.

[93] Dahl 1977, 183–88.

[94] Dahl 1977, 187.

[95] Cf. Rom 11,17.

[96] Rosenbloom 1978, 44.

[97] For a brief overview, see Hengel and Schwemer 1997, 357. Feldman (1993) offers a broad and thorough presentation.

[98] Dahl 1977, 184–86.

And Yhwh will become king over all the earth; on that day Yhwh will be one and his name one. (Zech 14,9)

The tension is here seen as *temporal* – at least on the last day God will have only one name. The exclusion of the Gentiles, which in practice has forced them into idolatry, viz. calling God by other names, and thereby counteracted the Sh°ma, is transient.[99]

A corresponding expression can be found in Isa 45,21b-23.[100] Thereby universal monotheism is seen as an eschatological goal. On the last day, there will be no religious difference between Israel and other nations,[101] but all men will know God by the same name, viz. worship the same God. Only then will true universal monotheism have been attained. However, such an eschatological solution of the tension does not clearly explain how this will be practically possible, viz. how to cope with the separating function of the law.

How is this discussion reflected in the Pauline writings? Was the attainment of universal monotheism instead of monolatry a central issue for him? To begin with, we must refer to Wright, who correctly emphasizes the central role of monotheism in Pauline thinking.[102] While living in close contact with the non-Jewish polytheistic environment, the belief in Israel's God as the one and only god was a central doctrine, which sharply differentiated Judaism from other religions.[103] It is not by accident that the Sh°ma, ἄκουε ᾿Ισραηλ· κύριος ὁ θεὸς ἡμῶν κύριος εἷς ἐστιν, became the confession, the characteristic means of identification for the Jews.[104]

When proclaiming his message to non-Jews, the belief in one God must have been a central issue in Paul's agenda, too.[105] Although he seldom discusses issues directly combined with the question of monotheism, references to the

---

[99] Cf. Thurén 1979, 98–99.

[100] "There is no other god besides me, a righteous God and a Saviour; there is no one besides me. Turn to me and be saved, all the ends of the earth! For I am God, and there is no other. By myself I have sworn, from my mouth has gone forth in righteousness a word that shall not return: 'To me every knee shall bow, every tongue shall swear.'"

[101] However, Israel's special status is not challenged (Isa 45,25).

[102] Wright 1992, 120–36; cf. also Becker 1989, 402–406 and section I 2C above.

[103] Although monotheistic thoughts existed even among the Greeks, see Dahl 1977, 179–82.

[104] Cf. Dahl 1977, 181.

[105] Cf. Grässer 1985, 237–50, discussed below.

idea of one God can be found throughout his letters.[106] For instance 1 Cor 10,19–22 reflects Paul's strong monotheistic attitude, and in this sense the picture conveyed by Acts 17,16.22–29 is well suited to Paul's character as presented in his letters.[107] In 1 Cor 8, he explicitly deals with monotheism and its consequences. I have suggested above that the problem with food offered to idols was partly caused by Paul's own standard proclamation. Monotheism was a central part thereof, but Paul had not earlier reckoned with the complications inherent in this proclamation in a Gentile setting.[108]

The lack of further specific discussions of monotheism may be due to the limited nature of our sources (letters to already Christian congregations). This may have obscured the central role of *theo*logy in Pauline theology and proclamation.[109] Another problem which clouds the issue consists in the difference between the agenda of modern theology and that of first century thinking.[110] Referring to W. Meeks, Wright states that questions pertaining to monotheism, idolatry, election, holiness, and their interaction, were then of great interest.[111]

However, contrary to Wright I doubt that Paul's "solution" was merely a product of a "Christian worldview".[112] Instead, it was closely connected to the law, and resembles the universal monotheistic goal in the OT. We can start by examining the rhetorical question in Rom 3,29–30.

---

[106] In 1 Cor 8,6, as well as in the hymns Phil 2,6–11 and Col 1,15–20, which are also evidence of Pauline thinking, Wright (1992, 129–32) sees as a modified version of the Sch$^e$ma, which he calls "christological monotheism"(1992, 136). Jesus the Messiah is situated within the monotheistic confession. (1992, 132).

[107] For the discussion about the possible historical background of the Areopagus speech, see e.g. Pesch 1986 and the radical dissertation of Gärtner (1955), who remarkably takes the dynamic nature of the text into account.

[108] See above section II 3Ab. Perhaps the main problem was the combination of Greek philosophical monotheism and Paul's Jewish monotheism.

[109] Grässer (1985, 258 n. 99) remarks that the lack of the most typical Jewish and Christian monotheistic expressions does not indicate a rejection of the theme.

[110] Wright 1992, 122.

[111] According to Wright, they "functioned as shorthand ways of articulating the points of pressure, tension and conflict between different actual communities, specifically, Jews and pagans" (Wright 1992, 122). To put it this way moderates of course the difference between a social and a theological perspective.

[112] Wright 1992, 136. He argues that Paul arrived at his Christian monotheism without the Torah, and sees this as a "significant by-product" in Pauline thinking. It seems however implausible that a Jew like Paul could arrive at any significant theological solution without the Torah.

Or is God the God of Jews only? Is he not the God of Gentiles also? Yes, of Gentiles also, since God is one; and he will justify the circumcised on the ground of faith and the uncircumcised through that same faith.

Käsemann rightly argues: "As merely the God of the Jews he would cease to be the only God. The full force of this revolutionary statement is seldom perceived."[113] But how is this force to be perceived? Käsemann misses the function of the rhetorical device utilized. For Rom 3,29 is not a statement, but a rhetorical question; therefore the answer cannot be surprising.[114] The audience is expected to know the answer very well. Thus Käsemann's claim that Paul here attacks a predominant rabbinic non-universal view is difficult to follow,[115] especially as the Jewish Christians in Rome were presumably unaffected by Pauline or rabbinic theology. It is more likely, that Paul refers to the OT and Early Jewish universalistic ideas, which are well attested. Only the consequences he presents are radical. The novelty in Paul's reasoning in Rom 3,29–30 is that the role of the Torah as a limitation marker has been replaced by faith and Christ.[116]

An unsociological, viz. theological, explanation is also provided by Ulrich Wilckens and Erich Grässer, who focus on the same rhetorical question. Wilckens argues, that to a good Jew the idea in Rom 3,29–30 sounds like a "blasphemische *abrogatio legis*".[117] According to him, for the Jews "Gesetz und Beschneidung markieren eine Grenze, die wohl zu überschreiten, aber nicht aufzuheben ist, ohne die göttliche Wahrheit der Erwählung anzutasten." But how does the law actually counteract monotheism?

Grässer explains Wilckens: Since God is one, and his Son one, the body of Christ must correspond to this unity – therefore there can be no difference between the Jews and the Gentiles anymore (cf. 1 Cor 10,17; Gal 3,26.28f). Everybody is a sinner and needs to be justified by God in the same way. The universal "Christusgeschehen" breaks down the old particularism (2 Cor 5,19).[118] The Torah does not fit into the new system. Grässer's explanation may sound more theological than exegetical, as it floats somewhat high above the text. Yet the suggested connection between monotheism, Christ, the law, and the relationship between the Jews and Christians is important.

---

[113] Käsemann 1980, 104.
[114] See Dahl 1977, 189.
[115] Cf. Dahl 1977, 182–88.
[116] Dahl 1977, 191; Moxnes 1980, 79–80.
[117] Wilckens 1978, 248, my emphasis.
[118] Grässer 1985, 256–58.

According to Grässer, the basis of Paul's faith was Jer 10,10: "But Yhwh is the true God; he is the living God and the everlasting King." The ultimate goal of Paul's mission and theology was that the Gentiles should learn the monotheistic faith, and praise the glory of the one God.[119] However, the exclusive Covenant between God and Israel, expressed in the Torah, could be considered an obstacle, since it ruled out other nations. Thus, according to Hays, the distinguishing function of the law rendered it incapable of serving the universal goal.[120] Although God was seen as the creator and ruler of all nations, he could be worshipped only by his own people.[121] Ever since the election of Abraham, other nations were practically excluded, and the law especially served as a fence around God's people, separating it from the Gentiles. The Jews enjoyed a special status, they had the Covenant, and were justifiably proud of it. But the eschatological task was, in accordance with Zech 14,9, to teach all mankind to call the Lord by this true name.

This very *theo*logical issue signified for the Jews, including Paul, far more than e.g. the cognitive monotheism of Greek philosophers. Idolatry or polytheism was seen as a sign of mankind's rebellion against the Creator (Rom 1,18ff), whereas calling God by his true name meant a return from the apostasy for the whole world, both the Jews and the Gentiles (Rom 3,21–30). This in turn has its practical consequences: a new way of life according to the will of God.

The monotheistic, universal goal is a characteristic feature of Paul's theology, and the unity of Jews and Greeks in Christ is a recurrent theme in the Pauline texts.[122] This is particularly emphasized in Romans. According to epistolary and rhetorical principles, the main purpose of a text or speech is presented at the beginning and end of the discourse.[123] Thus in 1,5 Paul introduces the aim of his mission: "obedience of faith among all the nations for the sake of [God's] name."[124] Correspondingly, in 15,6 Paul emphasizes that all

---

[119]  Grässer 1985, 237.241–42.250.

[120]  Hays 1996, 154.

[121]  "I am God over all earth's creatures, yet I have associated my name only with you; for I am not called 'the god of idolaters', but 'the God of Israel'" (*Exodus Rabbah* 29:4).

[122]  See Moxnes 1980, 78–99.

[123]  See Thurén 1995a, 269–74. Byrskog (1997, 42–44) demonstrates the rhetorical relationship between Rom 1,1–7 and 15,7–13. 14–33. He however claims that 15,14ff has a rhetorical "recapitulative function", and concludes that such a rhetorical category helps us to "fill out the gaps left by the epistolographic approach" (1997, 44). A reference to White (1972, 62–63.97–99) on the epistolary ἔγραψα formula would have proved helpful.

[124]  According to Dunn, the obedience of the Gentiles is an eschatological equivalent to the Jewish obedience under the Covenant (Dunn 1988, 18).

the Roman Christians ought to praise God's name together. The praise of the Gentiles is motivated by other OT citations in 15,9–12. Furthermore, the ἔγραψα formula in 15,14–16.18 presents the making of the "offerings of the Gentiles" acceptable to God as Paul's ultimate goal.[125]

But for Paul, there is one major obstacle: The Gentiles do not possess the Torah. As the barrier between them and the Jews or the God of the Jews, it must be eliminated before true universal monotheism is possible. On the other hand, since the Torah is holy and given by God, it cannot be described as a mistake or sin. A better solution was derived from the tradition. Here Paul can follow the eschatological idea of the prophets and proclaim the religious differentiation between Jews and Gentiles as temporal. The new addition of Paul is to proclaim the core of this difference, the Torah, transient, too (Gal 3,24).

For him, the validity of the law has expired in Christ. The coming of Christ was seen as a sign of the new era (Gal 3,19.24; 4,4–5) and the new covenant. It has executed its duty as a guardian for Israel, but now its mission is accomplished. As a result, the Gentiles are no longer cut off from God. In Rom 10,12–13 Paul writes: "there is no more difference between Jew and Gentiles[126] – the same Lord is Lord of all and is generous to all who call on him.[127] For: 'Everyone who calls on *the name* of the Lord shall be saved.'" Thereby the goal expressed in Zech 14,9 becomes reality: now God really will have but "one name".

This is for Paul a far better solution than to condemn the law as being sin (cf. Rom 7,7). But although the solution is not based on criticism of the use of the law, it is inevitable that the law can *now* be misused. Therefore, although still describing the law as holy and good, and as providing proper knowledge of sin (Rom 3,20), Paul recommends that it be rejected, even with strong rhetorical expressions,[128] like father and mother in the rhetoric of Jesus.[129] For according to this logic, to retain the holy law in the changed situation, to keep it as a way of salvation, counteracts the monotheistic goal of the OT.

Thus it seems feasible that a major, and maybe *the,* theological problem causing Paul's break with the law were tensions he saw within the Scriptures:

---

[125] Michel (1978, 458) argues that this could refer to thanksgiving. It is unclear whether "of the Gentiles" is a genitive of apposition or whether they are supposed to make the offerings (see Dunn 1988, 860–61; Fitzmyer 1993, 712–13).

[126] Note again Paul's hyperbolic rhetoric – in other cases he would not express himself thus.

[127] Cf. also 2 Cor 5,14–21; Rom 3,9.22.

[128] E.g. in 1 Cor 15,56. See above section II 3Cb.

[129] See above section II 3C, introduction.

not only his eschatological perception of two mutually exclusive ways to salvation, the law and the promise, but a contradiction within the function of the law itself: How is it possible that the law, when performing its proper task, counteracts the monotheistic goal of the OT? Paul adheres to the old eschatological solution, but with two reservations.

First, he defines the law of Moses as the main barrier between the Gentiles and the Jews. Second, he sees the coming of Christ as the realization of the prophesied eschatological era, when the Torah will no longer separate the Jews from the Gentiles, so that true monotheism is possible. Everybody can praise the name of the one God. Christ has opened the way to the God of Israel and to the universal salvation for all nations by dethroning the law. Paul therefore thinks the OT tension is resolved, and the way is free for God's ultimate goal, universal monotheism. The only element in Paul's solution, which cannot be derived from the OT, is the identification of Jesus as the Christ.

Ever since this identification, Paul understood that his task was to promote the great monotheistic goal by new means, which only now become available. From his point of view, not only the good Pharisees, like himself prior to the conversion, but especially the "Judaizers" in Gal, are enemies of true monotheism in their eagerness for the law, or – what historically may be closer to reality – even minor elements thereof. Their adherence to the law in the changed situation was no longer acceptable.

Summing up: The influence of non-theological factors on Paul's change of theological position is often emphasized. Their effect cannot be excluded, but nor can it be reliably assessed. Nevertheless when focussing on the ideological level, this is of minor significance. On this level, to Paul Christ meant real salvation. But he was also a radical solution to theological dilemmas, discussed in Early Jewish texts and presumably also by Paul. Yet even this solution remains unsatisfactory.

In this chapter we have argued that, from a theological perspective, Paul's revolt against the law derived not only from his contemporary discussion, but from tensions which he perceived within the roles of the law in the OT. It may be inferred that these discrepancies irritated him already as a Pharisee, and Christ then *triggered* Paul's solution to the problems. Active Gentile mission can be seen as an unavoidable result of this theological turn.

# D. Law and Boasting – a General Element of Paul's Solution

*Motto*: ὅπως μὴ καυχήσηται πᾶσα σὰρξ ἐνώπιον τοῦ θεοῦ (1 Cor 1,29)

## a. Introduction

The reception history of the Pauline texts shows that they have had continuous validity for various readers in different historical situations. As literature they have qualities important for readers untouched by their original setting. This is especially true concerning Paul's ideas about justification and the law: they served as a source of inspiration for e.g. Marcion, Augustine, Luther, Calvin, Barth, and Bultmann.

Thus the Pauline texts can be approached also from this literary angle. This perspective means that the qualities of the text *per se* are considered; they are seen as an independent phenomenon, living their own life, unconnected with the original historical situation and author. An ancient text can affect even modern readers by transcending historical boundaries. This means that Paul's rebellion against the law reflects general human interests, not just first century Jewish issues. This change of perspective is easily made, since the apostle himself often wrote in general categories. To scrutinize and expound these features of Paul's texts is a legitimate and important task for hermeneutics, as long as the reader is aware of the difference between the historical Paul and these general theological thoughts. However, such an undertaking may also lead to an interaction with the text, as it can also shed light on the ideology of the historical Paul. For the symptoms must bear witness to something; *ex nihilo nihil*.

Yet there has been a major obstacle to generalizing studies of Paul: the earlier "Weberian" picture of Jewish soteriology. It was based on scholarship guided by a specific ideological dimension and therefore resulted in a biassed, although not completely false, historical picture. Thus modern scholars attempting to avoid such tendencies have not only resulted in the other extreme in describing Jewish soteriology, but even worse, they have abandoned the general, non-historical dimension in Pauline thinking.[130] This is too heavy a price: it constrains our picture of Paul as a thinker and unnecessarily widens the

---

[130] See above section I 2B.

gap between exegetics and the modern use of Pauline texts. If we could identify more closely the causes, which resulted in the modern distorted picture of Jewish soteriology, we could use more precise medicine against the disease. The side-effects would thereby be minimized and the general thoughts in the Pauline texts could be considered afresh.

In my opinion, the cause was not only anti-Judaistic or antisemitic European tendencies, for careful and respectable scholars also supported this view. But even they were often influenced by the malicious habit of neglecting the dynamic nature of the Pauline writings. His persuasive expressions were taken at face value, which supported and perhaps contributed to the adverse picture of Jewish soteriology. But when this is recognized and appropriately countered, the justifiable study of Paul's "transhistorical" thinking can be started anew.

An important – and probably unintended – victim of the new perspectives on Paul has been the Bultmannian thesis, according to which the piety of the law reflects general human *boasting* before God. Boasting *per se* was seen as an expression of man's innate pride. The idea not only explains the later validity of Paul's thoughts, but may also be relevant to his break with the law.

For something is missing in the solutions presented above. If the alternatives "works" and "grace" represent exclusive lines of salvation, why should the latter be preferred? If the law was unable to save people, as they could not comply with its ordinances, why could not Christ or Spirit enable them to do so? And if the law created a boundary between Gentiles and Jews, why could not this feature alone be removed and the law be universally proclaimed? But an essential attribute of the law is that those who rely on it are able to boast of it, not only of possessing it, but also of complying with it. This is true irrespective of what actually happened in First Century Judaism. Thus I would ask, whether the old, unpopular idea, that Paul wanted to reject the possibility of human boasting, could enable us to glimpse a solution. For indeed he does severely criticize boasting, although on the other hand, we find sections where he himself assuredly boasts.

This problem is difficult to study, for several obvious reasons. Unfortunately it has traditionally been too closely connected with historical questions and with hermeneutical purposes: Since for Paul the Jews seemed to stand for a self-centered religious attitude, this was assessed as a true historical description of their religion. The Jewish religion was then used as a great example of man's universal negative, egotistic tendency to boast, to obtain salvation unaided.[131] When scholars later learned that such a picture of Judaism was untenable, and

---

[131]  Bultmann 1938, 649.

that even "boasting" in God and his law was a positive concept,[132] also the *Pauline* expressions which promoted such a distorted view were rejected. However, trends in modern research or hermeneutical expectations should not impede serious scholarship.[133]

The great theologians' interest in the Pauline discussion of boasting at least indicates that, as literature, Paul's texts have been read as opposing human pride, which in turn is seen as man's perverse attitude to God. Our task is not to challenge or support the theology of those religious thinkers, but to ask how does their picture reflect Paul's actual thoughts, or even contemporary Judaism. For although Paul is primarily creating his own negative alternative to his ideology, with no attempt to provide a reliable description of his contemporaries, already rhetorical effectivity requires some contact between the charges and real Judaism.[134]

According to the "traditional" Bultmannian interpretation, boasting (καύχησις) is for Paul principally a theological concept, articulating the foundation of human existence.[135] There are two mutually exclusive alternatives: the improper one is characterized by one's own flesh, other people, external things, and finally oneself, whereas acceptable boasting builds on the Lord. When Paul is forced to boast of himself, he not only calls it "foolishness", but boasts primarily of his own weakness.[136]

This explanation appears too theological and distant from the text-level. First, Paul's explanations about "foolishness" in 2 Cor 11 are to be identified as a rhetorical *praeteritio*, like the use of the third person in chapter 12, which is intended to justify unreserved, genuine self-praise and boasting.[137] It is typical

---

[132] Cf. Heckel 1993, 186–87; Eskola 1998, 230–31.

[133] In the post-Holocaust era such a *theological* move is understandable. Yet the purely *exegetical* study of Paul ought not to be obscured by political interests. We have to set aside questions about Paul's general validity, or modern hermeneutical needs. Paul may well be the "prince of thinkers", whose deep insights into human nature transgress historical and ethnic boundaries. Yet such expectations should not colour a study of his texts. If his theology fails to meet our demands, this should not affect the exposition of what he actually wrote.

[134] See above. There were limits for inventing charges against the opponent, see du Toit 1994, 411.

[135] Bultmann 1938, 648–54; Zmijewski 1981, 686–90.

[136] Zmijewski 1981, 690, Heckel 1993, 144–214.

[137] See section I 4E, esp. n. 49. For example, 2 Cor 11,10: "As the truth of Christ is in me, no one will take this boast of mine..." For discussion see Betz 1972 and Martin 1986, 398–99, who is nicely affected by Paul's rhetoric. Cf. also Heckel 1993, 190. Heckel generally attempts to explain Paul's proud expressions with irony, parody and good intention. Yet the fact remains that Paul often *is* boasting, also of himself.

of Bultmann to refuse to understand this rhetoric[138] – obviously on ideological grounds, for he was well acquainted with the ancient art of persuasion.[139] Second, the apostle has a generally positive attitude toward boasting, especially in 2 Cor.[140] He does not criticise boasting as an attitude, provided that it is justified, nor does he blame the law for making people boast.[141]

### b. Phil 3 and Rom 4

Yet the "theological" understanding is not without support. Boasting in Paul's language indeed pertains to personal achievements. Philippians 3,3–8 as a piece of *epideictic* oratory[142] is an interesting case. Paul does not apologize for his Jewish status or achievements.[143] He claims to have been blameless – an exclamation which can cause severe theological problems, as does all Paul's boasting, unless the rhetoric is considered.[144]

The presentation includes three phases, and this technique can be compared with the tactics in 1 Cor 8.[145] There Paul first does something which is well suited to affect his addressees, but is surprising for us: he presents a strong argument *for* eating food offered to idols (1 Cor 8,4: there is no god). Then, he moderates his stance (1 Cor 8,5–6: admittedly some "gods" exist, but they are nothing compared with our God), and not until the third argument do we find his own position (1 Cor 8,7ff: eating food offered to idols has bad effects). In 1 Cor 10,19–22 he finally states that faith in one God does not allow eating food offered to idols, on the contrary.

In Phil 3 we have a corresponding (although dissimilar) development of the argument. First, after a forewarning, Paul in an astonishing way boasts of his Jewish past and his achievements (Phil 3,4–6). In the second phase, he moderates his tone (7–8a): these great gains are minor compared with the big

---

[138] Bultmann 1938, 650–53.

[139] Cf. his dissertation (Bultmann 1910), which bears witness to a rhetorical education.

[140] A glimpse in a concordance is enlightening. See also e.g. Räisänen 1987, 173–74.

[141] See Westerholm 1988, 170–72.

[142] Hawthorne (1983, 130) remarks that Paul here discusses the typical epideictic *topoi:* descent, education, titles, citizenship etc.

[143] In agreement with Räisänen 1987, 175–76; against Eskola (1998, 225), according to whom Paul is ashamed of his Jewish background.

[144] It would be naive to see a theological tension between Paul's strong language and other passages, where all are adjudged as sinners, or to suspect a distinction between righteousness before men and before God. It is plausible that Saul actually considered himself as righteous according to the law. It was this righteousness, which he now assesses as σκύβαλα, not the lack of it.

[145] See also above section II 3Ab.

gain in Christ. They are not yet condemned; only in comparison with Christ can they be "counted as loss". But not until the third phase is Paul's actual thesis revealed (8b): the glorious Jewish past is nothing but σκύβαλα. For according to v. 9, boasting is somehow connected with own righteousness, which for Paul excludes righteousness by faith through Christ. The expression is however short and remains obscure, if interpreted alone.

But the fact remains that Paul *is* boasting. This is apparent, when the ideological contents are ignored and we examine only what Paul is doing. As in 2 Cor 11–12, Paul uses a transparent rhetorical trick to create an opportunity to boast without constraint of himself.

The idea of negative boasting is more clearly expressed in Rom 4,1–5, where Paul discusses the example of Abraham. He attempts to show, that relying on one's own achievements before God is an unacceptable alternative.

Rom 3,27–30[146] refers to Jewish boasting of the *possession* of the law in 2,17.23.[147] This appears to be Paul's main target, and has been studied above. In Rom 3,27–30 he excludes Jewish boasting of the status conferred on them by the law. This means in fact termination of one of the principal functions of the Torah. Boasting is *per definitionem* a social phenomenon, based on comparison with other peoples. The Jews had good reason to boast, since only they possessed the law, and the Gentiles did not.[148] But as seen above, this fully justifiable, glorious and joyful feature was in conflict with the universal monotheism, and thus questionable.

However, this is not the quality of the text which has inspired later interpretations; they rather build upon the idea, according to which *compliance with* the law is a source for boasting. Has this interpretation any historical roots? Did Paul mean such boasting, too? At least Paul himself boasts of his own works besides his Jewish nationality.[149]

The thesis in Rom 3,27 is followed by an *exemplificatio* in Chapter 4, where the role of works is discussed. Limitation of the semantics of boasting to refer only to possession of the law only, is at odds with this discussion. Therefore it

---

[146] "Then what becomes of boasting? It is excluded."

[147] In agreement with Sanders 1983, 33, Watson 1986, 133, Räisänen 1987, 170–71, and Dunn 1988, 185.191–92 (cf. also 118). For discussion, see Laato 1991, 229 n. 2.

[148] Although it is true to say, that Paul's criticism is aimed at the Jews' "Missbrauch" of their status, which has resulted in hubris (e.g. Laato 1991, 229–37), even such a criticism would hardly have led to rejection of the law itself.

[149] Phil 3,4–6; 1 Cor 15,10; 9,1f; 2 Cor 10,13–18.

is more likely that both meanings are included.[150] Yet it is difficult to interpret boasting here as man's innate detrimental pride *sensu lato*. The following Rom 4,2 implies, that one has reason to boast, if one is justified by works. In Abraham's case Paul claims that this did not happen. Then follows the rule in verses 4–5: he who works, has merits and consequently reason to boast (4,4).[151] This idea itself is not religious or spiritual. An honestly earned salary has nothing to do with the employer's grace. Boasting is not presented as something avoidable,[152] but as a right like a well-earned reward. In accordance with Gal, Rom 4,4 is a general maxim.

But Paul uses the example to prove that Abraham was not justified by works (or through the law, v.13–14), since he received justification in another way, viz. by faith/grace. Consequently, he did not boast.[153] Boasting should of course not occur, if we are dependent on "grace", for it implies that we cannot depend on our own merits. This was, according to Paul, the case with Abraham. Since both Jews and Gentiles stand in need of God's grace, none has reason to boast before him.

An alternative to boasting is thus not only faith, but also God's grace (1 Cor 15,10b). The Christian history of the word may have somewhat obscured its semantic field: in standard Greek χάρις is not equal to the Pauline, undeserved grace, but means something favourable in general.[154] The semantic limitation of grace to the opposite of personal merits is rather Pauline, although found already in Aristotle.[155] For instance, in 1 Peter 2,19–20 or in Philo (All III,77–78; see also 83) God's grace is seen as a result of man's righteous action. Interestingly enough, both Philo and James also discuss the *topos* of Abraham and thereby disagree with Paul.[156] A similar connection between Abraham's righteousness in Gen 15 and his fidelity in Gen 22 (the *Akedah*) is found also in 1 Macc 2,50–52 and 4Q225, which thus may reflect a standard Jewish interpretation.

---

[150] Cf. Westerholm (1988, 170), according to whom boasting of one's own achievements is the main topic of Rom 3,27–4,5. Dunn (1988, 191–92) finds here only "Jewish pride in their election and in their law".

[151] "Now to one who works, wages are not reckoned as a gift but as something due."

[152] In agreement with Räisänen 1987, 171.

[153] The whole passage seeks to show how even the Gentiles can participate in Abraham's promises. But even the Jews are considered to share in this heritage only because of the divine action (e.g. Rom 9,4).

[154] Liddell and Scott, s.v.; cf. Bauer and Aland, s.v.

[155] Aristotle, Rhetorica II 7,1385a. For the various aspects of the word, see Arichea 1978, 201–206; Berger 1983.

[156] Philo All III,83; James 2,20–24.

Another verse indicating the double basis of boasting is the accusing question in Rom 2,23: "You that boast in the law, do you dishonour God by breaking the law?" Paul maintains that one can justifiably boast of possessing the law only when complying strictly with its commands, and criticizes the Jews for being inconsistent on this point.[157] Naturally we can also ask, why then none has reason to boast according to Paul? The answer undoubtedly hangs together with his idea of man's universal guilt, presented in e.g. Rom 1,18–2,24 and 3,20.[158]

A final dimension of boasting is the crucial issue of *epideictic* rhetoric, the question of honour. Boasting of personal achievements as a social phenomenon unavoidably yields personal honour. Religious boasting can however prove problematic, as honour and glory should be given to God alone (à la Rom 11,36). Faith is a better option for Paul, as it gives credit to God and Christ, not to the believer.

## c. 1 Cor 1

Boasting as such is accepted by Paul, but in religious matters is for him a symbol of relying on personal merits as opposed to depending on God's grace – if we have reason to boast before God, no mercy is needed, and God receives no glory. In 1 Cor the main source of boasting seems to be wisdom. But how does this clarify Paul's attitude to the *law*?

An important point is 1 Cor 1,27–29.31: God has chosen things which "are nothing" in order "that no one may boast before God" (ὅπως μὴ καυχήσηται πᾶσα σὰρξ ἐνώπιον τοῦ θεοῦ). Freely quoting Jeremiah 9,24 Paul continues: "Let him who boasts boast in the Lord."[159] Others are put to shame (1 Cor 1,27). But does this sentence only refer to the Corinthian situation, so that the addressees should not boast of Apollos to the exclusion of Paul? In this case the warning has merely a paraenetic and communal function.[160] Such a practical perspective could mean that the negative boasting, viz. self-praise is an expression of factionalism.[161]

However, the ideological dimension of an utterance is not excluded by its practical function. On the contrary, Paul never discusses ideological matters

---

[157] Cf. Gal 6,4 discussed above.

[158] See e.g. Winninge 1995, 264–65; Eskola 1998, 125–28.

[159] The exact quotation would have been unsuitable for Paul, since Jeremiah actually urges people to do something which Paul opposes: boast of theological *knowledge:* "But let those who boast in this, that they understand and know me, that I am Yhwh."

[160] Räisänen 1987, 172–73.

[161] Thus Mitchell 1991, 91–95, esp. n. 145; p. 216.

without a specific purpose.[162] Thus defending the ideological interpretation, Schrage argues: "...doch ist καυχᾶσθαι nicht 'a form of ethnic and national self-identification'." Instead, he prefers an highly theoretical, theological maxim: "Es gehört vielmehr zur Grundsünde des Menschen übehaupt, in Eigenmächtig-keit und Leistungsstolz seine wirkliche Situation zu verkennen."[163]

But how can the situation and theology be combined? We can consider the immediate context. In the rhetorical structure of 1 Cor, this sentence is unlikely to present a sharp polemical argument in the current Corinthian situation. Instead, a modest interpretation is to be preferred.

First a small observation: The question of the authority of different teachers is not a major issue in the rest of 1 Cor. But here, at the beginning of the letter, Paul's *ethos* is challenged and needs to be strengthened, so that it can be used later as an argument.[164] Consequently, after raising the unpleasant question of quarrels in the congregation (1 Cor 1,10–13) Paul attempts to set himself above such matters. The solemn style of the section is well suited to this goal.[165]

Second, the main argument: The saying occurs at an early stage of the argumentation in 1 Cor. Therefore Paul at least seems to follow a general line, seeking a "meeting of minds". The addressees are assumed to agree with him. Only thereby can he continue the argumentation, and later refer back to the maxim. In other words, the discussion about foolishness and wisdom at the end of chapter 1 serves as a theoretical or theological introduction to the letter. Paul first discusses the issue of human wisdom and pride and boasting thereof, but with no direct reference to the actual situation. Not until the addressees are expected to agree, does he attempt to show that boasting in oneself is an underlying factor in the congregation, demonstrated in many ways, such as factionalism, negligence of the interests of other, and lack of mutual love. All these are discussed later in the letter.

The fact that the principle in the context can be applied to a practical question, and is used "against" the addressees, is evident to us, but not necessarily to those who heard or read it for the first time. They were invited to dwell on the problem of boasting and glory on a general level, before its relevance to them was clearly revealed. Here, as in 1 Corinthians in general, the issues prompted by the question of different teachers or other practical problems, are larger than they appear.

---

[162] See above sections I 2 and 4A.

[163] Schrage 1991, 213 n. 650, as an answer to Mitchell. Recent commentaries may still have wholly lost the concrete situation (e.g. Fascher 1987, 106–107; Fee 1987, 84).

[164] E.g. in 1 Cor 7,40; 14,36–37.

[165] Schrage (1991, 204) praises the rhetorical quality of the section.

Thus verse 29 is to be taken as a general, widely accepted rule, which should not immediately resemble an argument in a crucial question. Instead, as a short and loaded expression, its usage resembles the role of 1 Cor 15,56, which probably referred to Paul's previous teaching as a reminder to the addressees.[166] Likewise, the idea of denying human boasting before God is hardly an *ad hoc* doctrine of the apostle, and can be studied even as a separate issue.

In the discussion of wisdom, verse 21 is crucial: "For since, in the wisdom of God, the world did not know God through wisdom, God decided, through the foolishness of our proclamation, to save those who believe." Here "foolishness" represents Paul's gospel of Christ crucified (v. 23), whereas "wisdom" denotes its counterpart. The commentators usually refer either to God's creation or to his plan.[167] But although at odds with the metaphorical language here, even the Torah as God's true wisdom can be included on the theoretical level beyond the actual text. For this suits Pauline thinking: the Gospel is usually proclaimed, not only instead of wisdom, but also instead of the law.

Speaking of foolish and shameful things before God, Paul not only refers to the Corinthians' social status, or his own rhetoric, but above all the crucified Christ (1,20–23). The *Christusgeschehen* was deliberately chosen in order that no flesh may boast before God. The gospel of the crucifixion of Christ is presented as the alternative to human boasting of wisdom, power, "being something", or – we could add – (works of) the law.

The opposition to human boasting in religious matters appears to be a Pauline pattern of speech, which he can apply to different issues. A corresponding, closely related figure is the image of yeast affecting "the whole batch of dough". In Gal 5,9 Paul used the metaphor against obedience to the slightest (μικρά) element of the law, whereas in 1 Cor 5,6–8 (where boasting is also mentioned) it is utilized against unethical behaviour! Unlike in Gal, the exposition is now enlarged and placed in its Passover setting.

Behind both patterns of speech there are patterns of thought, or in other words, the rhetoric is closely related to the ideology. The metaphor of yeast reflects Paul's absolutism, whereas at least in 1 Cor, boasting likewise stands for a general attitude. In Phil 3,3 the opposite of boasting in Christ is to "have confidence in the flesh". Perhaps the old ideologized, existentialistic interpretation of boasting is not inappropriate, when we focus only on what Paul says and does, and the underlying ideological level, but disregard the alleged historical references to ancient Judaism on the one hand, and 20th century philosophical discussions on the other.

---

[166] See above section II 3Cb.
[167] See Schrage 1991, 179–81.

## d. Gal 6

One of the strongest arguments against Bultmann's thesis is that it is not based on Galatians, although this letter incorporates Paul's "most vehement attack" on the law. Galatians is said to contain "absolutely no polemic against man's boasting".[168] This claim could be refuted forthwith by referring to the above-mentioned basic rule for New Testament scholarship: when studying the theology of a short document, *e silentio* is not a particularly strong argument. But if the idea of boasting is lacking in Gal, can it be a central theme in Paul's thinking about the law?

To be sure, the term καύχημα/ καυχᾶσθαι appears in Galatians 6,4.13–14. Yet, according to Hübner, its position at the end of the letter indicates the dearth of its relevance for Paul.[169] Thereby a basic rhetorical concept is however misunderstood. In the rhetorical structure of the letter the end of chapter six belongs to the *peroratio*, in which the author is supposed to present his message in a concise form (*recapitulatio*). Thus verses 13 and 14 in particular belong to the weightiest part of the letter, which forthrightly summarizes the whole message.[170] And in this peroratory section Paul condemns the antagonists' boasting.

But does this pertain to human boasting in general? Paul's aim is to prevent the addressees from following the antagonists, who would boast of the Galatians, instead of Paul, who boasts of nothing save Christ, and particularly not of circumcision. To this end, somewhat offensive rhetoric is utilized: Paul "unveils" the antagonists' actual motivation. They are said only to want to be able to boast of the Galatians.[171] Such an *indignatio,* or negative description of the adversary, is not only a standard rhetorical device for attacking the opponent *ethos,*[172] but also sheds light on Paul's own attitude in the whole issue. Obviously Gal not only concerns theology, but is also a contest of power and fame.[173] Paul seems to suspect that even his addressees understand this, since he proclaims in 6,14, that he himself is not boasting about the Galatians, or anything other than the cross of Christ. Thus he is not in the game, but only trying altruistically to guide the addressees. Is this mere rhetoric? Or can we find some ideological background to this tactic?

---

[168] Räisänen 1987, 169; Hübner 1986, 88–91.

[169] Hübner 1986, 88.

[170] Betz 1979, 312–13.

[171] The verse hardly *informs* us objectively about the opponents' attitude to the law, but rather serves as a rhetorical contrast. Cf. below section II 2Ac.

[172] Betz 1979, 313; correctly also Hübner 1986, 89.

[173] Cf. above section II 2Adδ.

According to 6,4 everyone should boast only of what he is himself. Now in 6,14 Paul explains that he is not boasting of anything – thus he implicitly claims to be nothing himself.[174] Since the goal is to create a contrast to the blameworthy, selfish antagonists, it is clear that Paul is presented as a model Christian, fulfilling the rule of verse 4. The antagonists, in turn, break this rule by attempting to boast of what the addressees are.

But in creating this situation Paul is not just vilifying the antagonists and emphasizing his own virtue. He thereby gives the addressees a final teaching, a positive *exhortatio*, where he himself stands as the model. A good Christian ought to follow him, not the crooked teachers. They should act as nobly as does the apostle. This means: even they should not boast in themselves or anything else but the cross of Christ. 6,15 does not appear abrupt but is germane: There is no ground for pride in the circumcision, since it "is nothing". The only thing that "is", is the new creation in Christ, viz. the result his impact on the Galatians.

Now, when the question about boasting is presented according to rhetorical conventions as an open, revealing, and summary *peroratio* of the epistle, it must have a close connection with the main issue of the text. And indeed, Paul boasts about *being* a new creation in Christ: he alone in 2,20–21 and together with his envisioned addressees in 3,26–29. Although the word "boast" does not appear until chapter 6, the idea of boasting also occurs in chapters 2 and 3.

The overall strategy of Gal builds on *status definitionis*[175]: the first step is to redefine the addressees' interest in circumcision, aroused by the antagonists, as general willingness to follow the law as a way to God. Only thereby can Paul claim that their new interest nullifies the cross and grace of Christ – and their outcome, this right boasting. As a result, the addressees as true Christians should not follow the antagonists, viz. not base their relationship to God on circumcision or any other obedience to the law, but on Christ.

It is possible to draw further ideological conclusions and claim that reaching righteousness by own means leads to boasting of own achievements before God, and precisely therefore excludes Christ (cf. Gal 2,21).[176] This is the consequence of the *peroratio*. However, Paul does not explicitly draw this

---

[174] Paul boasts only in the cross of Christ, but this does not contradict the rule in verse 4, as he claims to *be* crucified by this cross.

[175] For the *status*, see Martin 1974, 32–36. See also above section I 4C, end.

[176] "I do not nullify the grace of God; for if justification comes through the law, then Christ died for nothing."

conclusion in Galatians. Thus, Hübner is right to maintain that the idea is "noch nicht ausgesprochen" in Galatians,[177] although its roots are clearly visible.

Did Paul avoid expressing this idea for some rhetorical reason? For me it seems more plausible, that we here actually witness a development in Paul's theology.[178] Whereas boasting in Gal ensued from the contest with the antagonists, and its role as the ultimate factor behind the whole theological question was only a rhetorical climax, Paul may well have developed the idea later in Romans to a theological principle. Yet Rom is hardly much later than Gal.

We can see that the criticism of boasting in religious matters, somewhat obscurely articulated in Gal, becomes more explicit in Rom. But even then its philosophical nature is less clear than in later interpretations. For Paul does not present boasting as a universal human vice, but only as a *sign* of reliance on something other than God's undeserved grace, and of following an alternative – and unviable – route to salvation. We should also note that although boasting before God is said to exclude his grace, boasters are never cursed as the preachers of the "another gospel" in Gal 1,6–9.

In Rom there is but one section, where boasting *per se* has distinct negative connotations. In 11,17–24, where Paul discusses the relationship between Jews (or Jewish Christians?) and Gentile Christians – not only theoretically, but perhaps particularly meaning the congregations in Rome – he asserts that the Gentiles should not boast. Boasting is here opposed to fear, and associated with abandonment of God's grace.

### e. Conclusion: Boasting, Judaism, and Paul

Boasting in the law cannot be described as a central issue on the rhetorical surface of Pauline texts. The application of the question in later theology is also an issue, which must be discussed in another context. But the topic is essential for the study of Paul's theology. The theologians' use of Paul as a source of inspiration in this question indicates, that on the ideological level boasting perhaps plays a major role.

In his texts, Paul speaks much of boasting. Maybe the issue was a sore point for the apostle personally. At least he often compares himself with other teachers, especially with the original apostles. Sometimes he obviously cannot resist the temptation to boast, which he justifies with transparent rhetorical camouflage. Or in kinder terms: both the issue of honour and the topics of his

---

[177] Hübner 1986, 91.

[178] Thus I agree here with Hübner. Yet I suggest that the idea was more mature already in Galatians.

boasting belong to epideictic rhetoric – Paul struggles thereby for authority and *ethos*.

But the issue has for him a general theological dimension, too. On the ideological level, the ground for personal boasting before God is "being something". Boasting signifies for Paul not just possessing the law, but also strict observance to it, and striving for his own righteousness. Theoretically, boasting of human righteousness is possible. It is not caused by the law, but enabled by it. God is said to have chosen another, exclusive way to salvation, in order to prevent such boasting. According to Paul, no combination is possible.

Paul does not actually discuss the reason for God's aversion to human boasting[179] before him, but the epideictic question of glory may be relevant. 1 Cor 1,31 and 2 Cor 10,17 hint in this direction by referring to Jer 9,23–24: "Let the one who boasts, boast in the Lord." Such boasting gives glory to God, whereas boasting of one's own knowledge, or anything else personal, glorifies the boaster. Undoubtedly God is presumed to disapprove of the latter alternative.[180]

It is no wonder that Paul's rhetoric and theology have served as a source of inspiration for later theologians. The exclusive options of relying either on oneself or on external help, and giving glory to oneself or to God, are easily incorporated in different theological or philosophical systems.

Here history and ideology should be carefully separated. We do not need a return to the 19th century picture of first century Judaism.[181] But our knowledge of different forms of this religion must not obscure *Paul's* thinking. It is important to recognize that Paul did not attempt to persuade his addressees, that the Jews actually corresponded his implied opponents. If, by referring to what the Jews and the Christian "Judaizers" really thought, we refuse to see Paul's rhetorically coloured opponents, we lose the dark background against which he highlights his own specific theology. Some characteristic features may thereby be obscured.

Attempts to "defend" Early Judaism against Pauline vilification may also lead to a distorted historical picture of this religion. No defence is needed. The problem with the Jewish view of the law opposed by Paul was, that it did not

---

[179] Actually there is a contradiction: first all human boasting is prohibited, then people ought to boast in the Lord (see Heckel 1993, 175–76). The tension however is not theological but due to the expression: in both cases human pride before God is seen as inadvisable.

[180] For the OT background and the Jewish understanding of Jer 9,22f, see Heckel 1993, 162–72.

[181] See Deines 1997, 40–299.

fall into place in his absolute scheme, where the choice lay between two exclusive alternatives. Indeed, the Pauline "grace alone" religion is hardly a correct description of perhaps any form of his contemporary Judaism.

Like many Early Christian authors, the first century Jews – at least the majority – hardly believed in man's total incapability to do good and choose the right way, but were less extreme. Irrespective of how the religious thinking of the Judaism of that time, or some section within it, are reconstructed, it is difficult to believe that they agreed with Paul's extreme theology. Among the Church Fathers, John Chrysostom shares his radical view of the law, but he may be an exception.[182] It is historically insincere to characterize Paul's contemporary Judaism as similar to the religious system he was promoting, apart from the identity of Christ, or even worse, as identical with the ultra- or quasipauline position criticized (and possibly rhetorically exaggerated) by James.

Insofar as there is theology behind the rhetoric of Gal, Paul assessed *any* deviation from his own principle as a "yeast" spoiling the whole religion. Any human component in soteriology was dismissed by Paul as trusting "in the flesh". This factor is the fault he found in real Judaism. And from this point of view, he could then draw caricatures of his Jewish or Judaizing opponents. These pictures were not fair, but nor were they necessarily obnoxious. For later scholars, who did not understand the original rhetoric, they created either a biassed picture of the opponents or an opportunistic picture of the Apostle. From Paul's – and his addressees' – point of view, they were just effective. That is: good rhetoric.

We have thus found an additional, but perhaps also a more profound answer to the question, what was wrong with the law, and also with Early Judaism, according to Paul. Beside giving glory to God, they enabled human boasting, which for him was a sign of relying on "the flesh". And such a combination was intolerable.

---

[182] See his commentary on Galatians, PG 61,615.628-31.643.647-48.665.668-69.672-73. Chrysostom's analysis of Gal is a masterpiece of ancient rhetorical criticism. A comparison with his approach and results is useful for modern scholars. See further Thurén 2000a.

# Part III
# Paul Derhetorized?

# Chapter 1

# Summary

Paul's theology concerning the law and the origins thereof have served as a test-case for a dynamic approach to Pauline theology. The applicability and usefulness of the approach might have been better demonstrated by studying a minor, custom-built problem. Yet my goal was not so much to highlight the method *per se* as to show how it can contribute to a serious classical problem. The question of the law and Paul is indeed large and controversial, but I hope that some new perspectives have been provided.

Paul speaks of the law in various ways in different letters. The dynamic approach emphasizes that a comparison of his comments must not only observe the situation of each letter as a whole, but also the communicative and interactive function of the part of speech in which these expression occur, and even the possible functional role of each expression. We should always ask, how each expression is designed to affect the addressees. Only thereby can the theoretical thinking behind the actual expressions be discerned, for Paul freely adjusts his manner of speech in order to convince his addressees. It is difficult to determine the degree to which these utterances actually represent the apostle's theology.

Summarizing, we can state that for Paul the law is still holy and of divine origin – this is denied nowhere in his texts. Yet the law is no longer valid for the Christians who should not even attempt to comply with it: it expired when Christ appeared. When attempting to persuade the addressees of this state of affairs, Paul can use strong language about the law. However, this alone does prove that his basic attitude towards it has changed.

Many seemingly contradictory or obscure expressions can be clarified when their persuasive functions are taken into account. Thus e.g. the requirement of the law is still valid, but it is fulfilled by other means, viz. by the Spirit. It is essential to acknowledge Paul's hyperbolic mode of expression. This may be effective persuasion, but complicates any characterization of his theology, for utterances on the same subject may appear very different, when used for different purposes.

Yet Paul's theology is not a solid, tension-free theory, which is only expressed in different ways. Obviously the often overstated and exaggerated way of speech has its equivalent in his thinking. But I would go so far as to suggest that theology is always rhetorical by nature. Theology like any ideology means that concepts must be simplified and expressed in absolute terms in order to facilitate their understanding in both theory and communication. This does not mean compromising the truth. It only suggests that modern (and even some ancient) readers' expectations concerning the nature of Paul's expressions are not always met.

The validity of the law is a case in point. On the one hand Paul can declare that the Christian is totally free from the law, just as he can say that the Christian is free from sin and already resurrected with Christ in baptism. This language springs from persuasion: such simple, astounding declarations are more effective than complex theoretical announcements. It is not mere rhetoric: Paul actually believes that these statements are true. But they are expressed not as philosophical statements, but as means of persuasion.

On the other hand, however, death, sin, and the law still exist as obvious realities even for Paul, and in 1 Cor he has to correct the addressees, who have taken his rhetoric too literally. For although the Pauline Christians already walk with Christ in an everlasting life, they are mortal also according to Paul, since they are flesh and blood. This idea is mentioned also in Rom 7, and denotes a division not in the law, but in the Christian. The law thus unavoidably continues to affect the Christian, despite Paul's 'rhetorical' Gospel. But such a role is presented in 1 Cor 15,56 in an extremely negative light.

Finally the intriguing question of the origins of Paul's changed view on the law was studied. The issue is difficult to approach, since Paul never directly addresses it. Yet something can be said.

It was suggested that non-theological explanations provide only superficial answers to the problem. In contemporary Judaism, there were many theological factors, which could contribute to Paul's solution, even though they did not directly question the role of the law. Such are the problems with sin and the fate of Israel, which prompted an amendment of the theology, and the idea of a new covenant, which could serve as a frame of reference for such a change. The increasing universal tendencies within Judaism too encouraged a revision.

As these issues did not suffice to affect the Torah, we sought more profound reasons in the OT. Notwithstanding, Paul in his letters seldom *discusses* OT passages or sayings, but uses them chiefly as evidence for his theses. This is natural, since a profound theoretical discussion is seldom good persuasion. Yet this does not prove that OT did not serve as a basic source for his theological thinking. On the contrary, as a Pharisee he probably held OT as essential and authoritative for his theology.

Paul's texts indicate that he had found two conflicting issues in the OT: the two lines of salvation and particularism contra universalism. Irrespective of any original meanings of corresponding OT passages or of contemporary Jewish interpretations, for Paul the alternatives in both questions were mutually exclusive. This interpretation corresponds to his hyperbolic way of thinking.

In both cases the role of the Torah was primary for Paul; it was responsible for the tension. Despite the positive characteristics, such as a divine origin and an important role for Israel between Moses and Jesus, the Torah was an addition, which became a rival for the promise. It also created a boundary around Israel, thereby counteracting the universal monotheism. It is important to acknowledge that Paul never condemns his fellow Jews or their interpretation for these problems. For him they are inherent in the OT.

But all these tensions could perhaps have been resolved without sacrificing the law. The fact that all these factors resulted in the end of Torah's validity, indicates that the change was attributable chiefly to the problematic nature of the law itself, as according to Paul, especially when it provoked positive pride and joy, it enabled trust in something other than God alone – such epideictic topics are enumerated in Phil 3,5–6. Boasting was a sign and symbol of this trust. This, in turn, excluded God's absolute glory.

Chapter 2

# Concluding Remarks on the Dynamic Perspective

Now some final thoughts can be offered about the problem-field as a whole.
Why has Paul's theology of the law been so difficult to approach for modern
scholars? This survey points out two main reasons, and hints at third.

First, modern readers have difficulties in interpreting Paul's rhetorical
expressions and tactics. This is not only due to our ignorance of the communicative conventions of his time, but to a second, deeper deficiency: The
modern theological readers' attitude to the text reflects a static model, where
the text seeks only to transmit conceptions – it is not seen correctly as a
dynamic tool for persuasion. This does not mean belittling of theology. But the
difficulty of describing such systems of thought behind the text must be
recognized.

Why has Paul been read with such prejudices? I venture to suggest, that the
main reason is the role played by his texts in Christian communities. They were
widespread in the Early Church because of their theological content, and they
continue to serve as a major source of Christian doctrine. But their original
setting and – what is even more important – their original persuasive character
was obscured long ago. This is not to deny that the Pauline texts may well
constitute such a source. But the readers should at least recognize their original
nature.

Second, I do not claim that the controversy concerning Paul's theology of
the law is due solely to the above-mentioned problems in communication, or
to his peculiar way of thinking. Another main reason is undoubtedly the
contents of the theology itself. It seems that the apostle's view of the law is
simply too radical for most people to accept. As mature, responsible, somewhat
static sociological entities, often on good terms with the surrounding society,
the churches and other religious communities need a positive attitude to
contemporary legislation. And even in a religious context the law seems to
function very well: consider e.g. the classical "three uses" of law.

In contrast to this practical necessity, Paul's attitude has not been adopted
by Christian communities generally. As a substitute for ethics based on the law
Paul presents the will of God expressed in the *paraenesis*, and instead of
negative or positive sanctions, or even joy and gratitude, he mostly refers to the
Spirit as producing fruit or creating a new life. These ideas have seldom been

acceptable to later theologians. While they would still hail the apostle as the great theologian of Christianity, conflict with Paul's actual writings was inevitable. It is not easy to combine Paul's radical theology and his somewhat mystical ethics with a practical approach to the law. The solution has been usually to avoid the confrontation and obscure Paul's thoughts so that the discrepancy is hard to perceive. In dogmatics, it is typical that the concept of "law" is first defined in terms very different from the Pauline, but then the definition is supported be reference to the apostle.

Recent critical exegetical research has correctly seen the unacceptability of such obscuration and /or harmonizing tendencies. However, we still run the risk of falling into the same trap. Instead of only describing or criticizing what Paul actually says about the law, and defining the possible theology behind his writings, modern scholars too may wrestled with an *ideal* Pauline theology. Such modern attempts to "save" or "destroy" the reputation of Paul's teaching as logical or cohesive are not intellectually acceptable.

I hope to have demonstrated, that Paul's view about the law *per se* is fairly clear and solid, if it is inferred from the conditions of communication, in which his statements occur, and the internal dynamics of his texts. Indeed, his search for consistency in theology was a major reason, maybe *the* reason, for his revolt against the law. But he never wrote a theoretical essay on this topic. Unnecessary problems begin, when the interpretation neglects the dynamic nature of his letters.

# Literature

ALTHAUS, P., *Römerbrief* (NTD 6; Göttingen: Vandenhoeck & Ruprecht, 10th edn, 1966).
ANDREWS, M.E., *The Ethical Teaching of Paul* (Chapel Hill: North Carolina UP, 1934).
ARICHEA, D., Translating 'grace' in the New Testament, *The Bible Translator* 29 (1978) 201–206).
AUSTIN, J.L., *How to Do Things with Words* (Oxford: Oxford UP, 2nd edn,1976).
AVEMARIE, F., *Tora und Leben:* Untersuchungen zur Heilsbedeutung der Tora in der frühenrabbinischen Literatur (Texte und Studien zum antiken Judentum 55, Tübingen: Mohr-Siebeck, 1996a).
AVEMARIE, F. and H. LICHTENBERGER (eds.), *Bund und Tora*: zur theologischen Begriffs-geschichte in alttestamentlicher, frühjüdischer und urchristlicher Tradition (WUNT 92; Tübingen: Mohr-Siebeck, 1996b).

BAMBERGER, B., *Proselytism in the Talmudic Period* (rev. edn, New York: KTAV, 1968).
BARCLAY, J.M.G., 'Mirror-Reading a Polemical Letter: Galatians as a Test Case, *JSNTS* 31 (1987) 73–93.
BARCLAY, J.M.G., 'Do we undermine the Law?': A Study of Romans 14.1–15.6, in Dunn 1996a (287–308).
BARTH, K., *Kirchliche Dogmatik* (vol. 2, Zürich: Zollikon, 1948).
BAUCKHAM, R., *Jude, 2 Peter* (WBC 50; Waco: Word, 1983).
BAUER, W.K. ALAND and B.ALAND, *Wörterbuch zum Neuen Testament* (Berlin: de Gruyter, 1988).
BECKER, J., *Paulus: Der Apostel der Völker* (Tübingen: Mohr-Siebeck, 1989).
BEKER, J.C., *Paul the Apostle* (Edinburgh: Clark, 1980).
BERGER, K., χάρις, *EWNT* III (eds. H. Baltz and G. Schneider; Stuttgart: Kohlhammer 1983, 1095–1102).
BERGER, K., *Formgeschichte des Neuen Testaments* (Heidelberg: Quelle & Meyer, 1984).
BERGER, K., Paul the Theologian, *Int* 43 (1989) 352–65.
BETZ, H.D., *Der Apostel Paulus und die socratische Tradition* (BHT 45; Tübingen: Mohr-Siebeck, 1972).
BETZ, H.D., *Galatians* (A Commentary on Paul's Letter to the Churches in Galatia, Hermeneia; Philadelphia: Fortress, 1979).
BETZ, H.D., The problem of rhetoric and theology according to the apostle Paul, in *L'Apôtre Paul* (ed. A.Vanhoye; BETL LXXIII; Leuven: Leuven UP, 1986) 16–48.
*BIBELEN*: Den helige skrift (Oversettelsen 1978, Oslo: Det Norske Bibelselskap, 1980).
BILLERBECK, P., *Kommentar zum Neuen Testament aus Talmud und Midrash* (vols. I and III, München: Beck, 1922; 1926).
BITZER, L.F., 'The Rhetorical Situation', *Philosophy and Rhetoric* 1 (1968) 1–14.
BOERS, H., The Problem of Jews and Gentiles in the Macro-Structure of Romans, *SEÅ* 47 (1982) 184–96.

BOERS, H., *The Justification of the Gentiles. Paul's letters to the Galatians and Romans* (Hendrickson: Peabody, 1994).

BOTHA, J., On the "Reinvention" of Rhetoric, in *Koninkryk: Gees en Woord* (ed. J.C. Coetzee; FS L. Floor, Pretoria: NG Kerkboekhandel, 1988) 1–18.

BOTHA, J., *Subject to Whose Authority?* Multiple Readings of Romans 13:1–7 (Atlanta: Scholars, 1994).

BRADLEY, D.G., The TOPOS as a Form in the Pauline Paraenesis, *JBL* 72 (1953) 238–46.

BRAUN, H., Römer 7, 7–25 und das Selbstverständnis des Qumran-Frommen, *ZThK* 56 (1959) 1–18.

BREUER, D., *Einführung in die pragmatische Texttheorie* (UTB 106; München: Fink, 1974).

BRINSMEAD, B.H., *Galatians as a Dialogical Response to Opponents* (SBLDS 65; Chico: Scholars, 1982).

BROOTEN, B.J., Paul and the Law: How Complete was the Departure? *The Princeton Seminary Bulletin* 1 (1990) 71–89.

BRUCE, F.F., *1 & 2 Thessalonians* (WBC 45; Waco: Word, 1982).

BÜCHSEL, F., κατάρα, *THWNT* I (Stuttgart: Kohlhammer, 1933) 449–51.

BÜHLMANN, W. and SCHERER, K., *Stilfiguren der Bibel: Ein kleines Nachschlagewerk* (Biblische Beiträge 10, Fribourg:, Schweizerisches Katholisches Bibelwerk, 1973).

BULLMORE, M.A., *St. Paul's Theology of Rhetorical Style:* An Examination of 1 Corinthians 2:1–5 in the Light of First Century Graeco-Roman Rhetorical Culture (San Francisco: International Scholars Publications, 1995).

BULTMANN, R., *Der Stil der Paulinischen Predigt und die kynisch-stoische Diatribe* (Göttingen: Vandenhoeck & Ruprecht, 1910).

BULTMANN, R., Römer 7 und die Anthropologie des Paulus, in *Imago Dei* (Beiträge zur theologischen Anthropologie, FS Gustav Krüger, ed. H. Bornkamm; Giessen: Töpelmann, 1932) 53–62.

BULTMANN, R., καυχάομαι κτλ., *THWNT* III (Stuttgart: Kohlhammer, 1938) 646–54.

BULTMANN, R., *Theology of the New Testament 1–2* (New York: Scribners, 1951–52).

BULTMANN, R., *Das Evangelium des Johannes* (KEK 2; Vandenhoeck & Ruprecht, Göttingen 11th edn, 1950).

BULTMANN, R., Das Problem einer theologischen Exegese, in *Das Problem der Theologie des Neuen Testaments* (ed. G. Strecker; Darmstadt: Wissenschaftliche Buchgesellschaft, 1975) 249–77.

BULTMANN, R., *Der zweite Brief an die Korinther* (KEK Sonderbd.; Göttingen: Vandenhoeck & Ruprecht, 1976).

BYRSKOG, S., Epistolography, Rhetoric, and Letter Prescript: Romans 1.1–7 as a Test Case, *JSNT* 65 (1997) 27–46).


CARRACCI, A., POUSSIN, N., LORRAIN, C., ROSSHOLM LAGERLÖF, M., *Ideal Landscape* (New Haven: Yale UP, 1990).

CHADWICK, H., 'All Things to All Men' (I Cor. IX.22), *NTS* 1 (1954/55) 261–75.

COMBRINK, H.J., Translating or transforming – Receiving Matthew in Africa, *Scriptura* 58 (1996) 273–84.

CONZELMANN, H., *An Outline of the Theology of the New Testament* (London: SCM, 1969).

CONZELMANN, H., *A Commentary on the First Epistle to the Corinthians* (trans. J.W. Leitch; Hermeneia; Philadelphia: Fortress, 1975).

CRANFIELD, C.E.B., St. Paul and the Law, *SJTh* 17 (1964) 43–68.

CRANFIELD, C.E.B., *The Epistle to the Romans* (ICC; 2 vols.; Edinburgh: Clark, 1982–83).

DAHL, N.A., The Neglected Factor in New Testament Theology, *Reflection* 73 (1975) 5–8.
DAHL, N.A., *Studies in Paul* (Minneapolis: Ausgburg, 1977).
DALMAN, G., *Die Worte Jesu 1* (Leipzig: Hinrich, 1930).
DAUBE, D., *The New Testament and Rabbinic Judaism* (Jordan Lecture, 1952, London: Athlone 1956).
DEINES, R., *Die Pharisäer* (WUNT 101; Tübingen: Mohr-Siebeck, 1997).
DEISSMANN, G.A., *Paul: A Study in Social and Religious History* (London: Hodder and Stoughton 2nd edn, 1926).
DIBELIUS, M. and CONZELMANN, H., *The Pastoral Epistles* (trans. P. Buttolph and A. Yarbro; Hermeneia; Philadelphia: Fortress, 1972).
DONELSON, L.R., *Pseudepigraphy and Ethical Argument in the Pastoral Epistles* (Tübingen: Mohr-Siebeck, 1986).
DONFRIED, K.P., Introduction, 1977, in *The Romans Debate* (ed. K.P. Donfried; Edinburgh: Clark 2nd edn, 1991) xli–xlvii.
DONFRIED, K.P. (ed.), *The Romans Debate* (Edinburgh: Clark 2nd edn, 1991a).
DOTY, W.G., *Letters in Primitive Christianity* (Philadelphia: Fortress, 1973).
DRANE, J.W., *Paul: Libertine or Legalist?* (London: SPCK, 1975).
DUNN, J., The New Perspective on Paul, *BJRC* 65 (1983) 95–122.
DUNN, J., Works of the Law and the Curse of the Law (Galatians 3.10–14), *NTS* 31 (1985) 523–42.
DUNN, J., *Romans* (WBC 38ab, Waco: Word, 1988).
DUNN, J., *The Partings of the Ways Between Christianity and Judaism and Their Significance for the Character of Christianity* (Philadelphia: Trinity, 1991).
DUNN, J., Prolegomena to a theology of Paul, *NTS* 40 (1994) 407–32.
DUNN, J., (ed.), *Paul and the Mosaic law:* the Third Durham-Tübingen Symposium on Earliest Christianity and Judaism (WUNT 89; Tübingen: Mohr-Siebeck, 1996a).
DUNN, J., Introduction, in Dunn (ed., 1996a) 1–6 (=Dunn, 1996b).
DUNN, J., In Search of Common Ground, in Dunn (ed., 1996a) 309–34 (=Dunn, 1996c).
DUNN, J., *The Theology of Paul the Apostle* (Grand Rapids: Eerdmans, 1998).
DU TOIT, A., 'Alienation and Re-identification as Tools of Persuasion in Galatians', *Neotestamentica* 26 (1992) 279–95.
DU TOIT, A., 'Vilification as a Pragmatic Device in Early Christian Epistolography', *Biblica* 75 (1994) 403–12.

ECKSTEIN, H.-J., *Verheissung und Gesetz: Eine exegetische Untersuchung zu Galater 2, 15–4, 7* (WUNT 86; Tübingen: Mohr-Siebeck, 1996).
ECO, U., *The Limits of Interpretation* (Bloomington: Indiana UP, 1990).
ELLIOTT, J.H., The Rehabilitation of an Exegetical Step-Child: 1 Peter in Recent Research, *JBL* 95 (1976) 243–54.
ELLIOTT, J.H., *A Home for the Homeless* – a Sociological Exegesis of 1 Peter, Its Situation and Strategy (Philadelphia: Fortress, 1981, 2nd edn, 1986).
ELLIOTT, N., *The Rhetoric of Romans: Argumentative Constraint and Strategy and Paul's Dialogue with Judaism* (JSNTS 45; Sheffield: Sheffield Academic, 1990).
ERIKSSON, A.,'Hellenistisk Retorik i Första Korinthierbrevet', *Nordisk Nytestamentligt Nyhedsbrev* 1/1994) 54–67.

ERIKSSON, A., *Traditions as Rhetorical Proof*: Pauline Argumentation in 1 Corinthians, CB 29; Stockholm: Almqvist & Wiksell, 1998).

ESKOLA, T., *Messias ja Jumalan Poika:* traditiokriittinen tutkimus kristologisesta jaksosta Room 1:3, 4 (with an English summary) (Helsinki: Suomen eksegeettinen seura, 1992).

ESKOLA, T., *Theodicy and Predestination in Pauline Soteriology* (WUNT 2.100; Tübingen: Mohr-Siebeck, 1998).

EVANS, C.F., *The Theology of Rhetoric: The Epistle to the Hebrews* (London: Dr. Williams' Trust, 1988).

FASCHER, E., *Der erste Brief des Paulus an die Korinther,* Erster Teil (1–7), ThZNT 7.I; Berlin: Evangelische, 1987).

FEE, G., *The First Epistle to the Corinthians* (NICNT; Grand Rapids: Eerdmans, 1987).

FELDMAN, L.H., *Jew and Gentile in the ancient world: attitudes and interactions from Alexander to Justinian* (Princeton: Princeton U.P., 1993).

FITZMYER, J., *Romans* (AB 33; New York: Doubleday, 1993).

FORBES, C., Comparison, Self-praise and Irony: Paul's Boasting and the Conventions of Hellenistic Rhetoric, *NTS* 32 (1986) 1–30.

FUNG, R.Y.K., *The Epistle to the Galatians* (NICNT; Grand Rapids: Eerdmans, 1988).

GABEL, J. and WHEELER, C., *The Bible as Literature* (Oxford: Oxford UP 2nd edn, 1990).

GARDNER, P., *The Religious Experience of Saint Paul* (London: Williams and Norgate, 2nd edn, 1913).

GARLINGTON, D.B., *'The Obedience of Faith': a Pauline phrase in historical context* (WUNT 2.38; Tübingen: Mohr-Siebeck, 1991).

GÄRTNER, B., *The Areopagus Speech and Natural Revelation* (Uppsala: Almqvist & Wiksell 1955).

GLAD, C., *Paul and Philodemus: adaptability in Epicurean and early Christian psychagogy* (SuppNT 81; Leiden: Brill, 1995).

GOPPELT, L., *Der Erste Petrusbrief* (ed. F. Hahn; KEK 12.1; Göttingen: Vandenhoeck & Ruprecht, 1978).

GOULDER, M., *A Tale of Two Missions* (London: SCM, 1994).

GRÄSSER, E., *Der Alte Bund im Neuen: exegetische Studien zur Israelfrage im Neuen Testament* (WUNT 35; Tübingen: Mohr-Siebeck, 1985).

GRIMM, H., *The Reformation Era 1500–1560* (New York: Macmillan, 1954).

GROSHEIDE, F.W., *Commentary on the First Epistle to the Corinthians* (NICNT; Grand Rapids: Eerdmans, 1953, repr., 1980).

*DIE GUTE NACHRICHT*: Das Neue Testament in heutigem Deutsch (Stuttgart: Bibelanstalt, 1971).

GUTHRIE, D., *Galatians* (NCB; Grand Rapids: Eerdmans, 1973).

HALL, R., The Rhetorical Outline for Galatians: a Reconsideration, *JBL* (1987) 277–87.

HARTMAN, L., Bundesideologie in und hinter einigen paulinischen Texten, in *Die Paulinische Literatur und Theologie* (ed. S. Pedersen; Århus: Aros, 1980) 103–18.

HARTMAN, L., *Kolosserbrevet* (KNT 12; Uppsala: EFS, 1985).

HARTMAN, L., On Reading Other's Letters, *Christians Among Jews and Gentiles* (eds. G.W. Nickelsburg and G.W. McRae; Philadelphia: Fortress, 1986) 137–46.

HARTMAN, L., Galatians 3:15–4:11 as Part of a Theological Argument on a Practical Issue, in *The Truth of the Gospel (Galatians 1:1–4:11)* (ed. J. Lambrecht; Rome: Benedictina, 1993) 127–158.

HAWTHORNE, G.F., *Philippians* (WBC 43; Waco: Word, 1983).

HAYS, R.B., Three Dramatic Roles: The Law in Romans 3–4, in Dunn (ed., 1996a) 151–64.

HECKEL, U., *Kraft in Schwachheit: Untersuchungen zu 2. Kor 10–13* (WUNT 2.56; Tübingen: Mohr-Siebeck, 1993).

HEITSCH, E., *Wollen und Verwirklichen, von Homer zu Paulus* (Abhandlungen der Geistes- und Sozialwissenschaftlichen Klasse, 1989:12; Mainz: Akademie der Wissenschaften und Literatur, 1989).

HENGEL, M., *Die Zeloten: Untersuchungen zur jüdischen Freiheitsbewegung von Herodes I bis 70 n. Chr.* (Leiden: Brill, 1961).

HENGEL, M., Die Stellung des Apostels Paulus zum Gesetz in den unbekannten Jahren zwischen Damaskus und Antiochien, in Dunn (ed., 1996a) 25–51.

HENGEL, M. and SCHWEMER, A.-M., *Paul between Damascus and Antioch: the unknown years* (trans. John Bowden; London: SCM, 1997).

HESTER, J., The Rhetorical Structure of Galatians 1:11–2:14, *JBL* 103 (1984) 223–33.

HESTER, J., Placing the Blame: the Presence of Epideictic in Galatians 1–2, in *Persuasive Artistry: Studies in New Testament Rhetoric* (FS G.A. Kennedy; ed. D. Watson; JSNTSS 50; Sheffield: Sheffield Academic, 1991), 281–320.

HOFIUS, O., *Paulusstudien* (WUNT 51; Tübingen: Mohr-Siebeck, 1989).

HOLLAND, G., 'The Self Against the Self in Romans 7:7–25', in *The Rhetorical Interpretation of Scripture, Essays from the 1996 Malibu Conference* (JSNTS 180; ed. D.Stamps, S. Porter; Sheffield: Sheffield Academic, 1999a) 260–71.

HOLMBERG, B., *Sociology and the New Testament* (Minneapolis: Fortress, 1990).

HOLTZ, T., *Der erste Brief an die Thessalonicher* (EKK 13; Zürich: Benziger, 1986).

HONG, I.-G., *The Law in Galatians* (JSNTS 81, Sheffield: Sheffield Academic, 1993).

HOWARD, G., *Paul's Crisis in Galatia* (SNTSMS 35; Cambridge: Cambridge UP, 1979).

HÜBNER, H., *Das Gesetz bei Paulus* (Göttingen: Vandenhoeck & Ruprecht, 1978).

HÜBNER, H., κατάρα, *EWNT* II (eds. H. Baltz and G. Schneider; Stuttgart: Kohlhammer, 1981) 658–59.

HÜBNER, H., Methodologie und Theologie I–II, *Kerygma und Dogma* (1987) 150–75; 303–29.

HÜBNER, H., *Biblische Theologie des Neuen Testaments 2* (Göttingen: Vandenhoeck & Ruprecht, 1993).

HURD, J.C., *The Origin of 1 Corinthians* (London: SPCK, 1965).

ILLMAN, K.-J., *I Jobs tecken: Europa och judarna* (Åbo: Åbo Academy, 1996).

ISER, W., *Der Implizierte Leser – Kommunikationsformen des Romans von Bunyan bis Becket* (München: Fink, 1972).

ISER, W., *The Act of Reading: A Theme of Aesthetic Response* (Baltimore: Johns Hopkins UP, 1978).

JERVELL, J., A Letter to Jerusalem, in *The Romans Debate* (ed. K. Donfried; Edinburgh: Clark 2nd edn, 1991) 53–64.

JERVIS, L.A., *The Purpose of Romans* (JSNTS 55; Sheffield: Sheffield Academic, 1991).

JEWETT, R., The Agitators and the Galatian Congregation, *NTS* 17 (1971), 198–212.

JOHNSON, L.T., The New Testament's Anti-Jewish Slander and the Conventions of Ancient Polemic, *JBL* 108 (1989) 419–41.

KAISER, W.C., *Toward Old Testament Ethics* (Grand Rapids: Zondervan, 1983).

KÄSEMANN, E., An Apologia for Primitive Christian Eschatology, *Essays on New Testament Themes* (SBT 41, trans. W.J. Montague; London: SCM, 1965) 169–95.

KÄSEMANN, E., *Commentary on Romans* (trans. and ed. Geoffrey W. Bromiley; London: SCM, 1980).

KELLY, J.N.D., *A Commentary on the Epistles of Peter and Jude* (Thornapple Commentaries, Grand Rapids: Baker, 1981).

KENNEDY, G., *New Testament Interpretation through Rhetorical Criticism* (Chapel Hill: University of North Carolina, 1984).

KENNEDY, G., *Aristotle on Rhetoric: A Theory of Civic Discourse* (New York: Oxford UP, 1991).

KNOX, W.L., *St Paul and the Church of the Gentiles* (Cambridge: Cambridge UP, 1939, repr. 1961).

KOSKENNIEMI, H., *Studien zur Idee und Phraseologie des Griechischen Briefes bis 400 n.Chr.* (Annales Academiae Scientiarum Fennicae, Ser.B., 102.2; Helsinki: Suomalainen tiedeakatemia, 1956).

KÖSTER, H., *Einführung in das Neue Testament* (Berlin: deGruyter, 1980).

KRAFTCHICK, S.J., *Ethos and Pathos Appeals in Galatians Five and Six: A Rhetorical Analysis* (Ph. diss, Atlanta, 1985).

KÜMMEL, W.G., *Römer 7 und das Bild des Menschen im Neuen Testament* (Zwei Studien, TB 53; München: Kaiser, 1974).

KUSS, O., *Paulus* (Regensburg: Pustet, 1971).

KUULA, K., *The Law, the Covenant and God's Plan, vol. 1., Paul's Polemical Treatment of the Law in Galatians* (Helsinki: The Finnish Exegetical Society; Göttingen: Vandenhoeck & Ruprecht, 1999).

LAATO, A., *The Servant of YHWH and Cyrus: a Reinterpretation of the Exilic Messianic Programme in Isaiah 40–55* (CB 35; Stockholm: Almqvist & Wiksell, 1992).

LAATO, A., *A Star Is Rising: The Historical Development of the Old Testament Royal Ideology and the Rise of the Jewish Messianic Expectations* (Atlanta: Scholars, 1997).

LAATO, T., *Paulus und das Judentum: Anthropologische Erwägungen* (Åbo: Åbo Academy 1991).

LANG, F., *Die Briefe an die Korinther* (NTD 7; Göttingen: Vandenhoeck & Ruprecht, 1986).

LATEGAN, B.C., The Argumentative Situation of Galatians, *Neotestamentica* 26 (1992) 257–77.

LAUSBERG, H., *Handbuch der literarischen Rhetorik* (2 vols.; München: Hueber, 1960).

LEESTE, T., *ΕΓΩ i Rom. 7:14–25. En undersökning av tolkningshistoriens huvudlinjer* (Stiftelsens för Åbo Akademi, 1980).

LICHTENBERGER, H., Das Tora-Verständniss im Judentum zur Zeit des Paulus. Eine Skizze, in Dunn (ed.,1996a) 7–24.

LIDDELL, H.G. and SCOTT, R., *A Greek-English Lexicon, with a Supplement* (rev. H. Stuart Jones and R. McKenzie; E.A. Barber, Oxford: Clarendon 9[nd] edn, 1966).

LITFIN, D., *St. Paul's Theology of Proclamation* (SNTSMS 79; Cambridge: Cambridge UP 1994).

LONGENECKER, B.W., *Eschatology and the Covenant: A Comparison of 4 Ezra and Romans 1–11* (Sheffield: JSOT Press, 1991).

LONGENECKER, B.W., Defining the Faithful Character of the Covenant Community: Galatians 2.15–21 and Beyond: A Response to Jan Lambrecht, in Dunn (ed.,1996a) 75–98.

LONGENECKER, R., *Paul, Apostle of Liberty: The Origin and Nature of Paul's Christianity* (Grand Rapids, Baker, 1976).

LONGENECKER, R., *Galatians* (WBC 41; Waco: Word, 1990).

LÜTGERT, W., *Gesetz und Geist, eine Unterzuchung zur Vorgeschichte des Galaterbriefes* (BFCTh 22.6, Gütersloh: Bertelsmann, 1919).

LUTHER, M., *Werke* (Kritische Gesamtausgabe [WA] XL; Weimar: Böhlau, 1911).

MAIER, G., *Mensch und freier Wille* (WUNT 12; Tübingen: Mohr-Siebeck, 1971).

MALHERBE, A., *Paul and Popular Philosophers* (Minneapolis: Fortress, 1989).

MARSHALL, I.H., *1 & 2 Thessalonians* (NCB; Grand Rapids: Eerdmans, 1983).

MARSHALL, P., *Enmity in Corinth: Social Conventions in Paul's Relations with the Corinthians* (WUNT 2.23; Tübingen: Mohr-Siebeck, 1987).

MARTIN, D., *Slavery as Salvation: The Metaphor of Slavery in Pauline Christianity* (New Haven, Yale UP, 1990).

MARTIN, J., *Antike Rhetorik: Technik und Methode* (Handbuch der Altertumswissenschaft 2.3; München: Beck, 1974).

MARTIN, R.P., *2 Corinthians* (WBC 40, Waco: Word, 1986).

MARTYN, J.L., Christ, the Elements of the Cosmos, and the Law in Galatians, *The Social World of the First Christians*, (FS W. Meeks; eds. M. White and L. Yarbrough; Minneapolis: Fortress, 1995) 16–39.

MARXSEN, W., *Introduction to the Old Testament* (trans. G. Buswell; Oxford: Blackwell, 1968).

MICHEL, O., *Der Brief an die Römer* (KEK 4; Göttingen: Vandenhoeck & Ruprecht, 1978).

MITCHELL, M., *Paul and the Rhetoric of Reconciliation* (HUNT 28; Tübingen: Mohr-Siebeck, 1991).

MITCHELL, M., Pauline Accommodation and 'Condescension' (συνκατάβασις): 1 Cor 9:19-23, *Paul Beyond the Judaism-Hellenism Divide* (ed. T. Engberg-Pedersen; Edinburgh: T&T Clark, 2000, forthcoming).

MITTERNACHT, D., *Forum für Sprachlose, eine kommunikationspsychologische und epistolär-rethorische Untersuchung des Galaterbriefs* (CBNT 30, Stockholm: Almquist & Wiksell International, 1999)

MOO, D.J., 'Paul and the Law in the Last Ten Years', *SJT* 40 (1987) 287–307.

MORRIS, L., *The First and Second Thessalonians* (NICNT; Grand Rapids: Eerdmans, 1959).

MORRIS, L., *The Gospel according to John* (NICNT; Grand Rapids: Eerdmans, 1971).

MULLINS, T.Y., Formulas in New Testament Epistles, *JBL* 91 (1972) 380–90.

MUNCK, J., *Paul and the Salvation of Mankind* (London: SCM Press, 1959).

MUSSNER, F., *Der Galaterbrief* (HTK 9; Freiburg: Herder, 1974).

NEUSNER, J., *Children of the Flesh, Children of the Promise* (Cleveland: Pilgrim, 1995).

NIDA, E., LOUW, J., SNYMAN, A., CRONJE, J., *Style and Discourse*, with special reference to the text of the Greek New Testament (Cape Town: Bible Society of South Africa, 1983).

NISSEN, A., *Gott und der Nächste im antiken Judentum,* Untersuchungen zum Doppelgebot der Liebe (WUNT 15; Tübingen: Mohr-Siebeck, 1974).

NOLLAND, J., *Luke 9:21–18:34* (WBC 35b; Waco: Word, 1993).

O'BANION, J.D., 'Narration and Argumentation: Quintilian on *Narratio* as the Heart of Rhetorical Thinking', *Rhetorica* 5 (1987) 325–51.

O'BRIEN, P.T., Thanksgiving within the Structure of Pauline Theology, Pauline Studies (Essays Presented to F.F. Bruce, eds. D.A. Hagner and M.J.Harris; Exeter: Paternoster, 1980) 50–66.

ODEBERG, H., *Fariseism och kristendom* (Lund: Gleerup 2nd edn, 1945).

OEPKE, A., *Der Brief des Paulus an die Galater* (3rd ed. by J. Rohde; Berlin: Evangelische 1973).

OLBRICHT, T.H. and PORTER, S. (eds.): *Rhetoric, Scripture and Religion:* Essays from the 1994 Pretoria Conference (JSNTS 131; Sheffield: Sheffield Academic, 1996).

O'NEILL, J.C., *The Recovery of Paul's Letter to the Galatians* (London: SPCK, 1972).

OLSSON, B., Ett Hem för Hemlösa: Om sociologisk exeges av NT, *SEÅ* 49 (1984) 89–108).

PATTE, D., *Paul's Faith and the Power of Gospel* (Philadelphia: Fortress, 1983).

PESCH, R., *Die Apostelgeschichte 13–28* (EKK 5.2; Köln: Benziger, 1986).

PERELMAN, CH. and OLBRECHTS-TYTECA, L., *The New Rhetoric: A Treatise on Argumentation* (trans. J. Wilkinson and P. Weaver; Notre Dame: University of Notre Dame, 1969).

PETERSEN, N.R., *Rediscovering Paul* (Philadelphia: Fortress, 1985).

PETZKE, G., Exegese und Praxis: Die Funktion der neutestamentlichen Exegese in einer christlichen oder nachchristlichen Gesellschaft, *ThrPr* 10 (1975) 2–19.

PIPER, J., *'Love Your Enemies': Jesus' Love Command in the Synoptic Gospels and in the Early Christian Paraenesis* (SNTSS 38; Cambridge: Cambridge UP, 1979).

POGOLOFF, S.M., *Logos and Sophia*: The Rhetorical Situation of 1 Corinthians (SBLDS 134; Atlanta: Scholars, 1992).

PORTER, S.E., The Theoretical Justification for Application of Rhetorical Categories to Pauline Epistolary Literature, *Rhetoric and the New Testament* (eds. S.E. Porter and T.H. Olbricht; JSNTS 90; Sheffield: Sheffield Academic, 1993) 100–22.

PORTER, S.E., Paul of Tarsus and His Letters, in *Handbook of Classical Rhetoric in the Hellenistic Period 330 B.C.-A.D. 400* (ed. S. Porter; Leiden: Brill, 1997) 533–85.

*PYHÄ RAAMATTU*, 1938 (Pieksämäki: Suomen Kirkon Sisälähetysseura, 1961).

*PYHÄ RAAMATTU*, 1992 (Helsinki: Kirjapaja, 1993).

RÄISÄNEN, H., *Paul and the Law* (WUNT 29; Tübingen: Mohr-Siebeck 2nd edn, 1987).

RÄISÄNEN, H., *Beyond New Testament Theology* (London: SCM, 1990).

REICKE, B., *The Epistles of James, Peter, and Jude* (AB 37; Garden City: Doubleday, 1964).

RHYNE, C.T., *Faith Establishes the Law* (SBLDS; Chico: Scholars, 1981).

RICHARDSON, P., Pauline Inconsistency: I Corinthians 9:19–23 and Galatians 2:11–14, *NTS* 26 (1980) 347–62.

RIDDERBOS, H.N., *The Epistle of Paul to the Churches of Galatia* (NICNT; Grand Rapids: Eerdmans, 1953).

ROHDE, J., *Der Brief des Paulus an die Galater* (THzNT 9; Berlin: Evangelische, 1989).

ROSENBLOOM, J., *Conversion to Judaism: from Biblical period to the present* (Cincinnati: Hebrew Union College, 1978).

SANDELIN, K.-G., *Die Auseinandersetzung mit der Weisheit in 1. Korinther 15* (Åbo: Åbo Academy, 1976).

SANDERS, E.P., *Paul and Palestinian Judaism. A Comparison of Patterns of Religion* (Philadelphia: Fortress, 1977).

SANDERS, E.P., On the Question of Fulfilling the Law in Paul and Rabbinic Judaism, *Donum Gentilicium* (eds. E. Bammel, C.K. Barrett, and W.D. Davies; FS D. Daube, Oxford: Clarendon, 1978) 103–126.

SANDERS, E.P., *Paul, the Law, and the Jewish People* (Philadelphia: Fortress, 1983).

SCHELKLE, K.H., *Paulus Lehrer der Väter*: Die altkirchliche Auslegung von Römer 1–11 (Düsseldorf: Patmos, 1959).

SCHIMANOWSKI, G., *Weisheit und Messias: die jüdischen Voraussetzungen der urchristlichen Präexistenzchristologie* (WUNT 2.17; Tübingen: Mohr-Siebeck, 1985).

SCHLIER, H., *Der Brief an die Galater* (KEK 7; Göttingen: Vandenhoeck & Ruprecht 4th edn, 1965).

SCHLIER, H., *Grundzüge einer paulinischen Theologie* (Leipzig: St. Benno, 1981).

SCHMIDT, H.W., *Römerbrief* (THKNT; Berlin: Evangelishce, 1972).

SCHMITHALS, W., *Paul and Gnostics* (trans. J. Steely, Nashville: Abingdon, 1972).

SCHNABEL, E., *Law and Wisdom from Ben Sira to Paul: a tradition historical enquiry into the relation of law, wisdom, and ethics* (WUNT 2.16; Tübingen: Mohr-Siebeck, 1985).

SCHRAGE, W., *Der erste Brief an die Korinther* (EKK VII:1–2; Solothurn: Benziger, 1991, 1995).

SCHREINER, T.R., 'The Abolition and Fulfillment of the Law in Paul', *JSNT* 35 (1989) 47–74.

SCHÜSSLER-FIORENZA, E., The Ethics of Biblical Interpretation: Decentering Biblical Scholarship, *JBL* 107 (1988) 3–17.

SCHWEITZER, A., *Die Mystik des Apostels Paulus* (Tübingen, 1930).

SCHWEITZER, A., *Johann Sebastian Bach* (Wiesbaden: Breitkopf & Härtel, 1908, 11th edn, 1990).

SCHWEIZER, E., *Der Brief an die Kolosser* (EKK XII; Zürich: Benziger, 1976, 2nd edn, 1980).

SCHWEIZER, E., *Das Evangelium nach Lukas* (NTD 3; Göttingen: Vandenhoeck & Ruprecht, 1982).

SCROGGS, R., Can New Testament Theology be Saved? *USQR* 42 (1988) 17–31.

SEELEY, D., *Deconstructing the New Testament* (Leiden: Brill, 1994).

SEID, T., *The Rhetorical Form of the Melchizedek/Christ Comparison in Hebrews 7* (Ph.D. diss., Brown University, 1996).

SEIFRID, M., *Justification by Faith* (SuppNT; Leiden: Brill, 1992).

SIEGERT, F., *Argumentation bei Paulus* (WUNT 34; Tübingen: Mohr-Siebeck, 1985).

SMIT, J., The Letter of Paul to the Galatians: a Deliberative Speech, *NTS* 35 (1989) 1–26.

STAMPS, D., Rethinking the Rhetorical Situation: The Entextualization of the Situation in New Testament Epistles, *Rhetoric and the New Testament* (eds. S. Porter and T. Olbricht; JSNTS 90; Sheffield: Sheffield Academic, 1993) 193–210.

STANTON, G., The Law of Moses and the Law of Christ – Galatians 3.1–6.2, in Dunn (ed., 1996a) 99–116.

STENDAHL, K., The Apostle Paul and the Introspective Conscience of the West, *Paul Among Jews and Gentiles and Other Essays* (Philadelphia: Fortress (1976) 78–96.

STOWERS, S., *The Diatribe and Paul's Letter to the Romans* (SBLDS 57; Chico: Scholars 1981).

STOWERS, S., Text as Interpretation: Paul and Ancient Readings of Paul, *New Perspectives on Ancient Judaism* (eds. J. Neusner *et al.*; vol 3, 1982) 17–27.

STOWERS, S., *A Rereading of Romans: Justice, Jews, and Gentiles* (New Haven: Yale UP) 1994.

STOWERS, S., Romans 7.7–25 as a Speech-In-Character (προσωποποιία), in *Paul and his Hellenistic Context* (ed. Troels Engberg-Pedersen; Minneapolis: Fortress, 1995) 180–202.

THEISSEN, G., *The Social Setting of Pauline Christianity: Essays on Corinth* (ed. and tr. By J.H. Schütz; ET; Philadelphia: Fortress, 1988).

THEISSEN, G., *Psychologische Aspekte paulinsicher Theologie* (FRLANT 131; Göttingen: Vandenhoeck & Ruprecht, 1983).

THIELMAN, F., *From Plight to Solution: a Jewish framework for understanding Paul's view of the law in Galatians and Romans* (SuppNT 61; Leiden: Brill, 1989).

THIELMAN, F., *Paul and the Law: A Contextual Approach* (Downers Grove: InterVarsity, 1994).

THIESELTON, A., Realized Eschatology at Corinth, *NTS* 24 (1978) 510–26.

THURÉN, J.,"Der Herr ist einer" in neutestamentlicher Sicht, *Der Herr ist einer, unser gemeinsames Erbe* (eds. K.-J. Illman and J. Thurén; Åbo: Åbo Academy 1979) 98–121.

THURÉN, J., Paulus och torah: Reflexioner kring Heikki Räisänens arbete 'Paul and the Law, 1983, *Judendom och kristendom under de första århundradena* (Stavanger: Universitetsforlaget 1986) 165–92.

THURÉN, J., *Galatalaiskirje. Filippiläiskirje* (Helsinki: Sley-kirjat, 1993j).

THURÉN, L., *The Rhetorical Strategy of 1 Peter With Special Regard to Ambiguous Expressions* (Åbo: Åbo Academy, 1990).

THURÉN, L., On Studying Ethical Argumentation and Persuasion in the New Testament, *Rhetoric and the New Testament* (eds. S. Porter and T. Olbricht; JSNTS 90; Sheffield: Sheffield Academic (1993) 464–78.

THURÉN, L., Risky Rhetoric in James? *NovTest* 37 (1995a) 262–84.

THURÉN, L., *Argument and Theology in 1 Peter: The Origins of Christian Paraenesis* (JSNTS 114; Sheffield: Sheffield Academic, 1995b).

THURÉN, L., Style Never Goes out of Fashion – 2 Peter Re-evaluated, *Rhetoric, Scripture and Theology* (eds. S. Porter and T. Olbricht; JSNTS 131; Sheffield: Sheffield Academic 1996) 329–47.

THURÉN, L., Hey Jude! Asking for the Original Situation and Message of a Catholic Epistle, *NTS* 43 (1997) 451–65.

THURÉN, L., Was Paul Sincere? Questioning the Apostle's Ethos, *Scriptura* 65 (1998) 95–108.

THURÉN, L., Was Paul Angry? Derhetorizing Galatians, *The Rhetorical Interpretation of Scripture, Essays from the 1996 Malibu Conference* (JSNTS 180; eds. D. Stamps and S. Porter; Sheffield: Sheffield Academic, 1999) 302–20.

THURÉN, L., Romans 7 Derhetorized, in *Essays from the 1998 Florence Conference* (ed. D. Stamps; Sheffield: Sheffield Academic, 2000, forthcoming).

THURÉN, L., John Chrysostom as a Rhetorical Critic – the Hermeneutics of an Early Father, *Biblical Interpretation* (2000a, forthcoming).

TOMSON, P., *Paul and the Jewish Law: Halakha in the Letters of the Apostle to the Gentiles* (Assen/Maastricht: Van Gorcum, 1990).

TOMSON, P., Paul's Jewish Background in View of His Law Teaching in 1 Cor 7, in Dunn (ed., 1996a) 251–70.

TOULMIN, S., RIEKE, R., JANIK, A., *An Introduction to Reasoning* (New York: Macmillan 2nd edn, 1984).

TROBISCH, D., *Die Entstehung der Paulusbriefsammlung* (NTOA 10; Göttingen: Vandenhoeck & Ruprecht, 1989).

TUCKETT, C.M., 'The Corinthians Who Say "There is no resurrection of the dead" (1 Cor15, 12)', in *The Corinthian Correspondence* (ed. R. Bieringer; Leuven: Leuven UP, 1996) 247–75.

VAN SPANJE, T.E., *Inconsistency in Paul?* (WUNT 2.110; Tübingen: Mohr, 1999).

VOLLENWEIDER, S., *Freiheit als neue Schöpfung: eine Untersuchung zur Eleutheria bei Paulus und in seiner Umwelt* (FRLANT 147; Göttingen: Vandenhoeck & Ruprecht, 1989).

VORSTER, J., The context of the letter to the Romans: a critique on the present state of research, *Neotestamentica* 28 (1994) 127–45.

VOUGA, F., Zur rhetorischen Gattung des Galaterbriefes, *ZNW* 79 (1988) 291–92).

WARNING, R. (ed.): *Rezeptionsästhetik, Theorie und Praxis* (München: Fink, 1975, 1989).

WATSON, D.F. and HAUSER, A.J., *Rhetorical Criticism of the Bible* – A Comprehensive Bibliography with Notes on History and Method (Leiden: Brill, 1994).

WATSON, F., *Paul, Judaism and the Gentiles* (SNTS MS 56; Cambridge: Cambridge UP, 1986).

WEDDERBURN, A.J.M., *Baptism and Resurrection:* Studies in Pauline Theology against Its Graeco-Roman Background (WUNT 44; Tübingen: Mohr-Siebeck, 1987).

WEDDERBURN, A.J.M., *The Reasons for Romans* (Edinburgh: Clark, 1991).

WEISS, J., Beiträge zur paulinischen Rhetorik, *Theologische Studien* (FS B. Weiss, Göttingen: Vandenhoeck & Ruprecht 1897).

WEISS, J., *Der erste Korintherbrief* (KEK 5; Göttingen: Vandenhoeck & Ruprecht, 1910).

WESTERHOLM, S., *Israel's Law and the Church's Faith:* Paul and His Recent Interpreters. (Grand Rapids, Eerdmans, 1988).

WHITE, J.L., *The Form and Function of the Body of the Greek Letter* (SBLDS 2; Missoula: Scholars 2nd edn, 1972).

WILCKENS, U., Zur Entwicklung des paulinischen Gesetzesverständnisses, *NTS* 28 (1982) 154–90.

WILCKENS, U., *Der Brief an die Römer* (EKK VI; 2 vols.; Köln: Benziger, 1978).

WILLIS, W., An Apostolic Apologia? The Form and Function of 1 Cor 9, *JSNT* 24 (1985) 33–48.

WILSON, J.H., The Corinthians Who Say There Is No Resurrection of the Dead, *ZNW* 59 (1968) 90–107.

WINNINGE, M., *Sinners and the Righteous: a comparative study of the Psalms of Solomon and Paul's letters* (CB 26; Stockholm: Almqvist & Wiksell, 1995).

WITHERINGTON, B.W. III: *Conflict and Community in Corinth:* A Socio-Rhetorical Commentary on 1–2 Corinthians (Grand Rapids: Eerdmans, 1995).

WOLFF, C., *Der erste Brief des Paulus an die Korinther*, Zweiter Teil (8–16) (ThZNT 7/II; Berlin: Evangelische, 1982).

WRIGHT, N.T., *The Climax of the Covenant*: Christ and the Law in Pauline Theology (Minneapolis: Fortress, 1992).

WRIGHT, N.T., The Law in Romans 2, in Dunn (ed., 1996a) 131–50.

WUELLNER, W., Der Jakobusbrief im Licht der Rhetorik und Textpragmatik, *LB* 43 (1978) 5 -66.

WUELLNER, W., 'Paul as Pastor: The Function of Rhetorical Questions in First Corinthians', in *L'Apôtre Paul: Personnalité, style et conception du ministère* (ed. A. Vanhoye; BETL 73; Leuven: Leuven UP, 1986) 49–77.

WUELLNER, W., Where is Rhetorical Criticism Taking Us?, *CBQ* 49 (1987) 448–63.

ZMIJEWSKI, J., Καυχάομαι κτλ., *EWNT* II (eds. H. Baltz and G. Schneider; Stuttgart: Kohlhammer 1981) 680–90.

# Sources

## Old Testament

## New Testament

## Other Ancient Sources

# Modern Authors

Althaus, P. 107
Andrews, M.E. 8
Arichea, D. 170
Austin, J.L. 24
Avemarie, F. 147

Bamberger, B. 157
Barclay, J.M.G. 11, 65
Barth, K. 110, 165
Bauckham, R. 34
Becker, J. 14, 20, 37, 38, 55, 85, 132, 134, 159
Beker, J.C. 3, 6, 8, 14, 15, 19, 20, 54, 55, 58, 115, 116, 121, 122
Berger, K. 29, 170
Betz, H.D. 26, 29, 32, 34, 39, 40, 43-44, 46, 47, 59-63, 65, 67, 69, 71, 78, 89, 113, 141, 156, 167, 174
*Bibelen* 15
Billerbeck, P. 45
Bitzer, L.F. 98
Boers, H. 9, 11, 19
Botha, J. 9, 29, 143
Bradley, J.D. 89
Braun, H. 118
Breuer, D. 24
Brinsmead, B.H. 59
Brooten, B.J. 86, 91, 133
Bruce, F.F. 32, 33, 40
Büchsel, F. 76
Bullmore, M.A. 105
Bultmann, R. 7, 8, 23, 40, 46, 117, 126, 128, 139, 165-168
Byrskog, S. 162

Carracc, A. 27
Chadwick, H. 32, 37, 40, 43
Combrink, H.J. 24
Conzelmann, H. 1, 2, 7, 30, 33, 34, 46, 104

Cranfield, C.E.B. 58, 60, 145
Cronje, J. 118

Dahl, N.A. 15, 107, 158, 159, 161
Dalman, G. 47
Daube, D. 41
Deines, R. 147, 177
Deissmann, G.A. 8
Dibelius, M. 46
Donelson, L.R. 7
Donfried, K.P. 9, 96, 99, 119
Doty, W.G. 11
Drane, J.W. 54, 94, 104, 105
Du Toit, A. 24, 26, 66, 67, 69, 72, 167
Dunn, J.D.G. 3, 8, 21, 29, 34, 45, 46, 53, 54, 59, 85, 96, 100, 107, 111-114, 116, 117, 121, 123, 127-129, 133, 139-141, 146, 147, 150, 151, 155-157, 162, 163, 169, 170

Eckstein, H.-J. 82, 93
Eco, U. 17
Elliott, J.H. 7
Elliott, N. 9, 97
Eriksson, A. 2, 102-105, 109, 114, 125
Eskola, T. 16, 53, 109, 129, 140, 147-150, 167, 168, 171
Evans, C.F. 68

Fascher, E. 172
Fee, G. 31, 101, 102, 104, 114, 115, 117, 125, 172
Feldman, L.H. 158
Fitzmyer, J. 110, 111, 121, 124, 163
Forbes, C. 40, 46
Fung, R.Y.K. 59, 62, 64, 65, 71

Gabel, J. 1
Gardner, P. 57, 74
Garlington, D.B. 147

*Modern Authors*

# Index of Subjects

# Wissenschaftliche Untersuchungen zum Neuen Testament

## Alphabetical Index of the First and Second Series

*Dunn, James D.G.* (Ed.): Jews and Christians. 1992. *Volume 66.*
– Paul and the Mosaic Law. 1996. *Volume 89.*
*Ebertz, Michael N.:* Das Charisma des Gekreuzigten. 1987. *Volume 45.*
*Eckstein, Hans-Joachim:* Der Begriff Syneidesis bei Paulus. 1983. *Volume II/10.*
– Verheißung und Gesetz. 1996. *Volume 86.*
*Ego, Beate:* Im Himmel wie auf Erden. 1989. *Volume II/34*
*Ego, Beate* und *Lange Armin* sowie *Pilhofer, Peter(Ed.):* Gemeinde ohne Tempel - Community without Temple. 1999. *Volume 118.*
*Eisen, Ute E.:* see *Paulsen, Henning.*
*Ellis, E. Earle:* Prophecy and Hermeneutic in Early Christianity. 1978. *Volume 18.*
– The Old Testament in Early Christianity. 1991. *Volume 54.*
*Ennulat, Andreas:* Die 'Minor Agreements'. 1994. *Volume II/62.*
*Ensor, Peter W.:* Jesus and His 'Works'. 1996. *Volume II/85.*
*Eskola, Timo:* Theodicy and Predestination in Pauline Soteriology. 1998. *Volume II/100.*
*Feldmeier, Reinhard:* Die Krisis des Gottessohnes. 1987. *Volume II/21.*
– Die Christen als Fremde. 1992. *Volume 64.*
*Feldmeier, Reinhard* und *Ulrich Heckel* (Ed.): Die Heiden. 1994. *Volume 70.*
*Fletcher-Louis, Crispin H.T.:* Luke-Acts: Angels, Christology and Soteriology. 1997. *Volume II/94.*
*Förster, Niclas:* Marcus Magus. 1999. *Volume 114.*
*Forbes, Christopher Brian:* Prophecy and Inspired Speech in Early Christianity and its Hellenistic Environment. 1995. *Volume II/75.*
*Fornberg, Tord:* see *Fridrichsen, Anton.*
*Fossum, Jarl E.:* The Name of God and the Angel of the Lord. 1985. *Volume 36.*
*Frenschkowski, Marco:* Offenbarung und Epiphanie. Volume 1 1995. *Volume II/79* – Volume 2 1997. *Volume II/80.*
*Frey, Jörg:* Eugen Drewermann und die biblische Exegese. 1995. *Volume II/71.*
– Die johanneische Eschatologie. Band I. 1997. *Volume 96.* – Band II. 1998. *Volume 110.*
*Fridrichsen, Anton:* Exegetical Writings. Ed.

von C.C. Caragounis und T. Fornberg. 1994. *Volume 76.*
*Garlington, Don B.:* 'The Obedience of Faith'. 1991. *Volume II/38.*
– Faith, Obedience, and Perseverance. 1994. *Volume 79.*
*Garnet, Paul:* Salvation and Atonement in the Qumran Scrolls. 1977. *Volume II/3.*
*Gese, Michael:* Das Vermächtnis des Apostels. 1997. *Volume II/99.*
*Gräßer, Erich:* Der Alte Bund im Neuen. 1985. *Volume 35.*
*Green, Joel B.:* The Death of Jesus. 1988. *Volume II/33.*
*Gundry Volf, Judith M.:* Paul and Perseverance. 1990. *Volume II/37.*
*Hafemann, Scott J.:* Suffering and the Spirit. 1986. *Volume II/19.*
– Paul, Moses, and the History of Israel. 1995. *Volume 81.*
*Hannah, Darrel D.:* Michael and Christ. 1999. *Volume II/109.*
*Hartman, Lars:* Text-Centered New Testament Studies. Ed. by D. Hellholm. 1997. *Volume 102.*
*Heckel, Theo K.:* Der Innere Mensch. 1993. *Volume II/53.*
– Vom Evangelium des Markus zum viergestaltigen Evangelium. 1999. *Volume 120.*
*Heckel, Ulrich:* Kraft in Schwachheit. 1993. *Volume II/56.*
– see *Feldmeier, Reinhard.*
– see *Hengel, Martin.*
*Heiligenthal, Roman:* Werke als Zeichen. 1983. *Volume II/9.*
*Hellholm, D.:* see *Hartman, Lars.*
*Hemer, Colin J.:* The Book of Acts in the Setting of Hellenistic History. 1989. *Volume 49.*
*Hengel, Martin:* Judentum und Hellenismus. 1969, 1988. *Volume 10.*
– Die johanneische Frage. 1993. *Volume 67.*
– Judaica et Hellenistica. Band 1. 1996. *Volume 90.* – Band 2. 1999. *Volume 109.*
*Hengel, Martin* and *Ulrich Heckel* (Ed.): Paulus und das antike Judentum. 1991. *Volume 58.*
*Hengel, Martin* und *Hermut Löhr* (Ed.): Schriftauslegung im antiken Judentum und im Urchristentum. 1994. *Volume 73.*
*Hengel, Martin* and *Anna Maria Schwemer:* Paulus zwischen Damaskus und Antiochien. 1998. *Volume 108.*

*Hengel, Martin* and *Anna Maria Schwemer* (Ed.): Königsherrschaft Gottes und himmlischer Kult. 1991. *Volume 55.*
– Die Septuaginta. 1994. *Volume 72.*
*Herrenbrück, Fritz:* Jesus und die Zöllner. 1990. *Volume II/41.*
*Herzer, Jens:* Paulus oder Petrus? 1998. *Volume 103.*
*Hoegen-Rohls, Christina:* Der nachösterliche Johannes. 1996. *Volume II/84.*
*Hofius, Otfried:* Katapausis. 1970. *Volume 11.*
– Der Vorhang vor dem Thron Gottes. 1972. *Volume 14.*
– Der Christushymnus Philipper 2,6-11. 1976, 1991. *Volume 17.*
– Paulusstudien. 1989, 1994. *Volume 51.*
*Hofius, Otfried* und *Hans-Christian Kammler:* Johannesstudien. 1996. *Volume 88.*
*Holtz, Traugott:* Geschichte und Theologie des Urchristentums. 1991. *Volume 57.*
*Hommel, Hildebrecht:* Sebasmata. Band 1 1983. *Volume 31* – Band 2 1984. *Volume 32.*
*Hvalvik, Reidar:* The Struggle for Scripture and Covenant. 1996. *Volume II/82.*
*Kähler, Christoph:* Jesu Gleichnisse als Poesie und Therapie. 1995. *Volume 78.*
*Kammler, Hans-Christian*: see *Hofius, Otfried.*
*Kamlah, Ehrhard:* Die Form der katalogischen Paränese im Neuen Testament. 1964. *Volume 7.*
*Kelhoffer, James A.:* Miracle and Mission. 1999. *Volume II/112.*
*Kieffer, René* and *Jan Bergman (Ed.)*: La Main de Dieu / Die Hand Gottes. 1997. *Volume 94.*
*Kim, Seyoon:* The Origin of Paul's Gospel. 1981, 1984. *Volume II/4.*
– "The 'Son of Man'" as the Son of God. 1983. *Volume 30.*
*Kleinknecht, Karl Th.:* Der leidende Gerechtfertigte. 1984, 1988. *Volume II/13.*
*Klinghardt, Matthias:* Gesetz und Volk Gottes. 1988. *Volume II/32.*
*Köhler, Wolf-Dietrich:* Rezeption des Matthäusevangeliums in der Zeit vor Irenäus. 1987. *Volume II/24.*
*Korn, Manfred:* Die Geschichte Jesu in veränderter Zeit. 1993. *Volume II/51.*
*Koskenniemi, Erkki:* Apollonios von Tyana in der neutestamentlichen Exegese. 1994. *Volume II/61.*
*Kraus, Wolfgang:* Das Volk Gottes. 1996. *Volume 85.*

– see *Walter, Nikolaus.*
*Kuhn, Karl G.:* Achtzehngebet und Vaterunser und der Reim. 1950. *Volume 1.*
*Laansma, Jon:* I Will Give You Rest. 1997. *Volume II/98.*
*Lange, Armin:* see *Ego, Beate.*
*Lampe, Peter:* Die stadtrömischen Christen in den ersten beiden Jahrhunderten. 1987, 1989. *Volume II/18.*
*Landmesser, Christof:* Wahrheit als Grundbegriff neutestamentlicher Wissenschaft. 1999. *Volume 113.*
*Lau, Andrew:* Manifest in Flesh. 1996. *Volume II/86.*
*Lichtenberger, Hermann:* see *Avemarie, Friedrich.*
*Lieu, Samuel N.C.:* Manichaeism in the Later Roman Empire and Medieval China. 1992. *Volume 63.*
*Loader, William R.G.:* Jesus' Attitude Towards the Law. 1997. *Volume II/97.*
*Löhr, Gebhard:* Verherrlichung Gottes durch Philosophie. 1997. *Volume 97.*
*Löhr, Hermut:* see *Hengel, Martin.*
*Löhr, Winrich Alfried:* Basilides und seine Schule. 1995. *Volume 83.*
*Luomanen, Petri:* Entering the Kingdom of Heaven. 1998. *Volume II/101.*
*Maier, Gerhard:* Mensch und freier Wille. 1971. *Volume 12.*
– Die Johannesoffenbarung und die Kirche. 1981. *Volume 25.*
*Markschies, Christoph:* Valentinus Gnosticus? 1992. *Volume 65.*
*Marshall, Peter:* Enmity in Corinth: Social Conventions in Paul's Relations with the Corinthians. 1987. *Volume II/23.*
*McDonough, Sean M.:* YHWH at Patmos: Rev. 1:4 in its Hellenistic and Early Jewish Setting. 1999. *Volume II/107.*
*Meade, David G.:* Pseudonymity and Canon. 1986. *Volume 39.*
*Meadors, Edward P.:* Jesus the Messianic Herald of Salvation. 1995. *Volume II/72.*
*Meißner, Stefan:* Die Heimholung des Ketzers. 1996. *Volume II/87.*
*Mell, Ulrich:* Die „anderen" Winzer. 1994. *Volume 77.*
*Mengel, Berthold:* Studien zum Philipperbrief. 1982. *Volume II/8.*
*Merkel, Helmut:* Die Widersprüche zwischen den Evangelien. 1971. *Volume 13.*

*Merklein, Helmut:* Studien zu Jesus und Paulus. Volume 1 1987. *Volume 43.* – Volume 2 1998. *Volume 105.*

*Metzler, Karin:* Der griechische Begriff des Verzeihens. 1991. *Volume II/44.*

*Metzner, Rainer:* Die Rezeption des Matthäusevangeliums im 1. Petrusbrief. 1995. *Volume II/74.*

– Das Verständnis der Sünde im Johannesevangelium. 2000. *Volume 122.*

*Mittmann-Richert, Ulrike:* Magnifikat und Benediktus. *1996. Volume II/90.*

*Mußner, Franz:* Jesus von Nazareth im Umfeld Israels und der Urkirche. Ed. by M. Theobald. 1998. *Volume 111.*

*Niebuhr, Karl-Wilhelm:* Gesetz und Paränese. 1987. *Volume II/28.*

– Heidenapostel aus Israel. 1992. *Volume 62.*

*Nissen, Andreas:* Gott und der Nächste im antiken Judentum. 1974. *Volume 15.*

*Noormann, Rolf:* Irenäus als Paulusinterpret. 1994. *Volume II/66.*

*Obermann, Andreas:* Die christologische Erfüllung der Schrift im Johannesevangelium. 1996. *Volume II/83.*

*Okure, Teresa:* The Johannine Approach to Mission. 1988. *Volume II/31.*

*Paulsen, Henning:* Studien zur Literatur und Geschichte des frühen Christentums. Ed. von Ute E. Eisen. 1997. *Volume 99.*

*Park, Eung Chun:* The Mission Discourse in Matthew's Interpretation. 1995. *Volume II/81.*

*Philonenko, Marc* (Ed.): Le Trône de Dieu. 1993. *Volume 69.*

*Pilhofer, Peter:* Presbyteron Kreitton. 1990. *Volume II/39.*

– Philippi. Volume 1 1995. *Volume 87.*

– see *Ego, Beate.*

*Pöhlmann, Wolfgang:* Der Verlorene Sohn und das Haus. 1993. *Volume 68.*

*Pokorny, Petr* und *Josef B. Soucek:* Bibelauslegung als Theologie. 1997. *Volume 100.*

*Porter, Stanley E.:* The Paul of Acts. 1999. *Volume 115.*

*Prieur, Alexander:* Die Verkündigung der Gottesherrschaft. 1996. *Volume II/89.*

*Probst, Hermann:* Paulus und der Brief. 1991. *Volume II/45.*

*Räisänen, Heikki:* Paul and the Law. 1983, 1987. *Volume 29.*

*Rehkopf, Friedrich:* Die lukanische Sonderquelle. 1959. *Volume 5.*

*Rein, Matthias:* Die Heilung des Blindgeborenen (Joh 9). 1995. *Volume II/73.*

*Reinmuth, Eckart:* Pseudo-Philo und Lukas. 1994. *Volume 74.*

*Reiser, Marius:* Syntax und Stil des Markusevangeliums. 1984. *Volume II/11.*

*Richards, E. Randolph:* The Secretary in the Letters of Paul. 1991. *Volume II/42.*

*Riesner, Rainer:* Jesus als Lehrer. 1981, 1988. *Volume II/7.*

– Die Frühzeit des Apostels Paulus. 1994. *Volume 71.*

*Rissi, Mathias:* Die Theologie des Hebräerbriefs. 1987. *Volume 41.*

*Röhser, Günter:* Metaphorik und Personifikation der Sünde. 1987. *Vol. II/25.*

*Rose, Christian:* Die Wolke der Zeugen. 1994. *Volume II/60.*

*Rüger, Hans Peter:* Die Weisheitsschrift aus der Kairoer Geniza. 1991. *Volume 53.*

*Sänger, Dieter:* Antikes Judentum und die Mysterien. 1980. *Volume II/5.*

– Die Verkündigung des Gekreuzigten und Israel. 1994. *Volume 75.*

– see *Burchard, Chr.*

*Salzmann, Jorg Christian:* Lehren und Ermahnen. 1994. *Volume II/59.*

*Sandnes, Karl Olav:* Paul – One of the Prophets? 1991. *Volume II/43.*

*Sato, Migaku:* Q und Prophetie. 1988. *Volume II/29.*

*Schaper, Joachim:* Eschatology in the Greek Psalter. 1995. *Volume II/76.*

*Schimanowski, Gottfried:* Weisheit und Messias. 1985. *Volume II/17.*

*Schlichting, Günter:* Ein jüdisches Leben Jesu. 1982. *Volume 24.*

*Schnabel, Eckhard J.:* Law and Wisdom from Ben Sira to Paul. 1985. *Volume II/16.*

*Schutter, William L.:* Hermeneutic and Composition in I Peter. 1989. *Volume II/30.*

*Schwartz, Daniel R.:* Studies in the Jewish Background of Christianity. 1992. *Volume 60.*

*Schwemer, Anna Maria:* see *Hengel, Martin*

*Scott, James M.:* Adoption as Sons of God. 1992. *Volume II/48.*

– Paul and the Nations. 1995. *Volume 84.*

*Siegert, Folker:* Drei hellenistisch-jüdische Predigten. Teil I 1980. *Volume 20* – Teil II 1992. *Volume 61.*

– Nag-Hammadi-Register. 1982. *Volume 26.*
– Argumentation bei Paulus. 1985.
  *Voume. 34.*
– Philon von Alexandrien. 1988. *Volume 46.*
*Simon, Marcel:* Le christianisme antique et
  son contexte religieux I/II. 1981.
  *Volume 23.*
*Snodgrass, Klyne:* The Parable of the Wicked
  Tenants. 1983. *Volume 27.*
*Söding, Thomas:* Das Wort vom Kreuz. 1997.
  *Volume 93.*
– see *Thüsing, Wilhelm.*
*Sommer, Urs:* Die Passionsgeschichte des
  Markusevangeliums. 1993. *Volume II/58.*
*Soucek, Josef B.:* see *Pokorny, Petr.*
*Spangenberg, Volker:* Herrlichkeit des Neuen
  Bundes. 1993. *Volume II/55.*
*Spanje, T.E. van:* Inconsistency in Paul?. 1999.
  *Volume II/110.*
*Speyer, Wolfgang:* Frühes Christentum im
  antiken Strahlungsfeld. Band I: 1989.
  *Volume 50.* – Band II: 1999. *Volume 116.*
*Stadelmann, Helge:* Ben Sira als
  Schriftgelehrter. 1980. *Volume II/6.*
*Stenschke, Christoph W.:* Luke's Portrait of
  Gentiles Prior to Their Coming to Faith.
  *Volume II/108.*
*Stettler, Hanna:* Die Christologie der
  Pastoralbriefe. 1998. *Volume II/105.*
*Strobel, August:* Die Stunde der Wahrheit.
  1980. *Volume 21.*
*Stroumsa, Guy G.:* Barbarian Philosophy. 1999.
  *Volume 112.*
*Stuckenbruck, Loren T.:* Angel Veneration
  and Christology. 1995. *Volume II/70.*
*Stuhlmacher, Peter* (Ed.): Das Evangelium
  und die Evangelien. 1983.
  *Volume 28.*
*Sung, Chong-Hyon:* Vergebung der Sünden.
  1993. *Volume II/57.*
*Tajra, Harry W.:* The Trial of St. Paul. 1989.
  *Volume II/35.*

– The Martyrdom of St.Paul. 1994.
  *Volume II/67.*
*Theißen, Gerd:* Studien zur Soziologie des
  Urchristentums. 1979, 1989. *Volume 19.*
*Theobald, Michael:* see *Mußner, Franz.*
*Thornton, Claus-Jürgen:* Der Zeuge des
  Zeugen. 1991. *Volume 56.*
*Thüsing, Wilhelm:* Studien zur
  neutestamentlichen Theologie. Ed. von
  Thomas Söding. 1995. *Volume 82.*
*Thurén, Lauri:* Derhetorizing Paul. 2000.
  *Volume 124.*
*Treloar, Geoffrey R.:* Lightfoot the Historian.
  1998. *Volume II/103.*
*Tsuji, Manabu:* Glaube zwischen
  Vollkommenheit und Verweltlichung. 1997.
  *Volume II/93.*
*Twelftree, Graham H.:* Jesus the Exorcist. 1993.
  *Volume II/54.*
*Visotzky, Burton L.:* Fathers of the World.
  1995. *Volume 80.*
*Wagener, Ulrike:* Die Ordnung des „Hauses
  Gottes". 1994. *Volume II/65.*
*Walter, Nikolaus:* Praeparatio Evangelica. Ed.
  by Wolfgang Kraus und Florian Wilk. 1997.
  *Volume 98.*
*Wander, Bernd:* Gottesfürchtige und
  Sympathisanten. 1998. *Volume 104.*
*Watts, Rikki:* Isaiah's New Exodus and Mark.
  1997. *Volume II/88.*
*Wedderburn, A.J.M.:* Baptism and
  Resurrection. 1987. *Volume 44.*
*Wegner, Uwe:* Der Hauptmann von
  Kafarnaum. 1985. *Volume II/14.*
*Welck, Christian:* Erzählte ‚Zeichen‘. 1994.
  *Volume II/69.*
*Wilk, Florian:* see *Walter, Nikolaus.*
*Wilson, Walter T.:* Love without Pretense. 1991.
  *Volume II/46.*
*Zimmermann, Alfred E.:* Die urchristlichen
  Lehrer. 1984, 1988. *Volume II/12.*
*Zimmermann, Johannes:* Messianische Texte
  aus Qumran. 1998. *Volume II/104.*

*For a complete catalogue please write to the publisher
Mohr Siebeck · Postfach 2030 · D–72010 Tübingen.
Up-to-date information on the internet at http://www.mohr.de*